WOMEN OF COLOR

**Recent Titles in
Contributions in Women's Studies**

Excluded from Suffrage History: Matilda Joslyn Gage, Nineteenth-Century American Feminist
Leila R. Brammer

The Artist as Outsider in the Novels of Toni Morrison and Virginia Woolf
Lisa Williams

(Out)Classed Women: Contemporary Chicana Writers on Inequitable Gendered Power Relations
Phillipa Kafka

"Saddling La Gringa": Gatekeeping in Literature by Contemporary Latina Writers
Phillipa Kafka

Representing the Marginal Woman in Nineteenth-Century Russian Literature: Personalism, Feminism, and Polyphony
Svetlana Slavskaya Grenier

From the Field to the Legislature: A History of Women in the Virgin Islands
Eugenia O'Neal

Women and Domestic Experience in Victorian Political Fiction
Susan Johnston

African American Women and Social Action: The Clubwomen and Volunteerism from Jim Crow to the New Deal 1896–1936
Floris Barnett Cash

The Dress of Women: A Critical Introduction to the Symbolism and Sociology of Clothing
Charlotte Perkins Gilman, Michael R. Hill, and Mary Jo Deegan

Frances Trollope and the Novel of Social Change
Brenda Ayres, editor

Women Among the Inklings: Gender, C.S. Lewis, J.R.R. Tolkien, and Charles Williams
Candice Fredrick and Sam McBride

The Female Body: Perspectives of Latin American Artists
Raysa E. Amador Gómez-Quintero, and Mireya Pérez Bustillo

WOMEN OF COLOR
Defining the Issues,
Hearing the Voices

Edited by Diane Long Hoeveler
and Janet K. Boles

Foreword by Toni-Michelle C. Travis

Contributions in Women's Studies, Number 189

GREENWOOD PRESS
Westport, Connecticut • London

Library of Congress Cataloging-in-Publication Data

Women of color : defining the issues, hearing the voices / edited by Diane Long
    Hoeveler and Janet K. Boles ; foreword by Toni-Michelle C. Travis.
        p.   cm.—(Contributions in women's studies, ISSN 0147–104X ; no. 189)
    Includes bibliographical references and index.
    ISBN 0–313–31414–4 (alk. paper)
        1. Minority women—Social conditions.   2. Ethnic groups.   3. Minority women in
literature.   4. Minority women educators.   I. Hoeveler, Diane Long.   II. Boles, Janet K.,
1944–   III. Series.
    HQ1161.W65   2001
    305.48′8—dc21   00–064053

British Library Cataloguing in Publication Data is available.

Library of Congress Catalog Card Number: 00–064053
ISBN: 0–313–31414–4
ISSN: 0147–104X

First published in 2001

Greenwood Press, 88 Post Road West, Westport, CT 06881
An imprint of Greenwood Publishing Group, Inc.
www.greenwood.com

Printed in the United States of America

The paper used in this book complies with the
Permanent Paper Standard issued by the National
Information Standards Organization (Z39.48–1984).

10 9 8 7 6 5 4 3 2 1

Contents

Foreword

Toni-Michelle C. Travis

In this new century women of color face a turbulent future because technology has increasingly complicated the pace of everyday life, and old assumptions about the roles of women, men, African-Americans, the dominant WASP culture, and the government have to be reassessed. Before speculating on the future, however, let me make some observations about the past that was characterized by American values in which white men had power and blacks, both men and women, were considered inferior. These cultural assumptions were accompanied by segregation, with legal barriers in the South and numerous impediments based on custom in the North. A challenge to this hegemony was made by the black community, and specifically by women who worked, formed self-help societies, and fought segregation, especially the practice of lynching. Some became schoolteachers because education was seen as a key factor in achieving upward mobility. The barriers posed by a segregated society were met through preparing students at institutions such as Howard University, to lead and to contribute to their communities. Women played pivotal roles in preserving and transmitting cultural values in a fairly cohesive community that was often physically segregated from the dominant culture. Women as individuals and through community organizations mobilized during the Civil Rights Movement to fight for civil and political rights.

Since the Civil Rights Acts of the 1960s and a number of Supreme Court cases, notably *Brown v. Board of Education*, we now refer to the United States as an integrated society. In reality, however, American society continues to operate on the complications of integration, rather than the abolition of segregation. Although the clearly defined physical barriers of Southern segregation are no longer visible, the media lead the American public to believe in the illusion of racial inclusion. We can see this in several sectors of society; for instance, there are visible and high-profile blacks in entertainment and professional sports, yet economic barriers continue to abound. Few blacks own sports teams or control the production aspects of entertainment. Very few blacks are in the inner circles of corporate America.

We know how many blacks are in the president's cabinet or on the Supreme Court because we can easily count the few by name. We know the names the blacks who teach at Ivy League universities. There are so few that we know when there is a vacancy or who has lost a position in a prestigious school. We even know names of the only elected black the governor, Douglas Wilder, and the only modern era senators, Carol Moseley-Braun and Edward W. Brooke. Yet, the press and the establishment would have all Americans believe that every citizen is truly included and treated on an equal basis. However, for a reality check, we have only to hear about the cases of discrimination at Dennys and Texaco. What is the status of black women in the post-Civil Rights era? Uncertain at best. There are new rules because of economic competition. White women came into the workforce; black women never left the workforce. Some gains were made under affirmative action, but the policy has come under severe attack by the proponents of a colorblind society. The California civil rights initiative passed, although the American Civil Liberties Union is challenging the abolition of affirmative action in the courts.

So where are black women and the African-American community as we enter the era of multiculturalism, in an age of diversity? There are new rules and new cultural groups that must be considered. With diversity comes the concept of difference. Often differences are based on race or gender. For women, roles are no longer rigidly defined. They now have choices regarding employment that give them the option of working part-time or full-time, or remaining at home. Previously closed career paths are now open; women can seek careers in law enforcement, scientific research, and the military and financial institutions. With these choices, working women find that they can become financially independent of men.

The Civil Rights Movement and the influx of non-European immigrants forever changed racial designations and the rules of racial etiquette. Since the 1960s Asians, Latinos, and Middle Easterners have confounded the federal definitions of race on census forms. There are now challenges as to who is black, who is white, who is nonwhite, and how do we know? Relying on common knowledge or visual identification is now an inadequate guide to racial designations. The biracial society is gone. The Rodney King-inspired riot in Los Angeles in 1992 made this very clear. But perhaps even more telling is how the jury in the second O. J. Simpson trial was described in racial terms. The television commentator referred to black jurors, white jurors, Latinos jurors, and mixed jurors. The latter referred to those blacks whose ancestry was a combination of black and another, non-white, racial group, and whites whose ancestry included a racial group other than black.

Affirmative action is being reexamined and will likely be restructured along class lines to exclude anyone above a minimum income level. Assimilation to Anglo values is being seriously challenged by those fighting the "English Only" Movement. The English language has always been a unifying force, but its centrality in assimilation is now being questioned. No longer can we accurately describe American society in black/white terms or by reference to those who are Catholic,

Protestant, or Jewish. Assumptions about ethnic or racial backgrounds are hardly obvious or clear-cut. As I teach, no longer can I assume, from looking at a class roll, that a student named O'Keefe will be of European descent. She was Korean-American. Fultz and Nieberg were both African-American. A Latino student who spoke Spanish also identified as Jewish. To observe the New Year means the Jewish or Christian dates but also the Vietnamese. Easter may be the Greek Orthodox Easter, which is one week later than the Roman Easter. Diversity abounds in new and very different combinations.

How should black women respond, so that they are not left on the short end of affirmative action and in the precomputer age of the typewriter? As in the past, black women must seek a formal education and encourage others to do so. After they master the basics in college their language and computer skills must be refined in order to communicate on the Internet or with neighbors. Travel is another way to expand horizons because it forces a comparison of customs and experiences. In terms of interaction, it is essential to judge every person as an individual. Mistakes, often-costly ones, can be made by assuming that someone is Spanish-speaking or Christian. For example, not everyone from Iran and India is Muslim or Hindu; many are Christian. Coalitions, although they are temporary and are based upon limited objectives, must be built. Look for models of successful diversity.

I will conclude by recounting a recent event at my university. The campus is quite diverse, and usually students retreat to the safety of their own cultural group. However, when a recent visitor, a Christian missionary, verbally attacked Muslim women, gays, and blacks, students came together against him. Interaction with those who are different can be disquieting, but there is always more to learn and understand. As with parachutes, minds work best when they are open.

Acknowledgments

The coeditors wish to acknowledge the financial support of Marquette University's Educational Opportunity Program and the McNair Scholars Program. In particular, we are grateful for the support of Myra George and the editorial assistance of Wendy Weaver, Dr. Michael Wreen, Keith Alexander, Michele Crymes, and Nathanial Ziarek.

Introduction

Diane Long Hoeveler

Alice Walker's autobiographical essay "In Search of Our Mothers' Gardens" recalls Jean Toomer's reaction to walking through the South during the early 1920s. He recounted what was for him a curious thing: "black women whose spirituality was so intense, so deep, so *unconscious*, that they were themselves unaware of the richness they held." These women were defined by the post-Reconstruction South as the "*mules* of the world," survived against all odds, largely by continuing to dream the dreams that their society never acknowledged, let alone vindicated. As Walker observed in her essay, however, these women were not the "saints" that Toomer wanted to believe they were, but were instead:

Artists driven to a numb and bleeding madness by the springs of creativity in them for which there was no release. They were Creators, whose lives were lives of spiritual waste, because they were so rich in spirituality-which is the basis of Art that the strain of enduring their unused and unwanted talent drove them insane. Throwing away this spirituality was their pathetic attempt to lighten the soul to a weight their workworn, sexually abused bodies could bear. [1]

Walker's efforts as a contemporary African-American artist creating in her own right and her own voice hover over any discussion of women of color in this country. But it is also important to remember that Walker's literary writings have been supplemented by her heroic efforts to recover the history and writings of Zora Neale Hurston, an early twentieth-century woman of color whose talents were buried by a society indifferent, if not hostile, to her visions. Hurston, the first woman of color to attend Columbia University in the Ph.D. program in anthropology and the first woman of color to hold a Guggenheim fellowship, died in obscurity as a maid. These facts say more than any of us would like to hear about the issues facing women of color in America today.

This volume collects thirteen original essays on a variety of topics related to the major issues confronting women of color in both the United States and Latin America today. Each deals with one or more of the groups of women who have been underrepresented in Women's Studies scholarship or have had their experiences misinterpreted. These groups include African-Americans, Latinas, Asian-Americans, and Native Americans, the four racial/ethnic groups also identified as the focus of discussion in D. Soyini Madison's *The Woman That I Am: The Literature and Culture of Contemporary Women of Color* (1994). Defining and attempting to recognize the category "women of color" has been an unusually vexed issue in the field of Women's Studies. In addition to Madison's study, which centers on the "dynamic of difference" among women of different racial and ethnic groups, Maxine Baca Zinn and Bonnie Thornton Dill also explore the topic in their *Women of Color in U.S. Society* (1994). For Zinn and Dill, color and race are less important as defining categories than is a shared history of oppression and an active commitment to resist sexist and racist classifications. Another strategy for defining the topic has emerged in Chandra Talpade Mohanty et al.'s *Third World Women and the Politics of Feminism* (1991). They include Arab women and women of other "new immigrant" groups in their discussion, opening up and complicating the U.S.-dominated groupings of recognized racial categories. For them, women of all colors (including white women) constitute "an imagined community based upon a common context of struggle rather than color or racial identifications."[2]

The first goal of Women's Studies scholars, beginning in the late 1960s, was to introduce courses focused on the history, literature, and philosophies of women into the curriculum, and then to infuse a new body of scholarship emerging from this new focus into the mainstream of American education. Since the mid-1980s, the focus has expanded to include the voices and agendas of women of color. With this movement has come a growing awareness that sisterhood is not only powerful and global, but also diverse and complex. Even the designation "women of color," coined to encourage identity and unity through a panethnic/pan-racial term, is problematic in that it can obscure the important differences among the groups encompassed by this label and may suggest a non-Euro-American female "Other" in contrast to a normative white women. This particular problem is the focus of *Other Sisterhoods*, edited by Sandra Kumamoto Stanley (1998), an extremely useful volume that provides a helpful overview of the controversies that have vexed the category of "women of color" since its origin in the mid-seventeenth century. For Stanley, there is "no homogeneous woman of color voice," only diverse voices trying to map "complex and multiple sites of representation" (8). Some of these sites are "borderlands" (in Gloria Anzaldúa's sense), others are "houses of difference" (in Audre Lorde's terms), and others are "migrations of the subject" (Carol Boyce Davies), "constraining walls of social location" (Zinn and Dill), or "cartographies of struggle" (Mohanty et al.). [3] This volume follows the strategies outlined by Stanley in that it is organized first around disciplinary approaches, then theoretical approaches, and finally practical approaches to the multiply voiced topic of women of color.

Although the contributors in this volume focus on women of color and concepts of difference, diversity, power, privilege, inclusiveness, and the intersections of race, class, and gender, the approaches used and the topics addressed areas varied as the cross-disciplinary and interdisciplinary field of Women's Studies itself. This book is not only in the mainstream of contemporary women's studies research, it is also firmly situated in a U.S. society that is struggling with demographic projections of a "majority minority" population in which the old majority of white/Euro-American peoples is now a minority. Consistently one theme emerges: the need to recognize the reality of contemporary life as a "border-crossing," a mixing of races and classes that has led to the complexities of life in America today-for both Anglo women and women of color.

The volume begins, therefore, with an essay by Nina Manasan Greenberg, a mixed race woman attempting to make sense of the intersections between race theory and identity politics in the academy. As a theoretical introduction to the volume, Greenberg's essay articulates three questions that she foregrounds as crucial in understanding the intersection of feminism and Women's Studies with race: "that race is a marker for power in America which is at once absolutely real and absolutely fictional; that a thorough examination of identity politics... is crucial for coalition building in women's studies; and that we must reimagine race in America if we are to capitalize on the potential power of feminist coalitions, in the classroom and in the broad field of Women's Studies."

Greenberg's essay is followed by Patti Duncan's theoretical discussion of feminism and the uses of silence as a political and literary strategy of resistance. She writes in reaction to Euro-American feminists who valorize voice and speech indiscriminately (e.g., in "speak-outs," "breaking silence," "lost voices," and "a different voice"). In societies where much speech is "free" and "protected," silence can be a means of insurrection. Duncan uses her personal experiences to explore the way racism reinforces heterosexism to erase or leave out of consideration those whom the dominant society does not want to recognize or acknowledge: the lesbian, gay, and bisexual as well as the colored or mixed in our midst. Duncan argues for "historicizing silence(s) [because they] may allow us to examine the consequences of simply mapping one set of theoretical assumptions that may apply to, for instance, gender, onto contemporary racial discourses."

In the third essay in the collection, "Women Networking with Their Neighbors: The Universal Thread of Civic Activism," Janet Boles explores the inherent tension between inclusiveness, multiculturalism, and a focus on differences that end up immobilizing the quest to unite and generalize about women's lives without appropriating others' identities. Must "diversity" be a synonym for "disunity"? She suggests civic activism as a female universal that bridges race, ethnic, and class differences, and embodies the ethic of caring and sharing of sisterhood as well as the essence of being human.

In the next essay of the first section of the collection, Lance Grahn explores the recent attacks on the legitimacy of Rigoberta Menchú's memoir (1983). After reviewing the criticisms made about the text, Grahn focuses on its enduring value as a body of testimony by a Central American woman. He also examines the work as a reflection of contemporary developments in social activism, educational reform, theological reformations, and filmmaking throughout Latin America.

Finally, for Grahn the memoir illustrates the premises and the means of rebellion among indigenous and dispossessed women: "Menchú and her family stand as exemplars of the popular endeavor for identity, dignity, and peace in the face of official intimidation."

Finally, in the last essay of the first section, Jorge Valadez presents a philosophical analysis of standpoint epistemology, arguing that the experiences of women of color can make a major intellectual contribution to epistemology because of their experience with men and with third world and non-Western cultures. The general view of standpoint theory is that those most marginalized in society are best positioned to perceive the world in a holistic and less biased manner; women of color make it easier to see the importance of race, class, ethnicity, and gender.

The second section of the collection, essays on literature and art created by women of color, presents a broad spectrum of issues and works. The theoretical introduction to this section, "Ethical Authority and Women Writers of Color," explores the controversial notion that literature can ever present "racelessness" by examining the arguments made in Toni Morrison's recent works about the Africanist presence in the white American literary imagination. In addition, Mary Sullivan-Haller examines the texts of the Argentine philosopher Maria Lugones and the work of African-American legal theorist Patricia J. Williams to understand the ethical issues involved in speaking from a "raced" perspective.

In the next essay, Laura Roskos looks at the intersections between the writings of Paule Marshall and the United Nations End of the Decade Conference in Nairobi and the Fourth World Conference on Women held in Beijing. For Roskos, "The impetus of the international women's movement seemed to shift from Western feminists to women of the Southern Hemisphere. Ten years later...the interdependencies of women from developed and developing nations became acknowledged fact." Exploring the evolution of that fact in the fictions of Paule Marshall is the focus of Roskos' essay.

Building on that shift from Western feminism to the southern hemisphere, Diane Long Hoeveler's essay focuses on one contemporary Mexican novel, *Like Water for Chocolate* by Laura Esquivel, and examines it as an example of what Homi Bhabha has defined as an expression of literary "hybridity," one dominant method by which colonized peoples mimic and thereby attempt to deconstruct, the strategies of Western hegemony. Hoeveler's essay, however, suggests that hybridity does not operate successfully in this "border [Mexican-Texan] work." Instead she identifies how Platonic, pagan, and Christian traditions intersect in the novel, not to produce a system of power for women, but a monolithic hybrid force that causes women to internalize their status as objects-virgins or whores-in each of these systems.

The essay by Rosetta Haynes shows how race, gender, and sexuality converge with textual experimentation in women's autobiographical writings. The writings of Cherríe Moraga, of Mexican heritage and a lesbian, are contrasted to those of Chinese-American Maxine Hong Kingston, both reveal what the critic Gloria Anzaldúa calls a "*mestiza* consciousness." Increasingly, as we have seen throughout the essays in this collection, women of color see themselves as "border women," hybrids, struggling between conflicting forces, colors, and traditions in their attempts to forge a new identity that is not limited to the stereotypes of the old "mule of the world."

Nancy Backes's essay looks at adolescent fiction by Paule Marshall, Toni Morrison, and Michelle Cliff in order to explore how "the other is constructed" in the adolescent African-American imagination. She asserts that for the black teenage girl, her "encounters with the other, specifically, white others,...push her back, keep her 'in her place,' force her to consider her status as she stands in the shadows of the other's illumination. Ultimately, both black and white girls chase and reject impossible ideals."

In the final essay in this section, "The Theater of New World (B)Orders," Jennifer Drake examines the avant-garde theater work of Coco Fusco, Guillermo Gómez-Peña, and Anna Deavere Smith. All of these performance artists have staged works that are intended to shock and offend their viewers: "The work of these artists consistently refuses monoculture as it redefines the "experimental" in relation to the grassroots and the "postmodern" in relation to histories of marginalized cultural production. It questions both separatism and assimilation as models for resisting domination. In both form and content, this art reconceptualizes 'America' and "American" so as to remind "Americans" that we have all been uprooted; we are all potential border crossers; and we are all the products of more than one culture.

In the third section of the volume, "Praxis," essays focus on bringing issues related to women of color into the university curriculum. These final two essays examine practical issues facing women of color in the academy. The first of these looks at curriculum reform and the role that women of color can play in the field of Women's Studies. The second essay looks at librarians and Women's Studies programs. Arlene Sgoutas' essay reflects the shift in Women's Studies from balancing and mainstreaming information about women to curriculum transformation that involves a radical paradigm shift which is dependent on the voices and experiences of women of color as bridges between gender and ethnic studies. Women's Studies focuses on unmasking patriarchy, and ethnic studies takes racism and colonialism as core concepts (and, some would say, is male-centered and heterosexist).

Arglenda Friday describes a potential symbiotic relationship between academic librarians and Women's Studies, and its possibility to increase the quality and quantity of materials by and about women and people of color. Librarians are primarily women who are liberal and feminist in terms of the norms of inclusivity and service to all potential clients. Female librarians are very aware that the minority of men in the profession are very privileged and do hold a disproportionate number of library directorships. And as frequent readers, librarians know that when the literary canon is debated and redefined, ethnic women writers have been central in that revision and expansion.

As Bertolt Brecht once famously observed, art is a hammer, not a mirror. In creating literary, visual, and performance works of art women of color are enacting both their oppression and their imagined and fantasized liberation. Theory and theoretical approaches to racial inequality can be brought to life, made concrete, only when they are embodied, and thus we need to examine literary, visual, and performance records for the enacted and visible record of tragedy and triumph. This volume, then, moves from theory to practice in an effort to reveal how triumphant that spirit of creativity is in women of color. "Saint" or "artist" each is a hyperbolic characterization. Women of color simply want a fair hearing as equals in the discussion.

NOTES

1. Alice Walker, "In Search of Our Mothers' Gardens," in *The Norton Anthology of Literature by Women: The Traditions in English*, 2nd ed., ed. Sandra M. Gilbert and Susan Gubar (New York: Norton, 1996), 2315.

2. D. Soyini Madison, *The Woman That I Am: The Literature and Culture of Contemporary Women of Color* (New York: St. Martin's Press, 1994), 2; Maxine Baca Zinn and Bonnie Thornton Dill, eds. *Women of Color in U.S. Society* (Philadelphia: U of Pennsylvania P, 1994) *passim*; and Chandra Talpade Mohanty, Ann Russo, and Lourdes Torres, eds, *Third World Women and the Politics of Feminism* (Bloomington: Indiana U P, 1991), 7.

3. See Sandra Kumanoto Stanley, "Introduction," *Other Sisterhoods: Literary Theory and U.S. Women of Color*, ed. Sandra K. Stanley (Urbana: Uof Illinois P, 1998), 1-19. Stanley's valuable introduction surveys the conflicted terrain of "women of color" studies, and helpfully points to a variety of theoretical positions that can be employed to analyze race, class, and gender issues.

PART I

THEORETICAL PERSPECTIVES ON RACE, GENDER, AND IDENTITY

1

Defining Differences: Feminism, Race Theory, and Identity Politics in the Academy

Nina Manasan Greenberg

Identity. Difference. Identity Politics. Differences. In feminist discussions, these terms serve as markers for several debates about the future, the nature of feminism, and Women's Studies. This essay will trace some of the debates that feminism must engage in by examining a few idiosyncratic political and naturalized identities and identifications. My starting points are three: the problem of self-identification, the resistance that the category of *"mestiza"* may offer to race, and the question of a feminist coalition. When I say "Women's Studies," however, I mean the academic (inter)discipline, and when I say "feminism(s)," I always mean feminism in the academy, which encompasses the study of feminism and Women's Studies, as well as feminist interventions into the academy.

In *Am I That Name? Feminism and the Category of "Women" in History*, Denise Riley traces the sometimes useful indeterminacy of the identity category "women" for feminism:

My own feeling is that "identity" is an acutely double-edged weapon-not useless, but dependent on the context, sometimes risky-and that the closeness between an identity and a derogatory identification may, again always in specific contexts, resemble that between being a subject and the process of subjectification. "Women" can also suffer from too much identification. Yet an aspect of any feminism in formation *is* that collective self-consciousness of "being women," and to deny the force of that elective identification would be mistaken, as mistaken as the supposition of its necessary fixity. (122)

Riley is cited here because her comments help to outline the concerns of this essay. She begins by denaturalizing the notion of identity. Rather than being something whose purpose is simple to describe, identity is a "double-edged weapon." It is something that can inflict violence and, she notes, something that is not easily predicted or controlled. Further, she cautions that it is something which changes according to the context, so that its meanings are never fixed but arenism, cannot be taken for granted by feminism. It is a term that can be imbued with possibly problematic meanings, or perhaps too much meaning. And yet she points out the necessity and power in the "collective self-consciousness" of self-identification. From Riley, we must take the charge that feminism depends upon, and yet suspects, identity and identification.

Cornel West develops this notion of self-identification when he discusses race with Jorge Klor de Alva and Earl Shorris. West asserts that people "identify themselves in certain ways in order to protect their way of life; in order to be associated with people who ascribe value to them and for purposes of recognition to feel as if one actually belongs to a group" (Klor de Alva 57). So, for West, self-identification is often a pragmatic gesture; it is (as Riley says) meaningful only in context, and it defines groups as it defines individuals.[1] This last sense forces us to wonder what feminism's "collective self-consciousness" about self-identification does to the sort of group and individual it produces.

In the context of teaching Women's Studies classes, many of us have found that almost every student claims not only that personal experience is a helpful tool in understanding gender and race relations, but in fact that experience is a *crucial* tool in understanding these relations.[2] And yet, in class, we speak only cautiously of our own experiences, preferring to speak of the experience of others, mediated by texts, in our attempts to make sense of some of the problems of feminism, of race theories, and of theories of identity. In addition to the problem of identity, Women's Studies classes often have another interest that may be of use for this essay: "defining differences." By setting "defining differences" in quotation marks, we mean to indicate several interrelated issues: the primacy of the theoretical notion of difference for feminist and race theories, the literal attempt to define difference as a term and concept in any context, and the ways that difference works to define its subjects. That is to say, I use "defining differences" to indicate a complex web of interrelations. Similarly, one of the things that is most difficult about taking on identity politics is the place of identity in the classroom. We have been long taught, as academics, that the personal has little place in the classroom. And yet, as academics involved in Women's Studies, we've also learned that "the personal is political," and that what we teach in the classroom has "real-world" effects.

For the purposes of this essay, personal experiences of definition and difference mixed with theorization about these notions. The goal is a small one: to raise and order *questions* about identity, difference, race, and feminism. The "*mestiza*" term is used in order to reflect on some categories prominent in identity politics, as an effort to examine categorization itself and its implications for Women's Studies and feminist theory. The "*mestiza*"-the woman of mixed origins-presents a useful starting point for changing the debates around race and Women's Studies and for putting the politics of identity into crisis. In this essay, the figure of the "*mestiza*" is used to discuss three main ideas: (1) that race is a marker for power in America that is at once absolutely real and absolutely fictional; (2) that a thorough examination of identity politics, especially insofar as it relates to race, is crucial for coalition building in Women's Studies; and (3) that we must reimagine race in America if we are to capitalize on the potential power of feminist coalitions, in the classroom and in the broad field of Women's Studies. In its current usage, "identity politics" refers to the tendency to base one's politics on a sense of personal identity. This "personal identity" can be multivalent; perhaps the most common identity politics today are those centered on identities like race, gender, religion, and sexuality. The term "identity politics" provides a foundation for two salient problems: the too common tendency to crudely define race and ethnicity in popular understanding, and the dependence of feminist theory and Women's Studies on self-identification and identity politics.[3] This essay focuses on the "*mestiza*," who is at once, irrevocably, white and other, because to be part white and part "other" constitutes a troubled relationship to the power structure.[4] Both as a feminist subject and as an object of feminist inquiry, the "*mestiza*" occupies at least two (usually opposed) positions at once; in her elemental state she is both "first" and "third" world, and so embodies the very oppositions that often are used to define the problems at hand.[5]

Judy Scales-Trent is a white-looking woman, a lawyer, who identifies herself as African-American: she calls herself "a white black woman." In her book, *Notes of a White Black Woman; Race, Color, Community*, she uses her own life to illustrate some of the difficulties that come with believing in the "seemingly discrete categories 'black' and 'white'" (2). Often mistaken for white, Scales-Trent concludes from her experiences that "'Race' is not a biological fact but a social construct, and a clumsy one, at that" (2).[6] Indeed, the gauges we have been taught to rely on, our eyes and our ears, are often extremely untrustworthy.[7]

Many popular understandings of race depend upon the equation of race with color, which is to say that much of race theory has to do with the specular.[8] But race is not simply black and white, neither literally nor figuratively. As mixed-race people like Scales-Trent often demonstrate, appearances can be deceiving. This suggests two things: first, that consistently, in everyday conversations and in academic forums, intelligent people who know better speak as if there were only two races in this country, black and white;[9] and second, that there is a common assumption that, perhaps because these are often regarded as the only two racial categories, race can be read off of bodies.[10] But as Scales-Trent declares, her mixed-race existence "raises troubling questions. Suppose race really *does* have nothing to do with color? What, then, is it all about?" (8).

On the one hand, to claim that race has *everything* to do with color is to claim that race is simply a biological fact or, even more elementary, that race is simply a way to categorize people. To claim that race has everything to do with color, then, is to relegate the category of race to the realm of the merely descriptive. Perhaps part of the reason that African-American women have become this academic site of alterity is that they are *seemingly* easily defined and imagined in a visually defined world. Painted black and white, African-Americans seem to be easily identified.[11] Despite the popularity of the category "of color," which is quite open, white (and nonwhite) Americans seem to have difficulty picturing who might count as "of color" beyond the bounds of black and white. This visually defined understanding of race often leaves out the "*mestiza*." But Scales-Trent is correct: we must remove color from our idea of what race is. To say, on the other hand, that "race really does have *nothing* to do with color," is to make clear what we already know: that race descriptions are not merely descriptive but prescriptive. Scales-Trent's suggestion that race has nothing to do with color can be taken one step farther: race, then, has everything to do with power relations. Race is one of the foremost sites of defining differences: the assignment of racial categories, at least the pretense, that is, of describing manifest differences between groups and individuals, works to solidify and create the very categories it claims merely to present.[12] We must wonder precisely what power relations those categories represent. If, as Trinh T. Minh-ha writes, "To raise the question of identity is to re-open...the discussion on the self/other relationship in its enactment of power relations,"[13] then which power relations, exactly, are enacted by the "*mestiza*," who is at once self and other, in the most irreconcilable way?

There are several nodes of power that have to do with identity and feminism. There is the affirmative action debate, currently under siege in California in particular. There is the ever problematic understanding of feminism as a primarily white, middle-class field of study and practice.[14] And then there is the struggle over the power to define and to imagine, and therefore to dictate our imaginings.

It has become standard to track data via descriptive questionnaires. As academics, we see them most often when we switch institutional affiliations and are asked to fill out countless forms from the personnel or "diversity initiatives offices" of the universities that interview us, hire us, or train us for our degrees. Indeed, versions of this questionnaire abound in many nonacademic forms we fill out on a regular basis as well: from driver's license applications to the U.S. Census forms.[15] One of the pieces of the questionnaire is The Race Question, which often reads something like this: "Self-identification by race is strictly voluntary. Circle one: Asian, Black, Caucasian, Hispanic, Native American (Indian, Eskimo, Aleut), Other (please specify)." On statistical information forms of this sort, required of universities by the U.S. Department of Education, fractions are not allowed. In fact, if one attempts to exist between categories, either by using "½" as an indicator in two of the available fields, or by checking "Other" and specifying, for example, "*mestiza*: half Asian and half Caucasian," the choice is generally made for one: one is defined as either Asian or Caucasian. In the complicated realm of "third world" feminism, the *mestiza*, the woman of mixed-race parentage occupies a similarly vexed and vexing position, for she is not "simply" anything: not simply white, not simply American, not simply "of color." I draw attention to the figure of the *mestiza* in these two very different contexts, that of the race question in its quotidian uses and that of "third world" feminism.

When I began graduate school in 1988, I was sent one of those all-too-familiar forms to fill out, one not unlike the pre-employment questionnaires sent out by virtually every university in the country. The form asked some easy questions: my year of birth, my campus address and phone number, my department affiliation, and my intended degree. My sex? F. Veteran? No. Disability? No. It asked a few harder ones; I remember struggling, for example, over my permanent address. And then came the ever-annoying "race/ethnicity" question.

My father is a very white white man, pale skin and distinct roots in the small Jewish community of Omaha, Nebraska. My mother is a Filipino woman, darker skin that she carefully keeps light, and a hint of Indang or Quezon City discernible in her grammatically perfect English. So I am a *"mestiza,"* in the dictionary sense of the word.[16] As I filled out The Form for the first time at Brown University in late 1988, I looked at the Race/Ethnic Origin choices; nothing for *"mestiza,"* and no "other" box to check. I put a ½ in "white" and a ½ in "Asian-Pacific Islander." When the form came back for verification, someone had chosen "White" for me. I wrote a politely nasty letter, asking, basically, "What about my mother?" The form came back a second time, this time with a different single box checked: "Asian Pacific Islander." I sent another politely nasty letter: What about my father? They stopped asking for my verification.

This experience, and experiences like it, have been as central as my read-ings in race theory and in my understanding of what is at stake when we speak of race in this country. As I will explain in a moment, there has always been a great deal at stake in terms of economics when we speak of race here. But, and I cannot emphasize this enough, all of these economic relations simultaneously mark (and mask) personal relations. In blithely assigning me to whatever unitary category theychoose, the problem is that bureaucrats not only misrepresent me, they also erase one of my flesh-and-blood parents.

There has been a distinct historical shift in classification of the *mestiza*, a shift in what counts as "of color" in America. The shift is pronounced: from the mulatto, who counted as "Negro" if only one in eight great-grandparents was black, to the twentieth-century affirmative action tendency to characterize mixed-race people as Caucasian, as "not the real thing," as if only the white parent counts.[17] From the one-eighth laws, one might understand that nonwhite origins are inescap-able, and perhaps the message that they must be escaped if one strives for privi-lege.[18] At the same time, the affirmative action tendency to count one who is equal parts white and non-white as White, particularly when that nonwhite part is not African-American and carries a similarly complicated message: the hegemony is at once acknowledging the privilege inherent in whiteness and implying that non-whiteness, via affirmative action, which is aimed at correcting inequalities, brings a measure of privilege. This is particularly problematic. As Karen I. Blu explains,

For Whites, blood is a substance that can either be racially pure or racially polluted. Black blood pollutes White blood absolutely, so that, in the logical extreme, one drop of Black blood makes an otherwise White man black...White ideas about "Indian blood" are less formalized and clear-cut...It may take only one drop of Black blood to make a person a Negro, but it takes a lot of Indian blood to make a person a "real" Indian.[19]

Taken in historical context, Blu's comments underscore the workings of privilege in race assignment. Insofar as making an "otherwise White man black" was once a way of making an otherwise free person a potential piece of property, the white-dominated U.S. has long had a habit of equating the smallest amount of black ancestry with black status. However, the tribal land-rights and privileges that may be accorded to Native Americans are (in theory at least) of high value today. Thus, it takes a great deal more (nonwhite) Native American "blood" to give a person Native American status.[20]

    This becomes all the more resonant in what was Newt Gingrich's America. Recently, the so-called culture wars have battled over the latest version of the White Man's Burden: the possibility that white men are now in positions of inferiority, constantly discriminated against because of who their forebears were, constantly victims of "reverse discrimination." There is a double measure of idiocy here; it is as if affirmative action were not created to right the wrongs of the past, that is, as if we have suddenly reached full parity between all races in the U.S. and as if the paltry and meager "privileges" of affirmative action can begin to compare with the privileges of white masculinity. It is an amazing con job: How many white men would really like to trade positions? Feminists can see the idiocy here, but it would be foolish to dismiss this logic, given the obvious power of its dangerous rhetoric.

    The *mestiza* as a problem of naming suggests a way to complicate this power of naming: in the way she problematizes categorization, she suggests an anticategory category, much in the way that Ellen Rooney describes Women's Studies as an antidisciplinary discipline. For Rooney, Women's Studies and African-American studies in some settings succeed in resisting the strong pull of the regularization of the academy insofar as its students often bring their political work to bear on their intellectual work, insofar as "a critique of knowledge production is never merely a side-effect of political activity outside the university," but is instead a part of the academic behavior of its university constituents, and insofar as "[f]eminist theory in the academy is constituted by the discovery that a politicized, theoretical intervention within the disciplines is unavoidable" (Rooney 20, 21). That is to say, feminist theory and Women's Studies demand that their constituents adapt a skeptical approach to the university. My hope is that the *mestiza* can bring a similar insistence on skepticism (albeit on a much smaller scale) to race theory and Women's Studies. As a concept so clearly opposed to easy classification by race, the "*mestiza*" helps to empty out or denaturalize identity-based categories, and helps remind us of the politics intrinsic to such naming.

    This is why formulations like Gloria Anzaldúa's "*mestiza* consciousness" must be resisted, despite their obvious appeals.[21] For to suggest that all "*mestizas*" share some sort of innate, unitary consciousness, to insist, as my students often do, that is some sort of universalized political attitude that has little to do with a specific definition involving one's parentage, is to strip away the power of the anticategory. In investing the term (or ones like it) with such humanism, one insists on the academy's meanings. Then, as Christina Crosby suggests, "The academy will recognize differences everywhere, cheerfully acknowledging that since everyone is different, everyone is the same" (140).

    At the same time, Ross Possnock points out some of the problems inherent in embracing a multiracial identity:

There is also worry [that] multiracialism's mockery of the binary opposition black or white might (finally convince Americans of the absurdity of racial classifications) but at the cost of dividing the black community and reducing its political power. This worry is part of a larger question: what sort of politics emerges out of an embrace of miscegenated subjectivity? An answer must somehow negotiate colliding imperatives, a postmodern one of fluidity and a political one of collective unity. (105)

Possnock poses a useful question here: What might be the effects of "multiracialism's mockery of the binary opposition black or white"? But his comment also points to the very failure in imagination: the tendency to see the world (through the U.S., of course) as made of two races, black and white, and to conflate all nonwhites with the black community. Possnock shows his lack of imagination: he can see multiracialism only in terms of the African-American community and its political power as a community. What of the other non-white races in this country? What of the possible dilution of "white" that multiracialism offers (as evidenced by the large number of respondents to the US census who chose "Hispanic" over "White" when finally given the option)? What of the possibility of political coalition between nonwhites and partial-whites that multiracialism offers? This led me to wonder what sort of politics emerges from such a binary understanding of racial subjectivity. What does a multiracial identity allow politically and imaginatively? Does it merely divide the disenfranchised, as Possnock suggests? Is what Possnock calls the "powerful bias to naturalize classification as identity" (105) so strong that it overdetermines the response to the problem of naming the *mestiza* illicit? [22]

The shift in the "defining definitions" of race and gender have important consequences for feminism. As Barbara Christian notes,

Often women of color are represented in [feminist] scholarship by Afro-American women, as if Chicanas, Asian Americans, or Native Americans, not to mention women living outside this country, did not have their own specific contexts. If we are to move beyond a stultifying and false unity toward a more accurate, rich inquiry into the worlds of women, and therefore to new ideas about how liberations might come about, we will have to do more than acknowledge or cite differences; we may have to see the intersections of our many differences as central to the quality of our work. (64)

Feminism has long been thought of as a single, unitary movement of theory, and, as such, has been accused of being a "white, middle-class women's movement." Historically this may have been true, one need only reread Betty Friedan to see how early radical feminism spoke to a limited audience. Today, however, feminists and others conceptualize feminism in greater varieties, rather than as a unitary monolith. Barbara Christian argues that this reconception of multiple feminism is important; it is a first step in what she calls "the growing tendency among feminist scholars, who are [often] still white, middle class, and apparently heterosexual, to move away from the universal unified simplistic Abstract to more complex inquiries [that] may result in more accurate, exciting, and transformative scholarship" (63). The next step, according to Christian, is to "move beyond a stultifying and false unity" by changing the ways that scholarship treats difference. We must not just list or cite differences, she says. Instead, we must see differences as "central to the quality of our work." In the light of the strong work in feminist theory and Women's Studies that engages differences as a matter of practice, Butler, Rooney, Minh-ha, Mohanty, Fuss, and hooks all leap immediately to mind as examples, Christian's call seems to be less about inventing a new practice and more about redefining one already in place. That is to say, Christian reminds feminist scholars that part of what makes us feminists is an insistence upon the politico-theoretical idea of differences. As she suggests, we need to see the intersection of our many differences as central to the quality of our work, then to ask what is at stake in our current understandings of race and gender, and how we are taught to conceptualize them as discrete issues.

Is this understanding of race a linguistic problem? Gilbert and Gubar, Lorde, Irigaray, hooks, and a host of others have convincingly shown how our basic language is problematic for feminism. Western languages are mired in patriarchy; in fact, are patriarchy. It is important that we see how Western languages and the popular discourses of race theory are also responsible for limiting our conceptions of race. We have been trying to see race in discrete categories (in black and white) when it clearly is not so simple. Every time someone assigns me a single race, I see a "failure in imagination." But this failure is less an individual one than a collective one: we must learn how to reconceptualize race. One way into such a reconception is to examine a specific subject position: feminist teacher.

In *The Alchemy of Race and Rights*, Patricia Williams discusses the interrelation between race, law, and feminism at length. It is an interesting book, written by the well-known African-American woman law professor as a series of anecdotes, and even anecdotes within anecdotes. I want to conclude by considering two brief excerpts from her book. For feminism has taught me just what Williams illustrates: that power relations in the classroom and in every aspect of "social life" are arbitrary; and that, despite their arbitrary nature, power relations have very real effects. This is important because race has everything to do with power. Williams's book develops this claim:

We, as law teachers, create miniworlds of reality, by the faith that students put in our tutelage of the rules of reality. We define the boundaries of the legitimate and the illegitimate, in a more ultimately powerful way than almost anyone else in the world. It is enormously important therefore to consider the process by which we include and the process by which we exclude. (88)

Here, Williams speaks as a law teacher, yet her comments apply to Women's Studies teachers as well. In first-year composition classes and in graduate seminars, Women's Studies teachers create "miniworlds of reality" by everything they do: by the reading materials they include or exclude in their syllabi, by the types of writing we consider valid or problematic, and by the ways they allow students to interact with each other and with themselves. By foregrounding identity politics they create their problematic: they are at once bound up by and bound to question the politics of identity.

This next story in Williams's book helps illustrate the perils of forgetting that we create these "miniworlds of reality" while it takes on the current obsession with so-called reverse discrimination:

I am always aware of the ex-football player/student whom I had told in class to read the cases more carefully; he came to my office to tell me that I had humiliated him in front of everyone and he was going to "get you, lady." At that, I ordered him out of my office, whereupon he walked down to the associate dean's office and burst into tears, great heaving, football-player sobs, the tears dripping off the tip of his nose, as it was described to me later. Now I admit that all of the possible ways in which I thought he might get me, this was the one for which I was the least prepared; but it could not have been more effective in terms of coalescing both the student body and the administration against me. I became the drill sergeant. A militant black woman who took out her rage on her students. Someone who could make a big man like him cry and cry hard. (96-7)

In this case Williams gives her student a gender and a size when she refers to him as a "big man," but no race. So we can read this particular parable of "reverse discrimination" as a physical, gendered parable, not a racialized one.[23] The overt lesson that the student body and the administration teach Williams here is that power is relational, and that in the context of law school, William's superior position as teacher is more powerful than the ex-football player/student his position as a physically large and presumably strong male. Indeed, Williams explains the situation by saying that her ability to frighten this man "lies in the power I wield as a teacher over all my students" (97). But note that this is only part of the answer. Her ostensible question is "How did my self-assertion become so powerful as to frighten, frustrate, or humiliate this man?" I'd like to suggest that her brief anecdote implies that there is much more at stake in this discussion.

Williams's surprise is understandable: given what the statement "I'm going to get you, lady" indicates, she must have been expecting either physical violence or an overt verbal attack. Instead, the student employs a wholly different and unexpected discourse: he cries in front of the dean. This rhetorical move is incredibly powerful, as is the cry of reverse discrimination. For, in a binaristic world of the oppressed and the oppressor, to take on one role is also effectively to assign the other. The student's taking the role of the weeping, feminized/unsexed oppressed, Williams only the role of the masculinized oppressor. Perhaps the real power of the cry of reverse discrimination lies in the discursive positions of (race and) gender that it rewrites. We might do well to follow the suggestion of Cherríe Moraga, who reminds her readers that to truly understand another person's oppression, one must remember one's own experiences of oppression. But, at the same time, as Moraga says, the danger lies in forgetting the specificity of each oppression. That is to say, a burly ex-football player and a law professor may each wield an enormous amount of power, but rarely in the same world. Women of color, as well as students and faculty in Women's Studies programs, depend upon self-identification to create intellectual and political communities. But does this dependence on definitions build walls within as well as outside of feminism?

NOTES

1. Yen Le Espiritu, "Colonial Oppression, Labour Importation, and Group Formation: Filipinos in the United States," *Ethnic and Racial Studies* 19 (1996), 30. Yen Le Espiritu adds to this discussion of ethnic identification by taking on the opposite mecha-

nism, identification by others: "In explaining ethnicization, the process whereby ethnic groups come into being in the first place, scholars have focused primarily on two factors: categorization and external threats...Categorization refers to situations in which a more powerful group ascriptively classifies another; and external threats can be defined broadly as 'outside pressure—social, political, or economic—exerted against a group because of its ethnicity'...Though important, this approach fails to recognize that the identities of immigrants (particularly immigrants of colour) have been shaped not only by the social location of their group within their host country but also by the position of their country within the global racial order."

2. I often teach "Mixed Origins and the Category of Identity." This course is wide-ranging in the type of texts we use texts range from memoir to manifesto, from poem to novel, from history to diatribe to film to television but narrow in focus. And virtually every text that we read, from Gloria Anzaldúa's *Borderlands* to Carol Camper's *Miscegenation Blues*, emphasizes the role of personal experience in theorizing power relationships (whether those power relationships are in the guise of families, of patriarchy, of love relationships, of law, or of the classroom).

3. A broader understanding of gender in general, and of men in particular, are of course important to feminist inquiry; I limit my discussion to women in this essay to provide specificity.

4. Iris Marion Young, "Gender as Seriality: Thinking About Women as a Social Collective," *Signs* 19 (1994), 719. In a 1994 article, Young says that "Elizabeth Spelman shows definitively the mistake in any attempt to isolate gender from identities such as race, class, age, sexuality and ethnicity to uncover the attributes that women have in common...The absurdity of trying to isolate gender identity from race or class identity becomes apparent if you ask a woman 'to distinguish the "woman part" of herself from the "class part," for example.' "Gender," Spelman argues "is a relational concept, not the naming of an essence."

5. I really use this sentence for want of a better short statement. By it, I mean to indicate feminisms that purport to be multicultural or that attempt to take race into consideration. And I choose the term "third world feminism" precisely because of the awkwardness it produces. In the US, it is often used to indicate feminisms that are not dominated by so-called white, Western feminism, even when those feminisms are produced by members of the so-called first world.

6. Clara E. Rodriguez, and Hector Cordero-Guzman, "Placing Race in Context," *Ethnic and Racial Studies* 15 (1994), 523. Rodriguez and Cordero-Guzman note that by the 1960s "Race as a biological construct was useless...race, as people experience it, is a cultural construct." That is to say, they argue that there is no cross-cultural conception of race; it varies from culture to culture. However, they use the example of the US as a place where "race is conceived as being biologically or genetically based," as opposed to Latin America, where race tends to be conceived as a thick mixture of bloodlines, class, physical type, and ethnic background.

7. It has been my experience that single-race people, especially whites, have a tendency to read light-skinned, mixed-race people as white, and dark-skinned, mixed-race people as African-American or "of color," while mixed-race people seem to easily identify the mixture in others.

8. For first-person accounts of encounters with those who believe they can read one's race from one's appearance, Lise Funderburg, *Black, White, Other: Biracial Americans Talk About Race and Identity*. New York: William Morrow, 1994. Judy Scales-Trent, *Notes of a White Black Woman; Race, Color, Community*. University Park: Pennsylvania State U P, 1995); and, Claire Huang Kinsley: "Questions People Have Asked Me. Ques-

tions I Have Asked Myself," *Miscegenation Blues; Voices of Mixed Race Women.* ed. Carol Camper. (Toronto: Sister Vision, 1994), 113-47.

9. Scales-Trent points out that by the year 2010, Mexican-Americans should out-number African-Americans in the U.S. And she reminds her readers that there are ra-cial/ethnic groups like Jews who do not neatly fit into the category of "white" despite their appearances to the contrary.

10 Obviously, one of the reasons that "African-American" has come to stand in for "nonwhite" in academia is that African -American studies is widely varied and well developed; its history as a field of study is longer than many other fields that comprise "ethnic studies."

11. When I speak of African-American women as this academic site of alterity I am referring to Christian's and bell hooks's appropriate complaints of African-American women's dual role as "token" voices for all women of color in political/academic circles, and as speaking subjects and as objects of academic/political inquiry.

12. My notion of prescription by description is indebted to Louis Althusser's "Ideology and Ideological State Apparatuses," in his *Lenin and Philosophy and Other Essays*, trans. Ben Brewster (New York: Monthly Review Press, 1971).

13. Trinh T. Minh-ha, "Not You/Like You: Post-Colonial Women and the Inter-locking Questions of Identity and Difference," presented at the conference "Feminism and the Critique of Colonialist Discourse Conference," University of California at Santa Cruz, April 25, 1987, 12. (qtd. Gloria Anzaldúa, ed., *Making Face Making Soul / Haciendo Caras: Creative and Critical Perspectives by Women of Color* (San Francisco: Aunt Lute, 1990.)

14 . It is, of course, true that U.S. feminism is often in the domain of white-middle class women. But I am a bit impatient at the mandatory repetition of this mantra, found in so many otherwise interesting feminist writings and talks.

15. Sam Roberts, *Who We Are: A Portrait of America Based on the Latest US Census.* (New York: Times Books, 1994). There is a disclaimer by the U. S. government in its materials for both the 1980 and 1990 censuses: "The concept of race as used by the Census Bureau reflects self-identification by respondents; it does not denote any clear-cut scientific definition of biological stock." But this has not stopped the production of books whose titles claim to be able to determine Who We Are with the census results. The 2000 Census will not include a multiracial category, but Americans of mixed ancestry will be able to list themselves in an many racial categories as apply rather than choosing only one.

16. For the purposes of this essay, which discusses feminism in today's white-dominated U.S., I am interested specifically in the *mestiza* whose mixed parentage includes Caucasian in the mix. Clearly, one can be a mixture of two or more nondominant cultures. However, insofar as such a mixture implies a very different relation to the power structures in the U.S., it is the subject for another time.

17. I must note that there is a great deal more here than I can attend to in this es-say. Among other issues, not all white/nonwhite mixtures are treated in the same fashion in the U.S. Perhaps in recompense for the one-eighth laws, African-American mixtures are more often accorded nonwhite status for affirmative action purposes than are many other mixtures. Class status adds a clear problem in accounting for protected status in affirmative action. And, of course, only some nonwhite races "enjoy" protected status.

18. Scales-Trent adds that the theory of "hypodescent" is an anthropological term meaning "racial mixed people are assigned the status of the subordinate group," and that today the "one-drop rule" for African-Americans, though generally not codified, is still "generally accepted by both black and white communities in the US" (4).

19. Quoted in Louis Owens, "Other Destinies, Other Plots: An Introduction to In-dian Novels," *Other Destinies: Understanding the American Indian Novel*, (Norman: U of

Oklahoma P, 1992), 331.

20. Owens further complicates this model by noting that Native Americans also have an unusual problem relating to their place in the world's literary imagination. He says that the "American Indian in the world consciousness is a treasured invention, a gothic artifact like the 'powwows' of Hawthorne..." and therefore supposed to be long-vanished (3).

21. Anzaldúa in fact invests the *mestiza* with innate politics, as if one's parentage can ever mandate one's politics, when she says,

La *mestiza* constantly has to shift out of habitual formations; from convergent thinking, analytical reasoning that tends to use rationality to move toward a single goal (a Western mode), to divergent thinking, characterized by a movement away from set patterns and goals and toward a more whole perspective, one that includes rather than excludes. (79)

Her language gives her away here; Anzaldúa assumes that one's politics can be understood from one's identity. In this quotation, as in much of her compelling book, her argument is that "*mestiza* consciousness" is more or less a result of being *mestiza*, rather than of political choice or interpellation. And where does this consciousness lead, for Anzaldúa? Directly to pluralism: Anzaldúa's *mestiza* "has a plural personality, she operates in a pluralistic mode" (ibid).

22. Ross Possnock, "Before and After Identity Politics," *Raritan* 15 (1995), 95-115. Possnock bases his argument in part on Walter Benn Michaels's suggestions that racial identity is almost unavoidable. Michaels writes, "Our sense of culture is characteristically meant to displace race, but part of the argument of this essay has been that culture has turned out to be a way of continuing rather than repudiating racial thought," ("Race into Culture: A Critical Genealogy of Cultural Identity," in Appiah and Gates, 61). He insists that antiessentialism is either ineffective or untenable, "US social relations have been and continue to be organized in part by race. My point has been to assert that this basicorganization is the consequence of a mistake, and that antiessentialist defenses of race amount to nothing more than new ways of making the mistake" (Walter Benn Michaels, "The No-Drop Rule," in Appiah and Gates, 412). Michaels seems to indicate that multiracialism, and mixed race identity, necessarily lead back to either essentialism or pluralism. I wonder, if these are the only possibilities. Or, as Judith Butler suggests, "There is also the possibility of a movement through the temporal and textual distance between what is written and what is read where difference is neither foreclosed nor domesticated," ("Collected and Fractured: Response to Identities," in Appiah and Gates, 446).

23. This is and is not true, actually, for part of the way Williams understands power relations is due to the unavoidable fact that she is not just a woman teacher, but an African-American woman teacher, no matter what the race of her student might be. See Patricia J.Williams, *The Alchemy of Race and Rights: Diary of a Law Professor* (Cambridge: Harvard U P, 1991).

2

The Uses of Silence:
Notes on the "Will to Unsay"

Patti L. Duncan

> From another epic another history. From the missing narrative. From the multi-tude of narratives. Missing. From the chronicles. For another telling for other recitations.
> --Theresa Hak Kyung Cha[1]

> Literary history and the present are dark with silences: some the silences for years by our acknowledged great; some silences hidden; some the ceasing to publish after one work appears; some the never coming to book form at all.

> These are not natural silence, that necessary time for renewal, lying fallow, gesta-tion, in the natural cycle of creation. The silences I speak of here are unnatural; the unnatu-ral thwarting of what struggles to come into being, but cannot. In the old, the obvious parallels: when the seed strikes stone; the soil will not sustain; the spring is false; the time is drought or blight or infestation; the frost comes premature.
> --Tillie Olsen[2]

> Silence. The condition or quality of being or keeping still or silent. The absence of sound...refusal or failure to speak out
> *(The American Heritage Dictionary)*

By calling this essay "The Uses of Silence," I invoke Audre Lorde's essay "The Uses of Anger: Women Responding to Racism," in which she discusses anger as an appropriate, viable, and useful response to racism. Anger, she writes, when "ex-pressed and translated in the service of our vision and our future is a liberating and strengthening act of clarification,... [It] is loaded with information and energy" (127). Lorde compares anger to other, less useful, responses to racism, such as reactionary defensiveness, hatred, and guilt. She suggests that guilt "is not a response to anger; it is a response to one's own actions or lack of action...It becomes a device to protect ignorance and the continuation of things the way they are, the ultimate protection for changelessness" (130). Thus, Lorde effectively reclaims an emotion previously regarded as negative, even harmful. She examines the ways in which anger, within specific contexts, is "loaded with information and energy," and, when used as a means of social and personal transformation, can liberate and clarify. Her words force me to examine my own reactions to racism, and I speak of racism in various forms, the racism I face as a mixed-race, Korean-American woman, and the forms of racism I see in operation against other people of color, which are not always identical to that which I struggle against. However, my anger against racism is often met with silence, sometimes my own, but more often the silence of others upon perceiving it. Making sense of these silences in relation to oppressive contexts is the primary motivation for this essay.

Lorde's analysis of anger in relation to racism also serves to expand and complicate definitions and understandings of both race and racism. Her focus on women's racism links race to gender, suggesting the ways in which such categories of identity are inextricably intertwined, and must be examined synchronously. In this essay, I recognize and acknowledge the many complex ways in which race and gender are structured in our culture, as well as the different forms that racism and sexism enact at various societal levels, from interpersonal interactions to larger sociostructural relationships. Upon careful review, however, there seem to be multiple silences at work in relation to race, gender, sexuality, and national identity. Such silences are suggestive of the various social and political possibilities and processes inherent in discussions of the critical intersections of categories of identity. Hence, I look to the silences within writings by women of color in order to interrogate their meanings to contemporary discourse about the relationships among race, gender, sexuality, and national belonging.

An examination of silence, in relation to the experiences of women of color in the U.S. opens questions regarding history, authenticity, and resistance to subjugation. As a postcolonial reconceptualization and reclamation of silence, this essay attempts to reinscribe its potential as a strategy of resistance. I suggest that an exploration of the uses of silence offers new insights into the ways in which silence operates as a form of discourse and as a means of resistance to hegemonic power. Interrogating and historicizing representations of silence within feminist and postcolonial writings and theories provides one significant site for reconsidering notions of language, translation, memory, and history, processes that remain crucial to liberatory political and social agendas.

Along with silence, I also explore the cultural meanings of speech in the U.S. often conceptualized as the opposite of silence. In fact the two are not binarily opposed, but have most often been understood through such a framework within Western culture. Both speech and silence must be examined for their implicit meanings, the assumptions that underlie our understandings of them, and the complicated associations they have for and with marginalized groups of people in the U.S. To demonstrate these points, I include in this essay a brief discussion of the multiple implications of speech and silence in Maxine Hong Kingston's *The Woman Warrior: Memoirs of a Girlhood Among Ghosts.* [3]

I use the terms "Asian-American" and "Asian-Pacific American" cautiously and rather self-consciously. Though I use these terms interchangeably, in some instances I also recognize the specificity implied by each term. Like Chandra Talpade Mohanty's statements, in "Under Western Eyes" about her decision to use the problematic term "third world woman," I recognize that while "[this] is the only terminology available to us at the moment," we must continue to question such designations. Mohanty suggests that she employs the term in order to designate a common context of struggle, and to link women from various social and geographical locations (52-54). In fact, and most notably, she pushes the term beyond geography, to demarcate a space that is social and political. Thus, "third world," in this context, suggests those women often defined as being outside the current mainstream notions of feminism--women of developing countries, women of color in the Western world, poor women, lesbian and bisexual women, in fact any women who choose to align themselves with "minority" women, who are situated within contexts of struggle, and/or who imagine themselves as part of a community committed to exploring the relationship among race, gender, class, sexual identity, and national belonging.[4] Thus, "third world women" implies a political definition--not an essentialist one. Similarly, Beverly Guy-Sheftall also advocates use of the term "Third World women," rather than or in addition to "women of color" in some contexts. She suggests that, although problematic, "third world women" may be more useful in moving out of the binary black/white framework so often implied by the term "women of color," and also situates feminist struggle within a global context.[5]

I use the term "Asian-American" in the broadest sense, to refer to North Americans of Asian descent.[6] Asian-American has been preferred by many activists in the U.S. since the 1960s, when the word "Oriental" was critiqued and then discarded as a derogatory term connoting exoticism and inferiority. Also in the 1960s, the hyphen was eliminated by some writers and activists in order to affirm Asian-Americans' sense of being American by avoiding the inference of split identities and not-quite-American status, as well as stereotypes of conflicted and tragically bifurcated Asian-American identities. Other women of color, such as Gloria Anzaldúa, offer critiques of terms for ethnic groups that place the ethnicity first, as an adjective, before the noun "American" (1987, 53-64). To Anzaldúa such a practice only conveys that, for example, "Mexican Americans" are neither Mexican nor American, but when push comes to shove, must identify more as "American" than "Mexican"; to her this is a form of "copping out." Yet other members of ethnic minority groups have suggested that by claiming "American" for ourselves, we assert our status as belonging, and we intervene into preconceived ideas about what "American", after all, means.

"Asian-American" as a term comes with its own set of problems. For instance, it masks differences among people of Asian descent based on national origin and national identity, region, class, generation, religion, and so on. It seems to imply some sort of unity among all Asian countries, which is not the case (in fact, there are long and complicated histories of colonization, war, and partitions among and within Asian countries). "Asian-American" does not specify immigration and generational differences, though a great deal has been written about, for instance, the issei, nisei, and aansei generations within Japanese American communities.[7]

Finally, use of the term "Asian-American" tends to marginalize certain groups and individuals that, at various historical moments, may or may not fall into this category legally, politically, or culturally. At the same time, "Asian-American" seems to center other groups. For example, it supposedly denotes those of Chinese, Japanese, Korean, Filipino, East Indian, Pakistani, Vietnamese, Thai, Burmese, Cambodian, Laotian, and Pacific Islander descent, among others. However, at various historical moments, people of South Asian descent have been considered other than Asian or Asian-American. Pacific Islanders currently face exclusion, marginalization, or simply being engulfed by the classification, Asian-American--"swallowed whole and remaining ever invisible among (East) "Asian-Americans" (Kauanui and Han, 377). People of mixed heritage fail to live up to the standard image implied by the term "Asian-American". In fact, according to Lisa Lowe, anyone who is not male, heterosexual, middle-class, of East Asian descent, and English-speaking does not qualify as "Asian-American" in the sense that the term is often coded. Similarly, Elaine Kim writes that historically, there have not been many ways to be "Asian-American": "The ideal was male, heterosexual, Chinese or Japanese American and English-speaking. The center of Chinese America was San Francisco or New York Chinatown, and the heart of Japanese America was in Hawaii or along Highway 99,...Asian-American history was about railroads, 'bachelor societies,' and internment" (12-13).

Asian-Americans, then, have been homogenized by mainstream American culture and by those who comprise the so-called norm within Asian-American communities. Members of dominant groups within the United States, who have argued for the exclusion of Asians from this nation, have viewed Asians as an expendable workforce and as interchangeable ("they all look alike"). Dominant groups within Asian America (e.g., East Asians, men, the affluent and middle-class, the English-speaking), in their attempts to represent the "model minority" of the United States, have also homogenized Asian-Americans, ignoring and erasing differences in gender, class, language, ethnicity, and even region and history. It is this homogenization of Asian-Americans that in some cases contributes to the oppression and cultural discrimination Asian-Americans face in the United States. Lowe suggests that we acknowledge the ways in which cultural definitions must change along with social and economic realities: "The boundaries and definitions of Asian-American culture are continually shifting and being contested from pressures both 'inside' and 'outside' the Asian-origin community" (66). She urges us to recognize the ways in which Asian America constitutes heterogeneous, hybrid, and multiple social locations.

I employ the term "Asian-American," then, with full awareness of its problematic political and social implications. As a strategic term and group identification, it lends itself to the illusion of unity, masking differences that, some argue, threaten the already precarious position of Asians in the United States However, recognition of such differences can also strengthen Asian-American communities, especially with careful consideration of the historical trajectories of the different experiences of Asian-Americans.

The notion of silence has long been a trope in liberation movements in the

United States, including women's liberation, gay and lesbian liberation, and civil rights movements of people of color.[8] Since the late 1960s and early 1970s, feminist and African-American, Asian and Pacific-Islander American, Native American, Latino/a, and Chicano/a activist leaders have advocated to their constituencies the importance of "finding a voice," of "speaking out" against oppression and injustice, and of moving away from the silences that may imply consent to subjugation as well as to the maintenance of dominant power.[9] The liberatory rhetoric of the gay and lesbian movement also utilizes notions of "speaking out" and "breaking silence" by linking those acts with the process of coming out. And finally, AIDS activists proclaim "Silence = Death" and demand that we "break the silence" imposed upon our lives. This rhetoric, its common appeal to "speaking out," "finding a voice," and "breaking silence," places its liberatory aspirations precisely within the discourses of speech, suggesting that speech itself represents liberation, whereas in opposition to speech, silence represents both the precondition and the very foundations of oppression.

Invisibility, loss, absence, repression, oppression, the unspoken, the unknown--these concepts continue to be equated with silence, whereas visibility, gain, presence, liberation, and "truth" are equated with the act of speech itself. As such, silence becomes antithetical to liberatory agendas and practices in the realm of political activism and in fields of scholarship. In these contexts, certain Eurocentric premises regarding social norms about speech and silence prevail. "Free" speech is supposedly one of the few protected "rights" of citizens. However, as Kyo Maclear suggests, the idea that all speech is "free" is open to critique. She notes the frequent operations of censorship and oppression, and questions the notion that democratic participation and representation are ensured through "speech." This speech is located in a Western philosophical tradition that posits, in the words of Maclear, "speech = agency = freedom" (8). Thus, subjectivity is defined in opposition to silence. Concurrently, speech is conceived to be a necessary condition for subjectivity.

Speech and silence are themes that continue to recur among feminist writings and in the writings of people of color in the United States Adrienne Rich, in her influential essay, "Taking Women Students Seriously" (1978), writes about women's silences in the classroom. She urges readers to consciously explore the actions and behaviors of women students, especially women's relationships to language, speech, and silence:

Look at the many kinds of women's faces, postures, expressions. Listen to the women's voices. Listen to the silences, the unasked questions, the blanks. Listen to the small, soft voices, often courageously trying to speak up, voices of women taught early that tones of confidence, challenge, anger, or assertiveness, are strident and unfeminine. Listen to the voices of the women and the voices of the men; observe the space men allow themselves, physically and verbally, the male assumption that people will listen, even when the majority of the group is female. Look at the faces of the silent, and of those who speak. Listen to a woman groping for language in which to express what is on her mind, sensing that the terms of academic discourse are not her language, trying to cut down her thought to the dimensions of a discourse not intended for her. (243-244)

To Rich, then, speech, assertiveness, even confidence, are discouraged in women during processes of socialization, because such qualities are assumed to be unfeminine, and therefore threatening to the status quo. For a woman to break free from such constraints requires grappling with and overcoming socialization and societal expectations of gender roles, and also language, because the very language that surrounds us is a male-dominated discourse, and of language of male domination over women. Similarly, Gloria Anzaldúa, nearly ten years later, writes that "language is a male discourse" (1987, 54). Recounting an experience of the first time she overheard two Spanish-speaking women use the word *nosotras* (a feminine rewriting of the generally masculine plural form, *nosotros*), she writes, "I was shocked. I had not known the word existed. We are robbed of our female being by the masculine plural" (54). Silences, in these two examples, result from gender socialization and cultural domination.[10]

bell hooks also urges women, especially women of color, to start "talking back," to challenge silences, in order to become subjects (and no longer objects) of our experiences and lives. Underlying her analysis of women's silences is a complex understanding of various differences that speech and silence may represent for members of different societal groups. "Within feminist circles," she writes, "silence is often seen as the sexist 'right speech of womanhood'--the sign of woman's submission to patriarchal authority" (1989, 6). However, while it might be accurate to suggest that white women have been silent (and silenced), hooks argues, women in black communities have not. The struggle for Black women, she suggests, "has not been to emerge from silence into speech but to change the nature and direction of our speech, to make a speech that compels listeners, one that is heard" (6). Thus, it is not simply that silence can and must be replaced with speech (any silence, any speech). Rather, as stated earlier, both speech and silence must be continually interrogated for their meanings, both explicit and implicit. As modes of discourse, they suggest certain assumptions about and associations for people of color in the United States.

Other writers, including Darlene Clark Hine, Paula Giddings, Evelyn Brooks Higginbotham, and Patricia Hill Collins, have discussed the politics of silence in the history of African-American women, where sexuality in particular represents an unspoken/unknown realm, for a variety of historical reasons. These silences of black women, although protective devices, have also had physical, psychological, and emotional consequences. Hine suggests that rape and/or the threat of rape influenced the development of a "culture of dissemblance" among them, within a context of institutionalized sexual violence against them. Defining dissemblance as "the behavior and attitudes of black women that created the appearance of openness and disclosure [while] actually shield[ing] the truth of their inner lives and selves from their oppressors" (292), Hine argues that this culture was an effect and "ideological consequence" of the consolidation of links between black women and illicit sexuality during the antebellum years. Thus, in the face of multiple attacks upon all aspects of black women's sexuality, dissemblance became a strategy of self-protection and a means of retaining some sense of self and control over their own bodies, sexuality, reproduction, and children (293-294). Though this culture of dissemblance became an effective tool for protection, and enabled Black women to assert agency over their own bodies and lives, Hine argues that one major consequence of such a culture has been the "absence of sophisticated historical discussion of the impact of rape (or threat of rape) and incidences of domestic violence on the shape of black women's experiences" (295). In addition, many black women, she argues, have felt "compelled to downplay, even deny, sexual expression" (295), in order to counter negative stereotypes. The silences, in this case, though strategic and useful, have had very real consequences.

Abdul JanMohamed refers to the institution of slavery in the United States as an "open secret" in which racialized sexuality functioned historically as a peculiar *silence*, a will to conceal, rather than a will to knowledge, in the Foucaultian sense. In JanMohamed's analysis, silence remains a force of oppression, whereby certain groups not only have been silenced historically, but also effectively written out of history itself. He argues for an "equal historical articulation" for African-Americans, in particular (116). Such an articulation must include not simply inserting African-Americans into history, but critically revising the methods and tools of historicization. Thus, he seems to suggest, it is only through articulation, an act of speech , that we can address the silences surrounding the historical oppression of African-Americans.

Audre Lorde asserts the necessity, for oppressed groups of people, to find ways to transform our silences into actions that may be part of various struggles to end domination. In her essay, "The Transformation of Silence into Language and Action," she writes, "My silences have not protected me. Your silence will not protect you...What are the words you do not have yet? What do you need to say?" (41). Describing the discovery that she had breast cancer, and her subsequent feelings about the possibility of death, Lorde states that she was "forcibly and essentially aware of [her] mortality...and what [she] most regretted were [her] silences" (41). It was "learning to put fear into a perspective," she writes, that gave her the strength to break those silences (41). That Lorde mentions fear is significant to her analysis of silence, for she suggests that fear is commonplace for marginalized and oppressed groups of people who, in fact, were "never meant to survive" (42). Breaking silences, to Lorde, does not mean living without fear, but simply speaking out despite the fears of censure, of contempt, of judgment, of challenge, of visibility, and even of annihilation. She argues that because of distorted and stereotypical images and interlocking systems of racism and sexism in this country, visibility is simultaneously the greatest source of vulnerability and the greatest source of strength for women of color (42).

Other writers also link speaking and silence to notions of visibility and invisibility. Mitsuye Yamada exhorts Asian Pacific Islander-American women to "make ourselves more visible by speaking out on the condition of our sex and race and on certain political issues which concern us" (71). Yet she cautions against the kind of visibility that is reducible to stereotypes and one-dimensional representations of "the passive, sweet...'Oriental woman'" (71). Thus, it is not that any visibility, or any act of speech for that matter, will do. Rather, speaking out and being seen must occur in very particular ways to be of any value to the kinds of societal transformations these writers advocate. In other words, language and visibility that can be reduced to stereotypical representations only contribute to the oppression of women of color. Anzaldúa, in her "Letter to Third World Women Writers," writes, "[the] woman of color is invisible both in the white male mainstream world and in the white women's feminist world,...the *lesbian* of color is not only invisible, she doesn't even exist. Our speech, too, is inaudible. We speak in tongues like the outcast and the insane" (165). In Anzaldúa's example, speech is not absent, but misunderstood, incomprehensible, or unnoticed altogether.

Also, entire fields of study seem intimately bound to the issues of speech and silence, and visibility and invisibility. Lesbian and gay historians rely on these themes and frameworks to discuss a history of sexual oppression in the United States.[11] For example, the editors of *Hidden from History*, an anthology that purports to "reclaim the gay and lesbian past," suggest that the first phase of this sort of history involves what they refer to as biographical reclamation.[12] In other words, first we must find and restore to history those gay and lesbian lives which heretofore have been missing, absent, invisible. Yet this notion of invisible, silent, isolated individuals living in shame and secrecy has been called into question in recent years. John D'Emilio and George Chauncey, among others, have attempted to dispel the myths of what Chauncey calls "isolation," "invisibility," and "internalization."[13] Chauncey, for one, seeks not to uncover previously hidden lives, but to restore to history a whole social world, "highly visible, remarkably complex, and continually changing" (1), a gay male world, with a distinctive culture and language, in New York City between 1890 and 1940. Others, like Jennifer Terry, argue instead for an "effective history" that might be attentive to "the ruptures and discontinuities in history," and useful as "an interventionist strategy...necessary to those positioned in the margins of dominant accounts" (56).

[This paradigm] involves what Foucault calls "historical sense"--a strategic awareness of points of emergence or "possibilities" existing at particular historical moments in the formation of particular discourses ...Effective history allows us to theorize a counterdiscursive position of history-telling which neither fashions a new coherence, nor provides a more inclusive resolution of contradicting "events" ...Effective history exposes not the events and actors elided by traditional history, but instead lays bare the processes and operations by which these elisions occurred. (56)

In other words, Terry emphasizes discursive "silences," those historical gaps or elisions, as the very sites upon which to interrogate history.

Lesbian, gay, and bisexual theorists and film critics search novels, films, and other cultural texts for any indication of lesbian or gay themes, "the love that dare not speak its name." For example, Deborah McDowell, Bonnie Zimmerman, and Teresa de Lauretis, to name a few, have attempted to reread familiar narratives for lesbian content, asserting the notion of "coding" as a significant representational strategy for lesbian and gay texts.[14] However, the assertion of "coded" representations relies on assumptions of silence, secrecy, and repression as an implicit and overarching framework for the production of lesbian and gay images and narratives.

Thus, the reliance on notions of "coded" representations tends to relocate queer subjectivities within dominant discourses that associate sexuality in general and homosexuality in particular with the unspoken and the unspeakable. Also, as Julie Abraham suggests, certain texts (and lives) can be read as "coded" or silenced "only if the lesbian novel is understood as *the* lesbian text" (24).[15] She writes:

The repression hypothesis from which coding derives implies that there were other, more direct ways for saying what was being said, of writing "about lesbianism," that the writer avoided because of social pressure. It implies, moreover, that we know the forms lesbian writing would take were it not for social hostility..."Coding" implies that heterosexual and lesbian writers occupied different literary worlds, and that public and private speech can be clearly differentiated. (25)[16]

Thus, the notion of coding precludes a more critical analysis of the roles and functions of silence, in more than simple causal relationships or easy binaries between speech/silence, visibility/invisibility, public/private, repression/liberation, and a host of other relationships that imply implicit vs. explicit "truths" are known, and that tend to homogenize marginalized persons.

Silence, conceptualized as antithetical to the liberation of oppressed groups of people, has most often been viewed as yet another method and symbol of oppression. However, such interpretations fail to recognize the different forms and meanings silence may take, as well as the ways in which speech acts, too, are limited and constrained. There are qualitative distinctions between being silent and being *silenced*. Similarly, as I have suggested, it is a quite different process to be silent then it is to be unheard. One may speak and simply not be listened to, understood, or taken seriously. Thus, even speech is structured by existent relations of power. As Maclear states, freedom of speech in the United States is not necessarily a protected right enjoyed by all members of society. Not all silences are the same; likewise, speech acts may be distinct from one another in their meanings, implications, and effects. Hence, we might ask: How effective are "speaking out," "finding a voice," "breaking silence," and "coming out" as liberatory rhetoric and political acts when such notions rely on the very discursive practices through which social and political domination occurs? How might silence also represent a means of political resistance to domination, rather than a means of compliance? And how might silence signify political and social agency, rather than solely the loss or lack of such agency?

Silence is not simply the absence of speech. In his influential *The History of Sexuality*, Michel Foucault questions the Western myth of sexual repression. He interprets the act of confession as part of a will-to-knowledge, a form of seeking "truth," whereby speaking is both demanded by and a demand for power. Power is both productive and prohibitive; in fact, prohibition, or not-speaking, is part of the production of power. Foucault's theory suggests that silence, too, is productive, and is not to be understood in opposition to speech, but as a part of discourse; silence in such a model may operate as a different way of saying.

In her essay "Not You/Like You: Postcolonial Women and the Interlocking Questions of Identity and Difference," Trinh T. Minh-ha identifies the "uses of

silence" as a form of difference that "undermines the very idea of identity" (372).
She writes: "Within the context of women's speech silence has many faces...Silence
is commonly set in opposition with speech. Silence as a will not to say or a will to
unsay and as a language of its own has barely been explored" (372-373). And in
Woman, Native Other: Writing Postcoloniality and Feminism, Minh-ha suggests
that "silence as a refusal to partake in the story does sometimes provide us with a
means to gain a hearing. It is a voice, a mode of uttering, and a response in its own
right" (83). Silence, rather than being outside of discourse, is very much within it,
functioning along with and in relation to what is said. However, silence may also
be misconstrued. Trinh goes on to suggest that without other silences, "[her] silence
goes unheard, unnoticed; it is simply one voice less, or more point given to the
silencers" (83). Thus, silence functions as a way of saying (and of unsaying) and
is related to ways of seeing (unseeing) and knowing (unknowing), but it is useful
only in contexts of other silences, whereby it signifies resistance rather than voice-
lessness.

      The relationship between speech and silence represents a site of power in
which subjectivities may be created, destroyed, or otherwise transformed. Yet, this
site is highly unstable, and those processes of subjectivity implied by speech/silence
are all the more tenuous. As Trinh highlights, the meanings of speech and silence
are always open to (mis)interpretation. And Foucault suggests that the act of
speaking, or confessing, does not necessarily lead to liberation from power; rather,
it acts as the very process by which power is produced. Also, as noted earlier,
within specific historical and cultural contexts, the production of "free" speech
remains regulated and controlled. Finally, notions of speaking tend to posit specific
conceptions of subjectivity. For instance, Sagri Dhairyam describes the binary
established in the field of queer theory between the "silent closeted native" and the
articulate (speaking) white queer (32). Her assertion suggests that for people of
color breaking silence and "coming out" may involve moving away from cultural
traditions--and spaces--and into (white) lesbian or gay subject-hood.

      More than simply a trope, then, silence for marginalized groups of people
in the United States and elsewhere is also a history, a reality, and a lived experience.
Silencing is a means of domination, and access to "free" speech is often limited.
Control of language is a constant and powerful tool in the acts of domination and
colonization. Within such political contexts, speaking and its association with
writing become crucial for the centering of previously marginalized subjectivities.
For instance, associated with the speech so central to feminism is the de-centering
of the neutral, unmarked (read: male) subject. For women, subjectivity, demarcated
by the "I" who speaks and writes, has always been disturbed by silence(s), gaps, and
elisions: the unrepresented, the unseen, the unsaid. Dichotomous thinking within
Western culture implies binaries such as man/woman, Western/Eastern, mind/body,
culture/nature, and subject/object.[17] Such oppositions generally privilege one part
of the dichotomy over the other, holding up, for example, men, the West, the mind,
culture, and the subject as superior. The terms, Collins states, gain meaning only
in relation to their counterparts. Those who occupy inferior subject positions are
often viewed in opposition to the "norms" of our culture, male, white, Western,

middle-class, heterosexual, and so on, and are therefore seen as society's "others," and accordingly objectified. The consequences of being rendered "other," in terms of language and the struggle for subjectivity, have been explored by feminist writers since at least the twentieth century.

My analyses are influenced by other feminist writings on the theme of silence, attributed by many to the early work of Tillie Olsen, both her talks at the Radcliffe Institute in the early 1960s and her text, *Silences*, published in 1965. In their introduction to the anthology, *Listening to Silences*, Elaine Hedges and Shelley Fisher Fishkin identify the theme of silence not only as "central to feminist literary inquiry," but also as a means to understand women's experiences on a multitude of levels (3). Citing works by Marge Piercy, Adrienne Rich, Joanna Russ, and Audre Lorde, Hedges and Fishkin document a recent history of feminist writings about silence. They suggest that whereas Olsen originally relied on the notion of silence in order to emphasize external impediments to and constraints on women's writing, related to "their more limited access to education, cultural pressures that dissuaded them from taking themselves seriously as artists, the fragmentation of their time amidst the duties and distractions of motherhood, or the workings of a male literary establishment that excluded them" (5), a new critical perspective, influenced by poststructuralist and postmodern theories, stresses as well the silences within and "intrinsic to" texts. Silences, according to this critical perspective, "might reveal reticences culturally imposed upon women, the workings of a repressed ideology, or, alternatively, women's deployment of silence as a form of resistance to the dominant discourse" (5).

In *A Room of One's Own* (1929), Virginia Woolf comments on the great "I" of literature and history:

It was delightful to read a man's writing again. It was so direct, so straightforward after the writing of women. It indicated such freedom of mind, such liberty of person ...All this was admirable. But after reading a chapter or two a shadow seemed to lie across the page. It was a straight dark bar, a shadow shaped something like the letter "I." One began dodging this way and that to catch a glimpse of the landscape behind it. Whether that was indeed a tree or a woman walking I was not quite sure. Back one was always hailed to the letter "I"...the worst of it is that in the shadow of the letter "I" all is shapeless as mist. Is that a tree? No, it is a woman. But...she has not a bone in her body (103-104).

Woolf highlights the gender politics of writing and language. The traditional "I" of Western literature and history, according to Woolf, represents (white) male subjectivity. This "I" looms large over our cultural landscape, blurring and over-shadowing the subjectivities of woman/women. Yet Woolf's solution asserts not a challenge to, or an undoing of, the assumed normativity of this "I," but rather a lack of sex consciousness, an *un*marking, a disavowal.

More recently, debates within feminist criticism have engaged issues of reading and writing "as" or "like" a woman, or a man.[18] These dialogues raise questions about the relationship between speaking and writing. Significantly, they also introduce issues of language, subject position, and subjectivity. For example, in *The Lesbian Body* (1973), Monique Wittig suggests that language is always political: to say "I" [*je*] one must be a subject. She proposes *j/e* to symbolize the impossibility of speech for the divided nonsubject:

The "I" [*je*] who writes is alien to her own writing at every word because this "I" [*je*] uses a language alien to her; this "I" [*je*] experiences what is alien to her since this "I" [*je*] cannot be "un ecrivain"...*J/e* is the symbol of the lived, rending experience which is m/y writing, of this cutting in two which throughout literature is the exercise of a language which does not constitute m/e as subject. *J/e* poses the ideological and historic questions of feminine subjects...If I [*j/e*] examine m/y specific situation as subject in the language, I [*j/e*] am physically incapable of writing "I" [*je*]. I [*j/e*] have no desire to do so. (10-11)

According to Wittig, in order to signify a *subject*, "I" cannot be partial or relative. "I" cannot be silent; "I" must speak.

It is precisely this "I," so troubling to white, Western feminists, that also presents problems (related yet significantly different) for people of color in the United States, and for "third world" women writers. For instance, young Maxine,[19] the narrator of Maxine Hong Kingston's autobiographical *The Woman Warrior*, cannot understand this English, this *American* "I." And her confusion over the "I" is underscored by her silence, by her inability to speak in school. It is when she learns that she is expected to speak that school and silence become miserable for her. She remains silent and feels ashamed of her silence: "I knew the silence had to do with being a Chinese girl" (166). And this silence, she writes, was "thickest--total" when the time in her childhood during which she covered all her school paintings with black paint (165).[20] This silence causes her misery and shame. Her "broken" voice, when she forces it out, is even worse, "weak," "frozen," and "ugly," described by a Chinese woman from her family's village as the quack of a duck (165, 192). Interestingly, the silence noted here is imagined as already existent, and problematic only in the context of enforced speech--in the American educational system. What is it about being a Chinese girl that colludes with and even produces silence, and makes speech so difficult? Kingston seems to suggest such possibilities as the United States school systems, processes of remembering, Americanization, and standards of femininity as underlying the production of silence for the narrator.

Indeed, critics have suggested that the Chinese "I" is strikingly distinct from the American "I," marking a cultural difference in experiences of subjectivity. In Judy Yung's analysis of Jade Snow Wong's autobiography, *Fifth Chinese Daughter* (1950), deference to parents and elders was ingrained in Wong and signified "her understanding of her proper place in the Confucian hierarchical order" (117). Though autobiographical, the book is written in the third person, identified by Wong as "Chinese habit." In fact, according to Wong, "in written Chinese, prose or poetry, the word 'I' almost never appears, but is understood...Even written in English, an 'I' book by a Chinese would seem outrageously immodest to anyone raised in the spirit of Chinese propriety" (117). However, as Yung points out, Jade Snow Wong does not follow such a practice in her second autobiography, *No Chinese Stranger* (1975), in which she begins in the third person singular, but changes to first-person midway through the text. Resonating with Virginia Woolf's experience, the change occurs after her account of her father's death, suggesting that in Wong's case, it was only after his death that she was able to assert her identity through first-person narration.[21] Such an example suggests the consequences of patriarchal oppression for women's subjectivity. Also of significance, however, in a Chinese-American woman's refusal to employ the first-person "I" in a narrative, is its equation with subjugation. Kingston writes that the Chinese word for the female "I" is "slave," signifying the relationship between Chinese women's speech and subordination (47). Thus, in questioning this "I," a symbol of subjectivity for American women, writers such as Kingston and Wong signify their refusal to be participants in their own degradation.

In educational institutions, as well as other locations of mainstream United States culture, a high premium is placed on speech and language. Pedagogical discussions of race and classroom dynamics often focus on the silence of Asian-American students and other students of color, generally chalked up to "their cultures," as though culture is static and temporal. In her essay "Not So Many Words," Maclear discusses her own silence in the classroom, and her experiences as an Asian Pacific Islander-American student. She writes that she was silenced by being made to feel that she, as a woman of color, had nothing of value to contribute to class discussions. Silences in the classroom, however, may also relate to the content of what is studied (particularly the lack of subject materials about women and people of color in the United States), as well as the absence of instructors or other students of similar racial, cultural, or class backgrounds. Maclear states that in her case, "racialized and gendered constructions of Asian women had functioned to serve up my silence as 'good 'n' natural,' as emblematic of my docility and obedience" (6). Her silence was perceived, then, as natural to Asian-American women, buttressing stereotypes of them as obedient, passive, and lacking in subjectivity. Yet in her analysis, Maclear states that she was not being "silenced" as much as she was unheard, "a more subtle and insidious form of exclusion" (7). Her statement suggests, once again, the distinct ways in which language and silence may be structured in society for members of various groups, according to subject position.

In, *Articulate Silences*, King-Kok Cheung discusses the multiple meanings of silences in works by Hisaye Yamamoto, Maxine Hong Kingston, and Joy Kogawa. She questions the placement of verbal and nonverbal forms of communication into hierarchical terms, suggesting that the meanings of silence must be culturally contextualized. Through her discussion of distinct forms of silence, including "rhetorical," "provocative," and "attentive" silences, she argues that the Asian-American women writers under consideration employ strategies of silence to engage directly with history, offering critiques of histories that homogenize them, exclude them, or efface their subjectivities.

For Wittig, speech is related to memory. She urges women to remember, and, if unable to remember, then to *rewrite* the past: "You say you have lost all recollection of it, remember...You say there are no words to describe this time, you say it does not exist. But remember. Make an effort to remember. Or, failing that, invent" (1969, 89; emphasis added).[22] Wittig links the absence of memory to an absence of language statement, resonant of Rich's assertion that the language available to us is a male-dominated language incapable of the full expression of women's ideas and thoughts. And for young Maxine, as well, the problem of memory is not simply a matter of forgetting. Rather, memory and history are themselves marked by peculiar silences. She wonders how she can have memories when she cannot speak, and is told by her mother that she, like the ghosts, has no memories (167). Indeed, Kingston's mother links her children's lack of memory to their lack of feelings, and interprets both in relation to her inability to communicate effectively with them (115). Here in the United States among the "barbarians,"[23] where the children speak English, Kingston's parents do not seem to hear them (123). Hong Kingston cannot remember because she cannot speak; yet she cannot speak because she cannot remember. Moreover, there are reasons why she is not *supposed* to remember. "We had so many secrets to hold in...immigration secrets whose telling could get us sent back to China" (182-183). Maxine's parents tell lies on a regular basis--they give false names, addresses, birth dates, former jobs. Significantly, exclusionary United States immigration procedures encouraged and even facilitated such "lies." Due to changing restrictions and injustices, Asian immigrants in particular often had little choice but to lie, in order to enter the country or to bring family members to the United States One major exempt status of the Chinese Exclusion Act, for example, effected the emigration of large numbers of "paper sons" and "paper daughters" to the United States In such cases, young people could claim derivative citizenship in order to enter the country by purchasing the name and family status of Chinese men already living in America (Yung, 106). In addition, those immigrants who had already entered the United States often created slots for new immigrants by falsely documenting children who did not exist, thereby further complicating familial histories and relationships.[24]

Also, in *The Woman Warrior*, parents keep truths about their lives and histories from their children, who are ghostlike in their status as Americans (183). This ghostliness of which Hong Kingston speaks represents generational differences, and linguistic differences, and is contextualized against the very real threat of immigration authorities and deportation, the possible betrayals of parents by children. America, writes Kingston, for her parents was full of ghosts (96). To her mother, Brave Orchid, it represents a country of toil and hardship (104). Both her mother and her father mythologize China as "home," and in so doing, they suspend both America and happiness for their children (99). However, though her parents fear America, they fear deportation and an enforced return to China even more, thereby justifying the many lies and secrets that must be maintained.

On the one hand, Maxine's parents keep secrets because the differences between the generations and the Americanization of their children are disturbing to them (183-184). The children's ghostliness comes to signify their status as Americans. On the other hand, as I have pointed out, there are valid reasons to lie to authorities. "Lie to Americans," her parents warn. The children are exhorted to hide such community embarrassments as crime, unemployment, and communism from Americans: "The ghosts won't recognize you...Ghosts have no memories anyway and poor eyesight" (184-185). Kingston relates memory to vision and sight, connecting what is known to what is seen (or cannot be seen, as the case may be). The immigration secrets she is forced to keep maintain her silence in ghostly America (183). Indeed, Maxine feels silenced by both the ghostlike immigration authorities and her parents who admonish her not to tell. "Don't tell," her parents say, although, as she narrates, she would not be able to tell, because she does not know. And, she writes, even the good things in their lives are considered unspeakable (185).[25]

Memory, and remembering, are key to subjectivity and speech in *The Woman Warrior*. Yet the subjectivities in question are culturally specific. Chinese women's voices in China, Kingston notes, are strong, even "bossy," and Chinese communication is loud and public (11, 172). Yet to be American-Chinese means becoming "American-feminine" "Some of us gave us...and said nothing...We invented an American-feminine speaking personality, except for that one girl who could not even speak up in Chinese school" (172). Whispering is the way to become American-feminine, and failing that performance, silence becomes a last resort. Interestingly, silence is marked as a trait peculiar to being a Chinese girl, it is also implicated in becoming American-feminine. Whereas Western theories of subjectivity might imply that American identity is structured around acts of speech, for Maxine, part of attaining status as an American girl is learning how to whisper, how to be silent. Doing so, and making her life "American-normal," must involve pushing speech and Chinese language outside of her reality (87). The achievement of American subjectivity, then, revolves around a process of disavowal of all things Chinese, including Chinese manners of speaking.[26]

Becoming American means learning to walk and talk differently. Kingston suggests that the loud, public modes of communication commonly employed by Chinese in China, the strong, even "bossy" tones of Chinese women, are inappropriate in American contexts, and that finding her American voice has meant learning to speak inaudibly, or not at all. And it is not just the loudness of the Chinese language, she writes, but the way the language sounds to American ears as ugly (171-172). Because femininity is associated with (white) Americanness by the girls in school, feminine subjectivity provokes cultural and familial crises. Adopting American-feminine traits means further distancing themselves from what is perceived as authentically *Chinese*. It also throws the notion of an authentic way of being Chinese into crisis. However, Kingston's words also suggest contradictory impulses. The Chinese-American girls in *The Woman Warrior* are configured as already silent, silence being an inherent and negative cultural trait. At the same time, they are loud and in need of domestication, *silencing*, in order to be perceived as properly American. If silence, for her, signifies a loss of full subjectivity, it also implies her resistance to the process of mainstream acculturation and Americanization that is so difficult for her and her family members. To what extent, in these examples, might silence also be a means of resistance to the seemingly impossible task of becoming American-feminine? What of that one girl who could not [would not?] speak up even in Chinese school?

Though this girl's silence may indeed represent her refusal to participate in the process of assimilation into American culture, Maxine cannot accept her actions. Her own silences cause her great suffering, at school and elsewhere. When she must speak, even in Chinese school, she describes her voice as small and having no impact (48). It is something that she cannot offer to Americans, whom she has been taught not to trust. But, she explains, she cannot entrust her voice to the Chinese, either: "They want to capture your voice for their own use" (169). In her narrative, she depicts, with excruciating detail, her painful interaction with the silent girl, her other self, according to some critics' interpretations,[27] in the school bathroom one day. Deciding that she will force this little girl to speak, she taunts her and physically torments her, pleading with her to make it stop by simply saying something. While the girl silently cries, the narrator calls her disgusting, weak, nothing. To assert her identity and presence, she must speak: "If you don't talk, you can't have a personality" (178-180). Speaking, then, is a means to demonstrate subjectivity, strength, and a personality. Not speaking becomes equated, for Kingston's child narrator, with being disgusting, weak, and a "nothing."[28]

Yet, examples from her narrative suggest otherwise. For the warrior woman of "White Tigers," the second chapter of *The Woman Warrior,* writing becomes the means of reporting that saves family and community. Fa Mu Lan marches into battle with her grievances carved onto her back. She remains silent, however, so that others will not realize she is a woman. Though her words are powerful, her silence maintains self-preservation. Kingston herself a woman warrior, suggests that it is the reporting--the writing--that signifies her vengeance and subsequent liberation, not necessarily her speech. In this sense, she is not unlike the Fa Mu Lan. What they have in common, she writes, are the words at their backs, representing their reporting of "crimes" and their vengeance (53). Thus, Kingston recognizes that speech is not the only method of resistance. In the United States, where she is socialized into silence, she finds some sense of freedom through her writing, carefully distinguished from speech, which, she maintains, is still difficult for her, even as an adult (165). As Cheung suggests, "It is clear that a quiet pupil can nevertheless be(come) an articulate writer" (89). Also, Kingston becomes aware that all acts of speech are neither guaranteed nor liberating.

The narrator's unnamed aunt, Kingston's father's sister who allegedly brought shame on the family name, is virtually erased from the familial history. For her, silence purportedly functions as a means of forgetting. Yet this aunt is not forgotten; her history is narrated to Maxine as a warning and a "story to grow up on" (5). To put her story into words, Kingston risks the censure not only of her family but also that of the deceased aunt's ghost. She writes, "My aunt haunts me...I do not think she always means me well" (16). Kingston is, after all "telling on her" (16). This telling, though illustrative of the multiple silences and secrets circulating within Kingston's family, frees neither the aunt nor Kingston. The retribution is symbolic, because the old villagers are by now dead, their identities buried within family secrets and immigration lies. And telling her aunt's story fails to counter the namelessness of this "No Name Woman," a situation suggestive of the repercussions of being unnamed, misnamed, or distorted through stereotypical representations in the United States, a condition Maxine herself experiences in the narrative. Finally, Maxine, who seeks intimacy with her mother through mutual speaking, is forced to question notions ascribing power and "truth" to speech. At one point, she explains, she believed that speaking and silence made the difference between sanity and insanity, commenting on the many "crazy" girls and women from her ancestral village--those who were unable to "explain themselves" (186). Incidentally, it is the girls and women for whom speech appears most difficult, who are subsequently labeled insane. Again, speech and silence are conceptualized as gendered means of communication, shaped by subject position, immigrant status, and sanity. Maxine believes that her mother cut her tongue in order to silence her, but Brave Orchid argues that she did it so that her daughter would never be "tongue-tied." She tells Maxine that she cut her tongue to free it, so that it would be able to move in any language (164). When Maxine counters, "'But isn't 'a ready tongue an evil'"?, her mother responds,"'Things are different in this ghost country'"(164). While Hong Kingston believes Chinese in China speak freely, and that to be American-feminine, she must be silent, her mother argues that speech is also necessary for them in the United States. By cutting her daughter's tongue, she attempts to free her daughter from linguistic limits and constraints. However, for Maxine, speaking is always painful, and not-speaking is generally accompanied by throat pain and teeth gnashing (101, 197, 200, 205).

In developing a list of over two hundred things that she wants to tell her mother about herself, Maxine narrates the details of her attempt to become closer to her mother through speech. Through her sharing with her mother all the truths about herself, her mother will be able, finally, to know and understand her. However, when she attempts to tell these things, nothing happens. According to Maxine, "I had talked, and she acted as if she hadn't heard" (199). When they fight over their consistent miscommunication, Brave Orchid, admits finally, that speech is not always necessarily accurate, and that language does not always convey the truth. In the telling, Maxine realizes that there is no "higher listener" (204). In fact, there is no listener but herself, which suggest to Maxine the limits of language and that fact that speech is always shaped by the laws and conditions around her. After repeatedly struggling against silence, Kingston cautions her readers to be careful about what we say. Sometimes, she suggests, it comes true (204).

Interestingly, many critics have commented on the so-called authenticity (or lack thereof) of this text, presumably missing the fact that Kingston herself introduces these themes as compelling questions.[29] For Kingston, Chinese identity is neither static nor essential. Rather, she is forced to constantly wonder what makes her Chinese-American. Is there, or can there be, such a thing? "What is Chinese tradition and what is the moves?" (5-6). Is silence inherently Chinese? Is speech? She suggests that such attributions are indeterminate: writing "I continue to sort out what's just my childhood, just my imagination, just my family, just the village, just movies, just living. Soon I want to go to China and find out who's lying" (205).

Paralleling Maxine's quest for something truly "Chinese," critics and readers of *The Woman Warrior* have sought the authentic "Chinese" memoir. For instance, Cheung writes:

Asian-American intellectuals have endlessly debated the "authenticity" of *The Woman*

Warrior. Those who attack Kingston for blurring the line between reality and fantasy seem unmindful of the narrator's insistent admissions of her own penchant for fabrication and her inability to discern fact from fiction. Even those on the author's side tend to defend her autobiography on the ethnographic ground that the narrator's experience accords well with their own. (78-79)[30]

Kingston herself comments, "After all, I am not writing history or sociology but a 'memoir' like Proust" (1982, 64). She makes it clear within the framework of her narrative that her memoirs involve truth, fiction, and fantasy. Describing the outlawed knotmakers of ancient China, whose knots were so complex that one even blinded its maker, she claims that if she had lived in China, she would have been an outlaw knotmaker (1975, 163). While her child narrator continues to search for "truth," Kingston recognizes the complicated relationships between fact and fiction, especially in terms of autobiographical writing or an "authentic" Chinese experience.

The narrator of *The Woman Warrior* constantly questions the possibility of such an authentic Chinese culture or experience. Recounting her parents' lies, she wonders how the Chinese have maintained a continuous culture for five thousand years: "Maybe they didn't; maybe everyone makes it up as they go along" (185). And maybe Kingston, too, makes it up as she goes along, *inventing* the past and her memories as part of a strategic renaming/remembering, the outlaw knots that reflect her own ambivalent relationship to remembering. The act of renaming (and, in some cases, inventing), however, relates directly to historical "silences" and distortions in the United States of the histories of people of color and other marginalized groups. Mohanty, in her essay "Cartographies of Struggle: Third World Women and the Politics of Feminism," writes that "not only must narratives of resistance undo hegemonic recorded history, but they must also *invent* new forms of encoding resistance, of remembering" (35). Following this line of thought, inventing the past enables new possibilities, new ways of conceptualizing lived realities:

Resistance is encoded in the practices of remembering, and of writing...The very practice of remembering against the grain of "public" or hegemonic history, of locating the silences and the struggle to assert knowledge which is outside the parameters of the dominant, suggests a rethinking of sociality itself. (38-39)

In other words, remembering our histories is part of resisting hegemonic discourses and master narratives. When our own histories are not available or accessible to us, when our pasts comprise a history of silence, we must rely on speaking and writing practices such as "remembering against the grain" and "invention." As Mohanty suggests, these new ways of thinking are directly related to "our daily practices of survival and resistance" (39). Yet, in what ways may silence also represent a way of remembering and of reinventing history?

Maclear provides an illuminating example. In her personal critical essay, she recalls an incident at a workshop on oral history and pedagogy. While a video oral history made by an Asian-Canadian man about the experiences of Japanese-

Canadians in internment camps during World War II, Maclear was struck by the testimony of an old man whose silences were more telling than his words. The pauses and unedited silences in the film represented to Maclear "the lapses and disjunctures attendant in processes of remembering" (9). She writes, "They guided me to what he was not telling and reminded me that some things will always remain unspoken--and unknowable" (9). Other viewers discounted the film as "too slow" and difficult to understand, taking the silences for absence, for "a lacking of sentiment and depth of reflection" (9). However, Maclear understood the silences as meaningful and as signification of the problems involved in reconstructing history. Implicit in the assumptions of the other viewers, who wanted more words and more explanations of the "experiences" in the camps, was a notion that somehow there can be a way to know the "truth" about the past--that history is more authentic when it is seen and spoken clearly. Maclear herself concludes with questions like, "Can silence ever be a self-evolved form of expression for people from oppressed groups? Given the material realities of racism, sexism, and other forms of institutionalized oppression, can we ever separate silence from mechanisms of domination that force us to 'be quiet' or that 'silence us'? Can we ever freely choose silence?" (11). In some instances, demonstrated by Kingston's narration, silence can be and has been, chosen as an expression and strategy of resistance.[31]

Thus, with speech comes silence, not simply the forgotten, the denied, or the disavowed, but also the refusal, the protest, or the resistance that silence might also signify. Historicizing silence(s) forces us to recognize its "many faces" and to validate the differences between varied contexts of time and place, as well as the *differences* among those discourses deployed by various social and political groups. Also, historicizing silence(s) may allow us to examine the consequences of simply mapping one set of theoretical assumptions that may apply to, for example, gender, onto contemporary racial discourses. Though I argue for the interrelatedness of these social categories, and attempt to refrain from compartmentalizing and/or overemphasizing their separateness, I also would like to move away from simple race-sex analogies and from arguments for universalizing theories of "difference." For example, "silences" in gay and lesbian history and "silences" in Asian-American women's history, though certainly connected, are not necessarily similar ways of unsaying.

Silence, then, is particular to lived realities and histories. It performs different functions and produces distinct interpretations in various contexts. It is not simply loss, lack, absence, or repression. As a will to unsay, it is also that which makes speaking or saying possible, as it constructs and shapes meaning. As Minh-ha suggests, it is "a language of its own [that] has barely been explored" (1990, 373). And we have not listened enough to this language of silence, to its ever-changing meanings, to its resonances of possibility.

NOTES

1. Theresa Hak Kyung Cha, *Dictee* (Berkeley: Third Woman Press), 1995, 81.

2. Tillie Olsen, *Silences* (New York: Delta/Seymour Lawrence 1965), 6.

3. My discussion of *The Woman Warrior* is not comprehensive, and does not include a comprehensive review of the literature. In fact, because of the great number of critical essays and texts about *The Woman Warrior*, nearly two hundred published sources, and several dozens of unpublished dissertations and theses, such a project is beyond the scope of this essay. Rather, I offer this discussion as a kind of "micro-analysis," demonstrating some of the themes central to my argument. Also, because Hong Kingston's text is perhaps the best known and most frequently studied text in Asian American literature, occupying a central space within the emerging "canon" of Asian American texts, it offers a unique vantage point from which to explore the issue of silence, an issue that I argue has relevance for most writings by Asian Pacific American women.

4. Here, I rely on the term "national belonging" rather than nationality, in order to draw attention to the fact that an individual may identify with a particular nationality (e.g., Asian Americans are, of course, Americans), yet he or she may not feel a sense of belonging. The social and political climate of the U.S. creates a problematic context for Asian Americans, for whom nationality and national belonging are not necessarily always the same thing.

5. Beverly Guy-Sheftall, Keynote Lecture, "Women of Color Across the Women's Studies Curriculum Conference", Marquette University, Milwaukee, Wisconsin, March 15, 1996. Notably, however, the term "women of color" implies a binary framework for race only because it is so often conflated with African American women, rather than used to mean all women of color (including Latina, Chicana, Native American, Pacific Islander, and Asian American women).

6. However, my main focus in this essay is specifically the U.S.

7. For example, Lisa Lowe points out the distinction between early Chinese immigrants to the U.S. in the 1850s, who were primarily poor laborers from the Canton Province, with men outnumbering women by ten to one, and more recent Chinese immigrants who come to the U.S. from Taiwan, Hong Kong, the People's Republic, or from other parts of the Chinese diaspora, including Malaysia and Singapore. Recent Chinese immigrants are heterogeneous in class backgrounds, and education and labor skills as well. See Lowe, 1996, 66.

8. Here, following Tejaswini Niranjana's careful rearticulation of "trope," I hope to indicate, as does she, a "metaphorizing that includes a displacement as well as a re-figuring" (5).

9. See, for example, *Sisterhood is Powerful: An Anthology of Writings from the Women's Liberation Movement,* ed. Robin Morgan (New York: Vintage, 1970); *The Black Woman: An Anthology*, ed. Toni Cade Bambara (New York: Mentor, 1970); *Roots: An Asian American Reader*, ed. Amy Tachiki, et al., (UCLA Asian American Studies Center, 1971); *Black Power: The Politics of Liberation in America*, ed. Stokely Carmichael and Charles Hamilton (New York: Random House, 1967); *By Any Means Necessary: Speeches, Interviews, and a Letter by Malcolm X*, ed. George Breitman (New York: Merit, 1970); Michele Wallace, *Black Macho and the Myth of the Superwoman* (New York: The Dial Press, 1978); Glenn Omatsu, "The 'Four Prisons' and the Movements of Liberation: Asian American Activism from the 1960s to the 1990s," in *The State of Asian America: Activism and Resistance in the 1990s*, ed. Karin Aguilar-San Juan (Boston: South End Press, 1994), 19-70; and *The Original Coming Out Stories*, ed. Julia Penelope and Susan J. Wolfe (Freedom, CA: The Crossing Press, 1980), in which the notion of "coming out" represents a significant

form of "breaking silence" and finding a voice.

10. Here I rely on Sandra Lee Bartky's definition of "cultural domination," in which she suggests that all parts of our culture, including our language, institutions, art and literature, are male-dominated and structured in such a way as to oppress women. See Bartky, *Femininity and Domination: Studies in the Phenomenology of Oppression* (New York: Routledge, 1990), 25.

11. I do not mean to posit a split between "writers of color" and "lesbian and gay writers," reinforcing the binary I am attempting to critique. Of course, writers like Anzaldúa, Lorde, Cherríe Moraga, and Barbara Smith write as lesbians of color, along with many others. I do think, however, that much of what has been regarded as "lesbian and gay history and theory" within the university has been white-centered and has paid scant attention to issues of race.

12. See Duberman, et al., "Introduction," especially pp. 2-3.

13. For example, although the Stonewall riots of 1969 are generally regarded as the beginning of not only an organized gay liberation movement but also a gay community in the U.S., both D'Emilio and Chauncey argue for a much more complex historical analysis, taking into account the bar communities and other subcultures of periods prior to Stonewall. See John D'Emilio, *Sexual Politics, Sexual Communities: The Making of a Homosexual Minority in the United States, 1940-1970* (Chicago: U of Chicago P, 1983); and George Chauncey, *Gay New York: Gender, Culture, and the Making of the Gay Male World, 1890-1940* (New York: Basic Books, 1994). In his introduction, D'Emilio writes about "a curious inconsistency . . . between the rhetoric of the gay liberation movement and the reality of its achievements. On the one hand, activists in the early 1970s repeatedly stressed, in their writing and their public comments, the intertwining themes of silence, invisibility, and isolation. Gay men and lesbians, the argument ran, were invisible to society and to each other. . . . A vast silence surrounded the topic of homosexuality, perpetuating both invisibility and isolation. On the other hand, gay liberationists exhibited a remarkable capacity to mobilize their allegedly hidden, isolated constituency, and the movement grew with amazing rapidity" (1-2). Also, Elizabeth Lapovsky Kennedy and Madeline D. Davis in their work *Boots of Leather, Slippers of Gold: The History of a Lesbian Community* (New York: Routledge, 1993), discuss a flourishing lesbian community in Buffalo, New York, from the 1930s to the 1950s, centered around bars and house parties. They refer to butch and fem constructions of identity, sexuality, and community as "pre-political forms of resistance" (190).

14. See, for example, Deborah McDowell, "'It's Not Safe. Not Safe at All': Sexuality in Nella Larsen's *Passing*," in *The Lesbian and Gay Studies Reader*, ed. Henry Abelove, Michele Aina Barale, and David M. Halperin (New York: Routledge, 1993): 616-625; Bonnie Zimmerman, "What Has Never Been: An Overview of Lesbian Feminist Criticism" in *The New Feminist Criticism: Literature and Theory*, ed. Elaine Showalter (New York: Pantheon, 1985), 200-224; and *The Safe Sea of Women: Lesbian Fiction 1969-1989* (Boston: Beacon Press, 1990); and Teresa de Lauretis, "Sexual Indifference and Lesbian Representation," also in *The Lesbian and Gay Studies Reader*, 141-158.

15. In her *Are Girls Necessary? Lesbian Writing and Modern Histories*, Abraham distinguishes between the "lesbian novel" and "lesbian writing." The lesbian novel, she suggests, is one of those texts "written, presented, and read as representations of lesbianism by lesbian, gay, and heterosexual writers and readers" (xiii). Compare this to lesbian writing, the "much larger body of lesbian-authored fiction--as well as poetry, drama, essays, journals, and so on--that is not 'about' female couples" (xiii).

16. Abraham also suggests that the concept of coding "provided the basis for an unproductive critical opposition between realist and modernist writing [which] furthered the

naturalization of the formula lesbian novel The critical emphasis on coding turns formal innovation into a defensive choice, a deliberately obscurantist gesture whose only function is to conceal taboo meanings" (See 25-26).

17. See Patricia Hill Collins, *Black Feminist Thought: Knowledge, Consciousness, and the Politics of Empowerment* (New York: Routledge, 1990), especially chapter four, "Mammies, Matriarchs, and Other Controlling Images," in which she discusses the cultural consequences of binary thinking.

18. See, for example, Peggy Kamuf, "Writing Like a Woman" in *Women and Language in Literature in Society*, edited by Sally McConnell-Ginet, et. al., (New York: Praeger, 1980): 284-299; Jonathan Culler, "Reading as a Woman" in his *On Deconstruction: Theory and Criticism after Structuralism* (Ithaca: Cornell U P, 1982): 43-64; Robert Scholes, "Reading Like a Man" in *Men and Feminism*, ed. Alice Jardine and Paul Smith (New York: Methuen), 1987, 204-218; Tania Modleski, "Feminism and the Power of Interpretation: Some Critical Readings" in *Feminist Studies/Critical Studies*, edited by Teresa de Lauretis (Bloomington: Indiana U P), 1986, 121-138; and Diana Fuss, "Reading Like a Feminist" in *Essentially Speaking: Feminism, Nature, and Difference* (New York : Routledge, 1989), 23-37.

19. Please note, in my discussion of Hong Kingston's *The Woman Warrior*, I use "Maxine" when referring explicitly to the narrator, or protagonist, of the text, and Hong Kingston when referring to its author. Because the text is largely autobiographical, this practice may seem confusing. However, I acknowledge, as Hong Kingston herself suggests, that her memoirs are based not only on fact, but on memory and imagination as well, reflecting the complicated relationship between history and fiction.

20. Again, the linkage between silence and Maxine's school experience in the U.S. In these paintings, she explains, the black paint represented a stage curtain, just before being opened (165). They were, to Maxine, "so black and full of possibilities" (165), suggesting the need to be seen and/or known. Also, as Hong Kingston herself suggests, this image of the black curtains "probably had its literal source in the blackout curtains of World War II, a war that not only threatened the United States but had for several years before the American entry devastated the Hong family's Chinese homeland" (Simmons, 8-9). And, as Cheung argues, the experiences of Japanese Americans during World War II most certainly had significant repercussions for other East Asian Americans (90-91). Because Japanese Americans were interned against their will for the duration of the war, viewed as a threat to U.S. national security, the status of other Americans of Asian descent also became tenuous. Cheung notes that for Maxine, this desire to assimilate into American culture as fully as possible is effected by her outright rejection of all things Chinese: Chinese language, Chinese school, new Chinese immigrants, even her own family (91).

21. See Yung, p. 334, n15, in which she explains Wong's transition to first-person narration in her second autobiography, *No Chinese Stranger*.

22. Cheung suggests that Kingston "emphasizes the difficulty of conveying reality by pointing out the omissions in received information and the lapses or discrepancies in her own memory" (11). To Cheung, memory is significantly related to history, particularly the "lost," distorted, and undocumented histories of Asian Americans.

23. In her conclusion to *The Woman Warrior*, Hong Kingston offers a significant "talk-story" of her own, "A Song for a Barbarian Reed Pipe," based in part on one of her mother's stories. While the beginning of the story is her mother's, she writes, the ending is her own (206).   In this narrative, she mythologizes her mother's experiences as a first-generation Chinese immigrant woman in the U.S. Ts'ai Yen, a Chinese poetess of ancient times, found herself captive in a land of foreigners, barbarians, who did not speak her language or understand her. Her own children adapted the ways of the barbarians; they

did not speak Chinese nor did they seem to care to learn. When this poetess finally told her story, however, her children eventually joined in to sing with her (209). This story, Hong Kingston writes, "translated well" (209).

24. Judy Yung provides an illuminating example, in her discussion of her own family history. In her introduction to *Unbound Feet*, she explains that during her research on Chinese American women's history, she discovered that her own family name, Yung, was in fact the result of a business transaction. In 1921, her father borrowed money to purchase the name, Yung Hin Sen, the "paper son" of Yung Ung, in order to enter the U.S. Whether there actually was a son in China named Yung Hin Sen or Yung Ung simply created a son, in order to sell his name and family status, is unclear. For Yung, however, the discovery that her own family name and genealogy were affected, indeed constructed, by such a historical process serves to further illustrate her arguments about the particular details of Chinese American emigration to the United States (3).

25. While lies to outside authority figures are justified, even enforced within her family, lies to parents represent betrayals. For example, in her narration of an exchange with her mother during a visit home as an adult, Maxine promises to return again soon for a visit. To this her mother replies with sarcasm and pain: "'Yes, I know you. . . . You're the one with the charming words. You have never come back. 'I'll be back on Turkeyday,' you said. 'Huh.'" (101). Maxine remains silent, reluctant to speak words that cause her mother such pain. This silence, deployed to protect her mother, causes Hong Kingston herself pain (symbolized by her aching vocal chords and gnashing teeth). Her "charming words," to her mother, represent lies and abandonment.

26. In the second chapter of *The Woman Warrior*, entitled "White Tigers," Hong Kingston relates the tale of Fa Mu Lan, the mythical Chinese woman warrior who was said to avenge her village by passing as a man in battle and leading her people to victory. To become the woman warrior, the narrator must first train for fifteen years, the span of her childhood, with an old man and woman on mountainous, dangerous terrain. She must learn to go hungry, to battle those who would do her harm, to run from that which she cannot confront, and to be quiet (23). Most of all, she must learn to expand her mind, so that she can understand paradoxes and make meaning of meaninglessness (29). This training, incidentally, resonates with Hong Kingston's own training to survive in the U.S. As an impoverished Chinese American daughter of immigrants, she too must learn to go hungry, to know when to fight and when to flee, to be quiet, fully aware of the multiple meanings of her silence, and to understand contradictions.

27. See, for example, Cheung, 88; Feng, 127; Simmons, 97.

28. Silence, for young Maxine, is also equated with ignorance and stupidity. When she confronts her mother toward the end of the text, she blames her for her own troubles with speech and language, suggesting that because her mother never taught her to speak English correctly, she now has a "zero IQ" (201). Incidentally, Cheung points out that it is not simply the other girl's silence that makes her despicable to Maxine, but also her "China doll haircut" (173). And, Hong Kingston writes, "If she had had little bound feet, the toes twisted under the balls, I would have jumped up and landed on them--crunch!--stomped on them with my iron shoes" (178). Thus, Cheung argues, Hong Kingston is angry and disgusted not only at silence, but at being Chinese. Her "gratuitous cruelty can be understood only in terms of Maxine's virulent self-contempt at being Chinese" (1993, 89). Sadly, at this point in the text, and in her life, Maxine "can become articulate in Western discourse only by parroting self-denigrating Western assumptions. Her tussle with her ethnic double represents a phase in the narrator's life when her racial self-hatred is most acute and her acceptance of white norms ostensibly complete" (Cheung, 1993, 90).

29. Asian-American male writers, in particular, such as Frank Chin, have excori-

ated Hong Kingston, calling her, according to Simmons, "a purveyor of 'white racist art,' [and] a latter-day 'Pocohontas,' selling out Chinese Americans to pander to white readers" (1).

30. As Cheung points out, critics have accused Hong Kingston of "reinforcing racist stereotypes and of falsifying Chinese myths and history" (1993; 77). Their criticism fails to grasp her artistry and the critical implications of her text, overlooking the ways in which she "resists the opposition of fact and imagination in the face of received falsehood and historical silence" (77).

31. To say that silence has been chosen, however, is misleading. The very notion of choice, especially "free" choice is problematic in a culture in which choices are limited for some groups of people.

3

Women Networking with Their Neighbors: The Universal Thread of Civic Activism

Janet K. Boles

The contemporary field of Women's Studies from its inception has had a commitment to inclusivity and multiculturalism. The preamble to the Constitution of the National Women's Studies Association (NWSA) states that Women's Studies is to be *about* and *for* all women, guided by a vision of a world free from sexism, racism, classism, ageism, and heterosexism. This concern is reflected in the NWSA structure that allots representation in governance to women of color, community women, lesbians, elementary and secondary teachers, and students and staff.

The dominance of Women's Studies by white, middle-class, heterosexual feminists, privileged by academic status, is widely conceded. As Zinn et al. note, most research about women is produced at prestigious institutions where women of color and working-class women are under-represented. As a result, privileged women teach concepts divorced from the realities of other women's lives to privileged students. Further ramifications of this are an assumption of the universality of women's oppression within the archetypal "passive, pampered non-working woman" of the feminist critique; the continuing analytical primacy of gender-based oppression even when the intersections of class, race, and ethnicity are considered; and the token inclusion of women of color in conferences and edited works within a single chapter or in footnotes, so that race and class are acknowledged, but not integrated, into the analysis.[1]

An exclusive interest in difference, however, can result in a dangerous fatalism about unbridgeable differences among women and their efforts to act outside homogeneous groups.[2] But some suggest that there is no shared sisterhood based on universal concepts, and that no underlying truths about women and gender are buried beneath the diversities of race, ethnicity, class, religion, and sexual preference. Sweeping generalizations about feminist commonalities may raise tensions along class and race lines or make Women's Studies more exclusionary by limiting or excluding many forms of women's experience.[3]

The search for unifying themes or universals is not without risk if it blurs, appropriates, or denies identity politics. This search can also involve losing control of one's own story, as witnessed by bell hooks' wry observation of the proliferation of anthologies of black women's writings, edited by white women with grants.[4] Historically, women have most frequently acted in homosocial groups with low levels of ethnic, racial, or class overlapping. It has also been suggested that the struggle of women of color for survival and liberation in the context of racism and sexism may make their lives and political struggles unique. Women of color identify with others of the same race and ethnicity, and may prefer to work on problems of race and gender with those most aware of the problem. And even within the setting of the same California city, contemporary feminists of different races participate in different feminist activities.[5]

Gender remains a core concept within Women's Studies, but, as Caraway suggests, scholars should start where people are, and not insist that a gender identity be based on shedding familial, regional, or religious local skins.[6] To be relevant for women of color, Women's Studies must acknowledge intersections of gender, race, and class as determinants of oppression, and not view gender as the primary form of oppression. Or, as hooks has written, a broad and whole feminist theory will emerge only from those who have knowledge of both the margin and the center.[7]

It is within the community and local politics that women have traditionally faced fewer cultural barriers and role conflicts; local issues are "people" issues, in which women are felt to have special expertise.[8] Certain women's issues are most appropriately handled at the local level or lend themselves to participation by those familiar with local conditions.[9] It is here that women enjoy greatest access to the political system. For example, because of the preponderance of local offices, city, county, and special district, the number of United States female elected officials serving at the city and county levels is many times greater than that of those serving in state and national offices.

Community politics as a female universal also holds the possibility of transcending Western epistemologies. For women worldwide there are communities of place (family, neighborhood, school, and church), of choice (friendships and identity groups), and of purposes based on shared situations that foster local political action.[10] Martha Ackelsberg has defined politics as webs of connection based in relationships rooted in workplace, residential, and racial or ethnic/cultural concerns, and with the goal of protecting and improving households, communities, and workplaces.[11] Those studying the women's movements around the world have found that small, local-level activist groups, acting through networks, committees, and caucuses, are more common than Western-style movements or organizations. In Latin America and the Caribbean, there are two types of women's organizations: the woman-created, neighborhood based groups with practical gender interests that use traditional roles as a moral claim for public activism to accomplish women's usual tasks, and feminist organizations that seek to change the relations between the sexes.[12] The United Nations classifies women's groups as either community-based, problem-solving groups or nongovernmental organizations with policy or program goals.

Grass roots politics as a female universal for Women's Studies is somewhat problematic, given some feminist ambivalence regarding unpaid or volunteer labor. The National Organization for Women (NOW) has taken the position that volunteer work contributes to women's low self-esteem because it confers little status and is society's alternative for those who have no employment choice. Conversely, Kaminer has suggested that the impulse to volunteer is a human one of sharing and caring, but one that has been gendered by society. She further notes that this critique is primarily voiced by upper-middle-class white feminists, in that women of color have always worked and their volunteer work has been essential to the community.[13]

In United States history, women's memberships in groups have closely followed social and cultural status. Depending on the issues and the sociopolitical context, women's groups may cross class, racial, and ethnic lines, but most have been homogeneous. In part, this is because most were local organizations based in pre-existing relationships of friendship, family, neighbors, colleagues, or common membership in other groups.[14]

The specter of white racism and classism is well documented. White female abolitionists came to these positions out of a religious and moral framework, and did not support social equality for African-Americans.[15] Similarly, efforts by white women to assist working women did not include black working women, who were viewed as job competitors. And, if anything, the white club woman's movement was more racist than men's clubs. However, some white women did race work in the nineteenth-century South through the suffrage movement, the YWCA, and churches, and did align themselves with working women in the settlement houses and trade unions such as the Women's Trade Union League (WTUL).[16] The women's arts clubs (1880-1930), were limited to white Anglo-Saxon Protestants of the urban middle class. Elites, non-WASPS, and working-class women did participate, but, in staging of pageants for the whole community, club women worked with women of color to include the music of Native Americans and African-Americans.[17]

Berg has argued that white women in these voluntary associations were not driven to control the poor. If early charity was restricted to "moral women," it was only because working with outcasts would have prevented their activities. As the groups became more established, these middle-class white women came to identify with those helped, and they reached out to all women. Such women came to recognize the diversity of the female population, and the problems of low pay for women in the labor force and domestic violence.[18] Currently, an emphasis on diversity has become a hallmark of national feminist organizations in terms of staffing, agenda-setting, and membership recruitment.[19] Many have added programs to address racism and have assigned a higher priority to working-class issues such as "sticky floor" employment issues, family leave, and welfare.

Women's voluntary associations arose from women's personal needs and the social context of urbanization. Women's clubs offered a route different from that of the suffrage movement, one that was more moderate, was consistent with "ladyhood," and, as such, was a safe haven. Many participants were middle-class WASPs; black and white women operated on separate, but often parallel, tracks.

And some worked with, not simply for, the poor. All women's clubs were deeply rooted in what Watts has termed "womanculture," the sum total of women's goals and activities within a woman-centered point of view. As such, nineteenth-century women's values were fifty to seventy-five years ahead of male Progressives' societal critiques of industrialization and modernization.[20]

Today, United States women, especially younger and lower-income women, continue to view the local arena as the most effective one for women's political activities.[21] A very comprehensive study of civic voluntarism in the United States, however, found that there is no gender gap in activity in voluntary organizations. The authors explain this unexpected finding in terms of the disadvantages that women face in free time and access to income and jobs that would allow them to develop and exercise civic skills. Even so, women currently belong to more different types of local organizations than do men. These include youth, religious, literary, discussion, and study groups. Again, these choices are driven by life experiences (e.g., educational involvement for mothers, human welfare goals for poor females).[22]

In 1797, women in New York City formed the Society for the Relief of Poor Widows with Small Children, which provided goods and services such as jobs and schools to "moral women." What appears paternalistic was also very personal and very brave, in that women risked their lives to visit homes hit by epidemics. White ethnic women and African-American women formed similar groups for mutual protection and self-help. Such societies organized schools, orphanages, homes for the elderly, soup kitchens, and employment services, based on much personal labor and minimal cash.[23]

Moral reform societies (involving temperance, anti slavery, women's rights, and prostitution) were formed to protect the home but, in practice, allowed women to navigate the city freely, even going into bars and brothels. More political tactics such as public speaking and petitions, were introduced. During this era, working-class women began to organize around wages and labor conditions, and African-American women formed the first female anti slavery societies. The Civil War soldiers' aid societies (for the purposes of providing food, nursing, and clothing) further expanded the role of women in the public sphere.

The Woman's Christian Temperance Union (WCTU) and the Young Women's Christian Association (YWCA), among others, emerged in the 1860s and 1870s. Missionary societies ministered to the urban poor, Native Americans, and Southern blacks. Schools, hospitals, day care facilities, hospices, and settlement houses were founded, and new reforms concerning prisons, sex education, and employment were advocated. During this era, racial, ethnic, and class cooperation were often possible.

This movement began with literary societies first developed by black, mostly middle-class women. They met in each others' homes to study art, music, history, geography, and literature, and to listen to scholarly papers presented by members. Gradually, they evolved from self-improvement to involving the whole community in culture and in founding many cultural programs and institutions of music, art, and drama. The clubs brought fine arts education to all children, raised money to buy instruments for immigrant children, and supported professional women in the arts with awards and concert dates.[24]

By 1880, women's voluntary associations had begun to focus on the dysfunctions of industrialization, and greater sensitivity to the working class emerged. The WTUL and settlement houses such as Hull House were formed. Women worked for protective labor legislation and abolition of child labor. Other goals centered on housing, public health, public education and kindergartens, visiting nurses, children's aid, and corruption in municipal government.

African-American women did not trail white feminists in mobilization, nor were their groups merely imitations of white models or responses to exclusion. Racially exclusive groups reflected a segregated society, but black women's voluntary organizations were true women's rights groups, not groups primarily organized around race. In 1816 the Salem Colored Female Religious and Moral Society formed without white assistance; in 1831 the Female Anti-Slavery Society of Salem, the first of its type, was formed by black women.[25] As early as the 1790s, Northern freewomen formed their own societies for mutual relief, self-education, and abolition, such as the Daughters of Africa, composed of Philadelphia washerwomen and domestics who pooled their coins to pay sickness and death benefits to their members. Black women formed missionary and temperance societies around their churches later than white women, but organized the first literary societies in the United States. Black women's anti-slavery societies proliferated, and after the Civil War, many Northern black women went to the South to teach black children and adults, and perform Christian mission work. Including the work of the black club women and subsequent municipal reform organizations, African-American women in voluntary organizations have been responsible for founding uncounted institutions: homes for the aged, hospitals, sanitariums, nursing schools and colleges, orphanages, libraries, gyms, and shelters.

And even though black women were historically much less likely to differentiate between the worthy and unworthy poor, class divisions were and are present; not all black women share the same social and economic interests. The National Association of Colored Women (NACW; motto; "lifting as we rise") was very middle-class; often uneducated, unskilled black women were viewed as in need of social and moral uplift, and thus not as part of the uplift process. At times class insensitivity emerged, as when an Atlanta settlement house had a millinery program. But often the classes have worked through separate organizations with different organizational styles, needs, and access to resources. Poor black women worked through churches, benevolent societies, and as female auxiliaries to fraternal orders. Working-class women raised money for Phillis Wheatley homes for black working girls and sometimes prepared black women for domestic service, one of the few positions then open to African-American women.

Middle-class black women's clubs flourished with the formation of the NACW; within twenty years of its founding, over a thousand clubs had affiliated, and worked with blacks of all classes to establish retirement homes, libraries, day nurseries, kindergartens, schools, settlement houses, health programs, theaters, and other fine arts and literary programs, and to improve the neighborhoods through installation of sewers and lights, paved streets, and housing rehabilitation. Black women also attacked racial violence, Jim Crow laws, restricted voting rights, and racial stereotypes. By the 1900s, there were black suffrage clubs all over the country, and black versions of the WTUL (the Women Wage-Earners Association) and the YWCA had formed in response to resegregation and racism.[26] Studies of contemporary community organizations confirm that black women outnumber black men in such organizations and do the bulk of community work. Black men may be the speakers, representatives, and confrontational negotiators, but black women are the center, mobilizing social networks, forming networks, and engaging in consciousness raising.[27]

The pan ethnic groups, Latino, Asian-Pacific, and Native American, have less extensive recorded histories of women's voluntary associations. Hewitt, however, found a specialization by class among Latinas in turn-of-century Tampa. Elite Latinas engaged in "charity" work, often Anglo associations; working-class Cubans participated within homosocial mutual aid societies; and middle-class Latinas participated in both and provided services for the ethnic community. Pardo, too, found an enduring class consciousness as Latinas in a middle-class suburban neighborhood used class markers (shirtless, tattooed Chicanos in a neighborhood store) to identify men who didn't "belong" (but were reporting to a previously unknown parole office located nearby). And Hardy-Fanta reconfirmed the female dominance of Latinas as participants and activists in Boston community organizations.[28] All three panethnic groups define feminism in terms of a struggle to serve the larger ethnic community and are strongly involved in the formation of community services and aid to immigrants, culture preservation, and the fight against racial stereotypes.[29]

It is a truism of social movement and interest group literature that participation in groups is dominated by the middle class, but numerous studies have shown that poor women, working-class women, and wealthy women have a rich history of networking with their neighbors. A study by Pope of the Brooklyn affiliate of the National Welfare Rights Organization (1967-1973), showed that women of color on welfare were able to establish lasting community institutions run by indigenous leaders. Likewise, Rabrenovic, studying community organizations in low-income neighborhoods, found that women in upstate New York successfully lobbied to close crack houses, for faster police response times, and for tougher drug sentences. In Chelsea, Massachusetts, Latinas mobilized against the takeover of the public schools by Boston University as an Anglo attempt to supplant their families and culture.[30]

Working-class women have come to dominate neighborhood organizations, based in family, workplace, and community networks. The lack of male participation in such groups has been explained as rooted in men's roles as workers and providers, and their experience as the dominant sex, both of which limit their time spent in the neighborhood, their concern for personal safety, and their emotional ties to neighborhood life.[31] These women enjoy contact and friendships with other women and have a developed class and gender consciousness. The National Congress of Neighborhood Women, an umbrella coalition of local women's community groups founded in 1974 around the unique problems of white working-class ethnic women, focuses on issues of housing, education, economic development, child care, and employment. The earlier protests of white ethnic women against integration of schools and housing, and their resistance to urban renewal, were termed racist, although there was also a motivation to preserve cultural and family values. Currently the group is racially and ethnically diverse.

Despite the envious and hostile response to wealthy, elite women within the democratic tradition, upper-class women have also been active, as donors and volunteers, in movements for better schools, parks, museums, music, conservation/preservation, hospitals and shelters, good government, and civic education.[32] Some activities are purely philanthropic or altruistic (hospitals, social services); others are to maintain an aristocratic and elite lifestyle (churches, private schools); still others are collective (museums, parks). By supporting the symphony, conservatories, and museums, wealthy women assure that Kinderconcerts and art and music lessons will be available for their own children (and that some will be free to "community" children). A homosocial group in a "classless society" uncomfortable with the rich has obvious appeal to elite women. These voluntary associations are also a means of combating the class/gender stereotype of the idle rich and of acting on a sense of *noblesse oblige*. However, the belief that anyone capable of giving aid should contribute to the community is one that may cut across class lines among women.

Utilizing grass roots politics as a female universal within Women's Studies has several advantages. Reconceptualizing the definition of politics to encompass women in voluntary associations assures that women's most important issues (safe neighborhoods, good jobs, day care and education, available health care) will be viewed as salient. Women's lives bridge workplace and community; centering politics on relationships, rather than interests, promises a more open, egalitarian perspective. Self-help, or "power to" rather than "power over," links the progress of women with that of the community.[33] In addition, grass roots activism offers the possibility of a "multicultural feminism," in which race, ethnicity, and class will be as important as gender for analyzing the social construction of gender. To value diversity, we must learn others' cultures, share our own, and understand why our issues and priorities are differently defined. Despite our pride in women at or beyond the glass ceiling, most women are still in low- income, low-status jobs, and local programs that deal with jobs, child care, violence, health care, and homelessness still resonate. Diversity and difference, rather than causing cleavages, can provide the context for more effective coalitions. Women have different resources and skills: legal and political connections in established institutions networking and collective approaches to survival; the ability to negotiate with bureaucracies; a style of speaking directly, strategizing, and acting, rather than talking an issue to death.

There is considerable documentation of the universality of grass roots activism among women. Even so, any essentialist "grass roots imperative" can be disquieting. Witness the appropriation of "different voice" language by lawyers for Virginia Military Institute (VMI) in arguing before the Supreme Court on behalf of single-sex admissions policies; women, the Court was told, employ "an ethic of care," and men, "an ethic of justice." Yet there is empirical evidence that women do relate differently to the community and to politics. Hardy-Fanta found that Latinas view politics as an interpersonal and interactive process, whereas Latinos see politics in terms of hierarchy and positions. For women, the key concepts are connectedness, collectivitiy, and community; they are conscious of a link between personal self-development and political activism. Or, as Mulder found in her interviews with men who did not participate in white, working-class neighborhood associations, men's traditional roles privilege work over home and, for men participation in community groups contradicts three male traits: self-reliance, action, and separation from women. Neighborhood meetings are viewed as social groups that sit and talk, not act. (Men, however, are more active in sports and patrolling activities of community organizations.) Home is a refuge for men, whereas women do not see this sharp separation of public and private spaces.[34]

Human motivation theory may be as helpful in explicating women's civic participation as feminist theories espousing "maternal thinking" or "an ethic of care," even though women's primary responsibility for home and children often serves to propel them into neighborhood politics. The best known of these theories is Abraham Maslow's five-tiered hierarchy of human needs: (1) the physiological (physical survival and sex); (2) safety (freedom from physical threat, job security, savings, and health insurance); (3) love and affiliation (emotional ties, friendship, group membership); (4) esteem (self-esteem and respect, sense of achievement, integrity, recognition and respect from others); (5) self-actualization (personal growth, attaining one's human potential).[35] For Maslow, these needs are met in order; as one is met, it ceases to be a motivator. Alderfer has modified Maslow's theory by suggesting that more than one need may simultaneously motivate an individual.[36] This view is preferable, in that the historical record implies this; further, it decreases the possibility that women of color and lower-income women will be disproportionately consigned to lower levels of human development. Women, in particular those of color, have used civic participation for group survival and coping. Working-class and low-income women have helped one another, knowing that they could be future recipients. More privileged women have acted to fill the gaps of government programs and helped to form the modern social welfare state.

Women's voluntary associations have promoted health care reform, workplace safety, and equity in pay, insurance, and pensions, and have placed personal issues of safety (temperance, racial and domestic violence, sexual assault, child welfare) on the public agenda.

Women's civic groups have created a sense of female solidarity and allowed some women to form alternative families for themselves through voluntarism and altruism. Many women in groups also believe strongly in the home and women's moral responsibility to provide guidance and education to the family, the community, and the less privileged.

Women in community work have also been motivated by a quest for the validation of women's experience, prestige, a sense of virtue, and civic power to change the system. The search for self-esteem has activated many women. Immigrant women have worked to preserve cultural values and feel good about them. Women of color have attempted to provide a positive image of themselves and to combat negative racial/ethnic stereotypes. Women of privilege have sought to advance the status and prestige of themselves and their families. Elite black women protested segregated train cars because they were forced to ride alongside whores and gamblers. Wealthy women fought the stereotype of Lady Bountiful while drawing upon the power base of fathers and husbands to attain their own goals. Although the activities of the white elite offer a greater opportunity for personal recognition through the society pages and "community service" awards, more recognition of grass roots women in voluntary service is currently available.

At the time of the clubwoman movement, women's self-improvement was more threatening to men than their social activism. Historically, women in local groups have been empowered to resist their confinement to the private sphere. Women learned to organize, administer, handle money, speak publicly, lobby, and travel. They set their own agenda and received psychic income.

If, as has been asserted, the end of democratic participation is to improve the individual, women's voluntary associations have played a major role in the development of American democracy. For many grass-roots women, their participation in organizations "changed their lives," as their female vision became a part of political discourse.

NOTES

1. Maxine Baca Zinn, Lynn Weber Cannon, Elizabeth Higginbotham, and Bonnie Thornton Dill, "The Costs of Exclusionary Practices in Women's Studies," *Signs* 11 (1986), 290-303. For a collection that is especially inclusive and aware of the impact of racism, sexism, classism, and homophobia, see Cathy J. Cohen, Kathleen B. Jones, and Joan C. Tronto, eds, *Women Transforming Politics: An Alternative Reader* (New York: New York U P, 1997).

2. Barbara Nelson and Najma Chowdhury, "Redefining Politics: Patterns of Women's Political Engagement from a Global Perspective," in *Women and Politics Worldwide* (New Haven; Yale U P, 1994), 9.

3. See Amrita Basu, "Introduction," in her *The Challenge of Local Feminisms: Women's Movements in Global Perspective* (Boulder CO: Westview Press, 1995) 1-21; Maxine Baca Zinn and Bonnie Thornton Dill, eds, *Women of Color in United States Society* (Philadelphia: Temple U P, 1994).

4. bell hooks, *Ain't I a Woman: Black Women and Feminism* (Boston: South End Press, 1981), 10.

5. Myra Marx Ferree and Beth B. Hess, *Controversy and Coalition: The New Feminist Movement* (Boston: Twayne, 1985); Janet A. Flammang, "Filling the Party Vacuum: Women at the Grassroots Level in Local Politics," in *Political Women*, ed. Flammang (Beverly Hills, CA: Sage, 1984), 108-9.

6. Nancy, Caraway, *Segregated Sisterhood: Racism and the Politics of American Feminism* (Knoxville: U of Tennessee P, 1991).

7. bell hooks, *Feminist Theory: From Margin to Center* (Boston: South End Press, 1984). For a white feminist's history of the lives of American Indian, African-American, and Mexican-American women in the United States over the last century, utilizing many of hooks's insights for such a study, see Karen Anderson, *Changing Woman: A History of*

Racial Ethnic Women in Modern America (New York: Oxford U P, 1996). On the same question, see Aída Hurtado, *The Color of Privilege: Three Blasphemies on Race_and Feminism* (Ann Arbor: U of Michigan P, 1996). But see a challenge to cultural diversity in Susan Moller Okin, *Is Multiculturalism Bad for Women?* (Princeton, NJ; Princeton U P, 1999). Okin argues that when culture or religion provides a rationale for controlling and demeaning women, it should not be valorized; instead, feminists should be advocates for its female victims.

8. Pioneering books on women's local activism and their rootedness in the family and community include Ann Bookman and Sandra Morgen, eds, *Women and the Politics of Empowerment* (Philadelphia: Temple U P, 1988); Nancy A. Naples, ed., *Community Activism and Feminist Politics: Organizing Across Race, Class, and Gender* (New York: Routledge, 1998); Nancy A. Naples, *Grassroots Warriors: Activist Mothering, Community Work, and the War on Poverty* (New York: Routledge, 1998); Penny A. Weiss and Marilyn Friedman, eds, *Feminism and Community* (Philadelphia: Temple U P, 1995).

9. Ellen Boneparth, "Resources and Constraints on Women in the Policymaking Process: State and Local Arenas," in *Political Women*. Janet A. Flammang, ed, (Beverly Hills, CA: Sage, 1984), 277-290; Janet A. Flammang, "Women Made a Difference: Comparable Worth in San Jose," in Mary Fainsod Katzenstein and Carol McClurg Mueller, eds., *The Women's Movements of the United States and Western Europe* (Philadelphia: Temple U P, 1987), 290-309.

10. Judith Garber, "Defining Feminist Community: Place, Choice, and the Urban Politics of Difference," in *Gender in Urban Research*, ed. Judith A. Garber and Robyne S. Turner (Thousand Oaks, CA: Sage, 1995), 24- 43.

11. Martha Ackelsberg, "Communities, Resistance, and Women's Activism: Some Implications for a Democratic Polity," in *Women and the Politics of Empowerment*. Ann Bookman and Sandra Morgen, ed., (Philadelphia: Temple U P, 1988), 297-313.

12. *Women and Politics Worldwide*, 18.

13. See Wendy Kaminer, *Women Volunteering* (Garden City, NY: Anchor Press, 1984); Marilyn Gittel and Teresa Shtob, "Changing Women's Roles in Political Volunteerism and Reform of the City," *Signs 5* (1980), 567-578.

14. Joan Acker, "Feminist Goals and Organizing Processes," in *Feminist Organizations: Harvest of the New Women's Movement*, eds. Myra Marx Ferree and Patricia Yancy Martin (Philadelphia: Temple U P, 1995), 137-144.

15. For an examination of the ways in which women manipulated racial ideologies in a quest for gender equality, see Louise Michelle Newman, *White Women's Rights: The Racial Origins of Feminism in the United States* (New York: Oxford U P, 1999). Also see Rosalyn Terborg-Penn, *African American Women in the Struggle for the_Vote, 1850-1920* (Bloomington: Indiana U P, 1998).

16. Nancy A. Hewitt and Suzanne Lebsock, "Introduction," in their *Visible Women: New Essays on American Activism* (Urbana: U of Illinois P, 1993), 1-13.

17. Karen J. Blair, *The Torchbearers* (Bloomington: Indiana U P, 1994).

18. Barbara J. Berg, *The Remembered Gate: Origins of American Feminism: The Woman and the City, 1800-1860* (New York: Oxford U P, 1978).

19. See Roberta Spalter-Roth and Ronnee Schreiber, "Outsider Issues and Insider Tactics: Strategic Tensions in the Women's Policy Network During the 1980s," in *Feminist Organizations: Harvest of the New Women's Movement*, ed. Myra Marx Ferree and Patricia Yancy Martin (Philadelphia: Temple U P, 1995), 105-127.

20. Margit Misangyi Watts, *High Tea at Halekulani: Feminist Theory and American Clubwomen* (Brooklyn, NY: Carlson, 1993), 172-174. See also Karen J. Blair, *The Clubwoman as Feminist: True Womanhood Redefined, 1868-1914* (New York: Holmes and

Meier, 1980); Anne Firor Scott, *Natural Allies: Women's Associations in American History* (Urbana: U of Illinois P, 1991).

21. Leslie R. Wolfe and Jennifer Tucker, "Feminism Lives: Building a Multicultural Women's Movement in the United States," in *The Challenge of Local Feminisms: Women's Movements in Global Perspective,* ed. Amrita Basu (Boulder, CO: Westview Press, 1995), 455.

22. Sidney Verba, Kay Lehman Schlozman, and Henry E. Brady, *Voice and Equality: Civic Voluntarism in American Politics* (Cambridge: Harvard U P, 1995).

23. Kathleen D. McCarthy; "Parallel Power Structures: Women and the Voluntary Sphere," in *Lady Bountiful Revisited: Women, Philanthropy, and Power,* ed. McCarthy (New Brunswick, NJ: Rutgers U P, 1990), 1-31.

24. Theodora Penny Martin, *The Sound of Our Own Voices: Women's Study Clubs, 1860-1910* (Boston: Beacon Press, 1987).

25. Caraway, *Segregated Sisterhood,* 125-126.

26. See the following for excellent histories and overviews of black women's civic activism: Lisa Albrect and Rose M. Brewer, "Bridges of Power: Women's Multicultural Alliances for Social Change," in their *Bridges of Power: Women's Multicultural Alliances* (Philadelphia: New Society, 1990), 2-22; Bernice McNair Barnett, "Black Women's Collectivist Movement Organizations: Their Struggles During the 'Doldrums,'" in *Feminist Organizations: Harvest of the New Women's Movement,* ed. Myra Marx Ferree and Patricia Yancy Martin (Philadelphia: Temple U P, 1995), 199-219; Patricia Hill Collins, *Black Feminist Thought* (Boston: Unwin Hyman, 1990); Darlene Clark Hine, "We Specialize in the Wholly Impossible: The Philanthropic Work of Black Women," in *Lady Bountiful Revisited: Women, Philanthropy, and Power,* ed. Kathleen D. McCarthy (New Brunswick, NJ: Rutgers U P, 1990), 70-95; Dorothy Salem: *To Better Our World: Black Women in Organized Reform, 1890-1920* (Brooklyn, NY: Carlson, 1990); ed. Dorothy Sterling; *We Are Your Sisters: Black Women in the Nineteenth Century* (New York: Norton, 1984); Paula Giddings, *When and Where I Enter: The Impact of Black Women on Race and Sex in America* (New York: Bantam, 1984).

27. Karen Sacks Brodkin, "Gender and Grassroots Leadership," in *Women and the Politics of Empowerment,* ed. Sandra Morgen and Ann Bookman (Philadelphia: Temple University Press, 1988), 77-94; Cheryl Townsend Gilkes, "Building in Many Places: Multiple Commitments and Ideologies in Black Women's Community Work," in *Women and the Politics of Empowerment,* ed. Sandra Morgen and Ann Bookman (Philadelphia: Temple U P, 1988), 53-76.

28. See Nancy A. Hewitt, "Charity or Mutual Aid? Two Perspectives on Latin Women's Philanthropy in Tampa, Florida," in *Lady Bountiful Revisited: Women, Philanthropy, and Power,* ed. Kathleen D. McCarthy (New Brunswick, NJ: Rutgers U P, 1990), 55-69; Mary Pardo, "Doing It for the Kids: Mexican American Community Activists, Border Feminists? in *Feminist Organizations: Harvest of the New Women's Movement,* ed. Myra Marx and Patricia Yancy Martin (Philadelphia: Temple U P, 1995), 356-371; Carol Hardy-Fanta, *Latina Politics Latino Politics* (Philadelphia: Temple UP, 1993).

29. Esther Ngan-Ling Chow, "The Feminist Movement: Where Are All the Asian-American Women?" in *Making Waves* (Boston: Beacon Press, 1989), 362- 377; Beatriz M. Pesquera, "There is No Going Back: Chicanas and Feminism," in *Chicana Critical Issues,* ed. Norma Alarcón et al. (Berkeley: Third Woman Press, 1993), 95-115; Sarah Slavin, ed, *United States Women's Interest Groups* (Westport, CT: Greenwood, 1995).

30. Jacqueline Pope, *Biting the Hand That Feeds Them* (New York: Praeger, 1989); Gordana Rabrenovic, "Women and Collective Action in Urban Neighborhoods," in *Gender in Urban Research,* ed. Judith A. Garber and Robyne S. Turner (Thousand Oaks,

CA: Sage, 1995), 77-96.

31. Michelle Mulder, "Reluctant Warriors: Working-Class Men, Women, and Neighborhood Politics," paper presented at the Annual Meeting of the American Political Science Association, Chicago, 1995. See also Kathleen McCourt, *Working-Class Women and Grass-Roots Politics* (Bloomington: Indiana UP, 1977).

32. Arlene Kaplan Daniels, *Invisible Careers: Women Civic Leaders from the Volunteer World* (Chicago: U of Chicago P, 1988).

33. Martha A. Ackelsberg, "Women's Collaborative Activities and City Life: Politics and Policy," in *Political Women*, ed. Janet A. Flammang (Beverly Hills, CA: Sage, 1984), 256; Siegrun Fox Freyss, "Women, Power and the Third Sector: Exploring the Service Delivery Potential of Feminist Interest Groups." paper presented at the Annual Meeting of the American Political Science Association, Chicago, 1995.

34. See Hardy-Fanta, *Latina Politics*, 36; Mulder, "Reluctant Warriors."

35. Abraham Maslow, *Motivation and Personality*, 2nd ed. (New York: Harper & Row, 1970).

36. Clayton P. Alderfer, *Existence, Relatedness and Growth: Human Needs in Organizational Settings* (New York: Free Press, 1972).

4

Bearing Subaltern Witness: Rigoberta Menchú's *Testimonio* and Our Human Identity

Lance Grahn

Since its publication in 1983, the memoir of Rigoberta Menchú, a young K'iche' (Quiché) Maya woman and activist, has elicited passionate reactions. On one hand, Latin American specialists and human and civil rights activists rightfully saw in it an eye-witness reflection upon the terrifying world of oppression and violence in revolutionary Guatemala. The journal made accessible to both professional and lay audiences a formidable grass-roots voice that represented human reality among the poor, the marginalized, the dislocated, and the misunderstood. As expressed in the opening paragraph, it represented a singular epitome of the Central American *testimonio*:

My name is Rigoberta Menchú. I am twenty-three years. This is my testimony. I didn't learn it from a book and I didn't learn it alone. I'd like to stress that it's not only *my* life, it's also the testimony of my people. It is hard for me to remember everything that's happened to me in my life since there have been many bad times but, yes, moments of joy as well. The important thing is that what has happened to me has happened to many other people too: My story is the story of all poor Guatemalans. My personal experience is the reality of a whole people.[1]

Born of the challenges and the dangers of growing up female, Indian, and poor in revolutionary Guatemala, it also expressed the potential and the hope of the author and her compatriots. It was a forceful declaration of personal dignity, class consciousness, and ethnic solidarity. It was, and remains, a moving and paradigmatic portrayal of the life and death struggles in Guatemala that arose out of the articulation of poverty, institutionalized racism and violence, militarized authoritarianism, and hope. Not surprisingly, then, *I, Rigoberta Menchú* became a standard text in Latin American and Women's Studies, including my own courses. On the other hand, Menchú and her book have been attacked over the past two decades with a nearly constant stream of, at worst, vitriolic denunciation and, at best, attempts to discredit their legitimacy. Pundits and scholars of the intellectual right, some quite willing to make a career of Menchú-bashing, have argued that Menchú's book was inaccurate, misleading, propagandistic, and hostile to United States interests. The popularity of this Indian woman's life story, therefore, evidenced the gullibility and politicization of academic leftists who, by foisting upon unsuspecting students their feminist, multicultural, and socialist agendas, undermined American education and values.

Dinesh D'Souza, for example, prefers to repudiate Menchú altogether: "Rigoberta is a 'person of color,' and thus a victim of racism. She is a woman, and thus a victim of sexism. She lives in South America, which is a victim of European and North American imperialism. If this were not enough, she is an Indian, victimized by latino [*sic*] culture within Latin America."[2] It has been difficult, however, to sustain this hateful criticism because it is so uninformed. D'Souza apparently does not know the difference between South America and Central America. He cannot distinguish between "ladino" (the predominant Spanish-speaking sector of Central American society of European descent) and "latino" (an adjective that refers to people and things Hispanic in the United States). As a result, the very racism, sexism, and anglo-centrism that he perpetuates indicates the usefulness of, indeed the need for, texts like *I, Rigoberta Menchú*.

Like D'Souza, David Stoll, an anthropologist who specializes in Guatemalan studies, is a professional Menchú opponent. He recently capped his on-going debate with her *testimonio* with the publication of *Rigoberta Menchú and the Story of all Poor Guatemalans* (1999). Agreeing "that it would be naive to challenge Rigoberta's account just because it is not a model of exactitude" (ix), Stoll nonetheless asserts that its incorrect detail, *not* its inaccurate portrayal of Guatemala's political violence and brutal dictatorship, defines the text as a collection of "romantic conceptions of indigenous peoples, mythologies that can be used to sacrifice them for larger causes" (xv). He implies that these causes are largely challenges to the hegemony of Western forms of knowledge. Subalterns are asserting their own voice, rather than allowing professional academics to speak for them. They are contextualizing their own stories in forms of colonial domination, instead of simply letting the facts speak for themselves. Thus, Stoll better disguises his discomfort with *I, Rigoberta Menchú*. After all, he is, at least superficially, arguing for an unbiased search for truth, a premise most academics hold dear. But, in the end, his attack on Menchú's memoir fundamentally coincides with that of the pundits: do not question or offer an alternative to the imperial control of knowledge and its interpretation by the male- and North Atlantic-dominated Western tradition. Other critics, such as Gayatri Spivak, have discounted subaltern narratives like *testimonios* by charging that the grass-roots voice is irretrievably disguised, if not silenced, by the codification of vocalization. Writing down the tale, they contend, actually undercuts the legitimacy and authenticity of that voice from below.[3] These commentators assert:

that First World intellectuals (inside the circuit of the international division of labor and thus unable to grasp the consciousness of the subject of exploitation who remains outside this circuit) continually construct the Third World subaltern subject...The First World intellectual's attempts to 'represent' and 're-present' the Third World subaltern subject are consistently inauthentic. Since the inauthentic subaltern cannot speak for the truly subaltern and the truly subaltern have no means by which to speak...'the subaltern has no history and cannot speak.'[4]

Correct in the recognition of the unavoidable impact of any kind of textual mediation: transcribing, translating, editing, publishing. Spivak's claim nonetheless too quickly and too easily dismisses the voice that can come into the First World only through some form of mediation. According to this argument, the lack of textual purity negates the voice altogether. Allowed to stand, such a dismissal based on allegations of theoretical inauthenticity would do our specializations, such as Latin American and Women's Studies, and most certainly our students considerable harm. For it would deny them access to "the other" and so leave them only with the voices of D'Souza's right-wing, privileged, and white male canon and Stoll's university-trained imperious social scientists.

Moreover, a rejection of mediated voices denies the subaltern her own agency. Menchú counters this negation, noting that she learned to speak Spanish so that other people would not be able to speak for her and usurp her voice (157). Furthermore, much of current ethnohistory illustrates that subalterns can, and do, manipulate, appropriate, and use for their own purposes and benefits the structures of colonial (or neo-colonial) oppression.[5] Mediated information and interpretation, therefore, can exhibit the forcefulness and effectiveness of subaltern action and the irony of the colonized turning colonial constructs on their heads. To be sure, most Latin Americanists realized that Menchú's claim of universality was not to be taken literally. They understood the textual dynamics of the *testimonio*; it was a K'iche' story told in Spanish to a Venezuelan anthropologist in Paris. Unmistakably based on fact, Menchú's story was a personal interpretation of her experiences. It was a constructed text. It was a purposeful narrative. But that is just the point: it is a first-hand account of the terror that convulsed Guatemala in the 1960s, 70s, and 80s.

The *testimonio* held value at the time of its publication in 1983, and still holds value now, for other reasons as well. First, its basic claims, if not every minute detail, have been overwhelmingly corroborated by a body of testimony from other Central American actors, including women. Second, *I, Rigoberta Menchú* reflects contemporary developments in social activism, educational reform, theological reformations, and film making throughout Latin America. Third, the narrative illustrates both the premises and the means of rebellion, particularly highlighting the agency of indigenous women. Consequently, Menchú and her family stand as exemplars of the popular endeavor for identity, dignity, and peace in the face of official intimidation.

Four years after *I, Rigoberta Menchú* appeared, Elvia Alvarado's personal story of life in revolutionary Honduras, *Don't Be Afraid, Gringo: A Honduran Woman Speaks from the Heart*, was published.[6] The commonalities between the two women were striking. Schooled only through the second grade but trained by the Catholic Church to organize women's groups to combat malnutrition, Alvarado came to question the wretched conditions she saw around her. She then became a political activist, emerging as one of Honduras's leading defenders of human rights and land reform. True to authoritarian form, the state responded with harassment, imprisonment, and torture, alleging that she represented a communist threat. But she exited the terror unbroken and continued the fight against poverty and oppression. Reminding the powerful that women, the poor, and the disenfranchised should not be feared, she continues to illustrate women's leadership in the battle for economic and political justice in Central America.

My own field research in Central America, including interviews with leaders of CoMadres (the Committee of Mothers and Relatives of Prisoners, the Disappeared, and Victims of Political Assassination of El Salvador, Monsignor Oscar Arnulfo Romero) and refugee communities in El Salvador, peasant women in highland Guatemala, base community leaders in Costa Rica, and human rights workers throughout Central America, has substantiated Menchú's and Alvarado's description of the oppressive and violent world in which the poor, the indigenous, and the socially conscious lived.[7] Looking over our shoulders for signs of the security forces that undoubtedly trailed us, my colleagues and I entered the San Salvador offices of CoMadres in February 1987. We sat in stunned sadness as we listened to the women report their efforts to determine the fate of their husbands and sons, looked at the photographs of victims of torture and murder, and saw the evidence of their commitment to investigate governmental human rights abuses while knowing they might be killed as a result. In 1984, CoMadres received the Robert F. Kennedy Human Rights Award, but the United States denied its leader, María Teresa Tula, an entry visa to attend the award ceremony at Georgetown University. She was later detained and tortured by Salvadoran security forces.

State responses to the charges leveled by the Salvadoran archbishop Oscar Arnulfo Romero and the Guatemalan bishop José Juan Gerardi further substantiate Menchú's account of rape, torture, and murder. On Sunday, March 23, 1980, Romero challenged the government on its human rights record, declaring, "We want the government to take seriously the fact that its reforms are of no service if they continue to leave the people so bloodied. Why, in the name of God, and in the name of this suffering people, whose cries rise up to the heavens every day in greater tumult, I implore them, I beg them, I order them in the name of God: Cease the repression!"[8] One day later, an assassin shot Romero through his heart while the prelate celebrated the Eucharist.

More recently, in April 1998, Bishop Gerardi was murdered in his residence just two days after his Office of Human Rights released its report, "Never Again," that detailed human rights abuses committed over the 36-year course of the Guatemalan civil war. Based on 6,500 interviews and testimonies, the report concluded that 200,000 people, far more than earlier estimates, died or were disappeared in the conflict. Ninety percent of the victims were unarmed civilians, and 75 percent of the fatalities were Maya Indians. Ninety percent of the atrocities were committed by government forces.

In 1992, the Nobel Peace Prize committee recognized Menchú's perseverance and influence, thus strengthening the international validation of her testimony. In its announcement of the award, the Committee cited "her work for social justice and ethno-cultural reconciliation based on respect for the rights of indigenous peoples." It then noted that

like many other countries in South and Central America, Guatemala has experienced great tension between the descendants of European immigrants and the native Indian population. In the 1970s and 1980s, that tension came to a head in the large-scale repression of Indian peoples. Menchú has come to play an increasingly prominent part as an advocate of native rights. Rigoberta Menchú grew up in poverty, in a family which has undergone the most brutal suppression and persecution. In her social and political work, she has always borne in mind that the long-term objective of the struggle is peace. Today, Rigoberta Menchú stands out as a vivid symbol of peace and reconciliation across ethnic, cultural and social dividing lines, in her own country, on the American continent, and in the world.[9]

A chronicle of human rights abuses and human bravery, Menchú's narrative was, too, a focal point of both the expression and the critical analysis of grassroots testimony and explication. Like Alvarado's book, Menchú's took the form of a *testimonio*. A specific literary category understood to operate simultaneously on two levels, the personal and the national (or global), the *testimonio* is an autobiographical reflection that seek both to inform and to persuade. Signaling the emergence of the popular sectors of Latin American national societies, it became a leading form of popular or revolutionary writing in the late twentieth century. It represented

a transformation of literary production that may well symptomize at least those forces tending toward an overall transformation in national social formations or even, at the extreme, modes of production. It is, then, a form which takes its place in the struggle for the middle sectors so often crucial in supporting and opposing revolutionary struggles. It may help constitute a new national narrative or deconstruct limited and excluding national constructs.[10]

And, so, Menchú's opening claim that her "story is the story of all poor Guatemalans," that her "personal experience is the reality of a whole people" characterizes the genre. Her objective of adding a typical voice from below to the national, even international, conversation on reconstituting a more democratic Guatemala is entirely consistent with the form.

Importantly, *testimonios* like Menchú's and Alvarado's fit within a larger context of the emergence of Latin American and Caribbean bottom-up and gendered perceptions of the world beginning about 1960. Early in that decade, for example, Carolina Maria de Jesus's famous journal of life in a Sao Paulo slum, *Child of the Dark* (New York, 1962) caused a stir that has yet to abate. In 1997, 1998, and 1999 more of her translated diaries have been published.[11] Clearly, readers continue to be captivated by the autobiographical accounts of a woman struggling to surmount urban poverty.

Likewise, in 1988 Jamaica Kincaid's biting critique of the neo-colonial underdevelopment of Antigua, *A Small Place*, appeared to popular and critical acclaim. Caribbeanists and Women's Studies faculty soon added this brief essay to many course reading lists in further acknowledgment of the capacity of women, the poor, and the formally uneducated, first, to understand their circumstances and, second, to challenge them. Kincaid bluntly declared, for example, "An ugly thing, that is what you are when you become a tourist, an ugly, empty thing, a stupid thing, a piece of rubbish pausing here and there to gaze at this and taste that, and it will never occur to you that the people who inhabit the place in which you have just paused cannot stand you" (17). Later in the book, she addressed the difficulties of reconstituting one's self as a neo-colonial subaltern:

I cannot tell you how angry it makes me to hear people from North America tell me how much they love England, how beautiful England is, with its traditions. All they see is some frumpy, wrinkled-up person passing by in a carriage waving at a crowd. But what I see is the millions of people, of whom I am just one, made orphans: no motherland, no fatherland, no gods, no mounds of earth for holy ground, no excess of love which might lead to things that an excess of love sometimes brings, and worst of most painful of all, no tongue. For isn't it odd that the only language I have in which to speak of this crime is the language of the criminal who committed the crime? And what can that really mean? (31-32)

Although her short discourse does not fully answer her own prescient query, she nonetheless concludes her critique on the more hopeful note of over-coming the rubbish of imperialism and neo-colonialism, finding freedom, and realizing one's own humanity. *Testimonios* also materialized at about the same time that religious and artistic movements celebrated the very human desire to establish purpose and dignity in life in the face of repressive socioeconomic structures. Liberation theology, with its emphases on lay participation, an experiential herme-neutic, a preferential option for the poor, and the reformulation of community, posited that sexism, racism, and classism were not Christian virtues but were instead evil vices. To quote again Archbishop Romero:

The terrible words spoken by the prophets of Israel continue to be verified among us. Amos and Isaiah are not just voices from distant centuries; their writings are not merely texts that we reverently read in the liturgy. They are everyday realities. Day by day we live out the cruelty and ferocity they excoriate. We live them out when there come to us the mothers and the wives of those who have been arrested or who have disappeared, when mutilated bodies turn up in secret cemeteries, when those who fight for justice are assassinated.[12]

Educational reform movements have also reflected a new, reformist activ-ism on behalf of the popular sectors of Latin American society as well. Paulo Freire's pedagogy of the oppressed with its accent on the connection between literacy and *concientización* (consciousness-raising) contended that education should be liberating in the here and now, that learning was a democratic and politi-cizing process, that teaching should result in transformative praxis. Informed by his reading of Marx and Catholic intellectuals, such as Maritain, Bernanos, and Mou-nier, and by his own experiences of poverty, exile, and imprisonment, Freire proposed that pedagogy should be about the practice of freedom, especially for the poor and marginalized who, without education, constitute "cultures of silence."[13]

Understandably rejected by authoritarian regimes in Latin America and Cold-War mentalities throughout the hemisphere, Freire's work nonetheless found effective expression in Latin American revolutions in the 1960s, 70s, and 80s. Learning to read and write became a hallmark of popular movements because literacy was a powerful vehicle for creative self-expression, for challenging the oligarchic monopolization of wealth and power, and for asserting a new national identity.[14] The connections between women and men striving to overcome their sense of powerlessness and to act in their own behalf, with Freire's work and influence, the liberation theology of Romero, and the *testimonio* movement, then, are not accidental.

The unfolding of a Latin American cinematic social conscience likewise testified to the power of grass-roots voices to affect national debates on major social issues. Film makers such as Luis Buñuel, Hector Babenco, and Victor Gaviria explored in dramatic fashion the realities of street children in Mexico City, Sao Paulo, and Medellin, respectively.[15] These directors brought to an international public the "loveless life" of girls and boys for whom violence and "gangs became the alternate means of socialization."[16] Raised in violence and depravation, it was through crime and gang membership that street children such as Ester, Ojitos, Pixote, and Rodrigo "inserted themselves into the symbolic and 'normative' world."[17] But as the films show, their violent behavior was in fact their attempt to confront and challenge their suffering in some way meaningful to them.

Similarly, several celebrated films that examined the strength of women in national struggles for self-identification and civil rights hit theaters around the world. In 1984, for example, María Luisa Bemberg released *Camila*, her evocative study of feminist non-conformity in authoritarian Argentina. Though set in the 1840s, the historical tale of the doomed love between the daughter of a wealthy rancher and a Jesuit priest stood as a sharp commentary upon the military dictatorship of 1976-1982. A year later, Luis Puenzo's striking study of one woman's battle to unravel the myths and lies that hid the terror of military rule in modern Argentina, *The Official Story*, won the Best Foreign Film Oscar. In the words of one viewer, "it perfectly expressed what we Argentines lived during those times of suffering. Everyone should see it to realize that what happened [ca. 1980] shouldn't happen again in any civilized country."[18] Menchú's *testimonio*, then, typifies popular and cultural responses to authoritarian practices in twentieth-century Latin America. It stands not in isolation from other forms of protest; rather it reflects a pattern of social and artistic reactions to terror. At the same time, Menchú uniquely and personally manifests the potential of the subaltern.

You will recall that Spivak asserted that "the subaltern has no history and cannot speak." By her life and in her story, Menchú has disputed that generalization. Notably, she argued that it is through her very history that she establishes her voice. She seized her past, her people's traditional and colonial past and her family's immediate past in the establishment of her voice.

She took what she found most useful in her past and gave it new meaning in the service of achieving her goals. Thus, in a very real way, she personalized and took ownership of her own mediated (and, therefore, to some outsiders, inauthentic) identity. She validated her mediated self as her real self.

For example, Menchú bluntly stated, "I am a Christian and I participate in this struggle as a Christian" (132). She, like her Christian co-religionists, adopted Catholicism, adapting to its teachings and demands, but all the while refusing to let it conquer a sense of cultural tradition and self-identity. In fact, her encounter with Christian scriptures emboldened her in her defense of Indian land and personhood. Noting correctly that "we don't need very much advice or theories, or documents: life has been our teacher," Menchú, like liberationists throughout the Americas, interpreted Christian scripture through a hermeneutic of praxis. "We came to a conclusion," she argued,

[t]hat being a Christian means thinking of our brothers and sisters around us, and that every one of our Indian race has the right to eat. This reflects what God himself said, that on this earth we have a right to what we need... . [We] realized that it is not God's will that we should live in suffering, that God did give us that destiny, but that men on earth have imposed this suffering, poverty, misery, and discrimination on us. We even got the idea of using our own everyday weapons, as the only solution left to us (132).

Clearly, Indian woman in Guatemala did not need Che Guevara or Karl Marx, nor did they need Paulo Freire or Oscar Romero, to tell them they did not deserve the injustice they encountered. Their own will and their own faith in themselves told them that. But, they saw in Christianity a theological and sociological logic that could be applied to combat the deleterious effects of historical Catholicism in their country. Menchú rightfully observed in her latest memoir, *Crossing Borders*, that European religions "have sometimes been used as weapons of oppression, and other times as weapons of conquest and colonization. Our experience, as indigenous peoples, is that religion was used as a powerful shotgun, a powerful machine-gun, a powerful arrow, to try to dismantle our cultures" (211). As intelligent "consumers" of Christianity, however, the indigenous also show how Catholic teaching could be used against itself: "we began to study the Bible as our main text." Menchu then goes on to explain that the biblical texts became relevant to the people only when they could recognize themselves and their lives in the Old and New Testament people and stories (*I, Rigoberta Menchú*, 131-132).

Menchú consequently challenged not only the military regime under which she and her family lived (and died), but also intellectuals who subsequently tried to silence her with various kinds of claims of purity. Her *testimonio* does not rest on its absolute factualness; it rests on an argument based on fact. Her activism and influence are not negated by some act of mediation. Otherwise, her own personhood would be negated because she herself admits that her sense of self is a mediated construct, formed in contact, conflict, and accommodation with the ladino world, its language, its dominant religion, and its economy. Her assertion of self as a woman, a daughter, a sister, an Indian, a Christian, a poor person, and a rebel is not diminished because she was persuaded to talk with Elisabeth Burgos-Debray by a man, Arturo Taracena, and became, after going into exile, a world traveler. The world she described was, in fact, the world she experienced.

Importantly, then, Menchú embodied and acted out one of the fundamental ironies of subaltern responses to colonialism: adapting to change and using the structures of conquest, such as religion and language, to battle against the maintenance of conquest. But Menchú also typified the power of tradition, especially the tradition of motherhood, in the fight for self-respect and social justice. Menchú, like the Mothers' Committee in El Salvador and Maria Luisa Bemberg in Argentina, asserted the dignity that traditionally came with being a wife and a mother, a sister and a daughter, and demanded societal respect for those roles. In so doing, she affirmed the gendered duality of the traditional Mesoamerican world-view and society. The cosmos rested on the contributions and involvement of both women and men. Menchú learned from her mother that women should demand their share within the polity, whether it be the community or the nation. In so doing, she maintained a centuries old spiritual and cultural conviction.

Menchú's emphasis on her mother's influence and on women's political agency paralleled too her appropriation of the Spanish language and Roman Catholicism. For in propounding maternal importance, she reflected Latin American *marianismo*. The flip-side and counterweight to *machismo*, *marianismo* represents the sociology of the Catholic theology surrounding the Virgin Mary, Mother of God. Women, especially mothers, by their very gender and sex, are accorded by society both limitations on personal expression and special status. They are assigned both inferior and superior societal roles. Women are less than men legally, governmentally, familially, and ecclesiastically, but they are deemed to be superior to men in terms of character and virtue. Women are viewed as uniquely perseverant, humble, dutiful, and kind.

Significantly, the idealization of the role of mothers with the Virgin Mary bridges the pre-Columbian past and the revolutionary present. Menchú acknowledged that her mother has the same attitude toward women as women have had in the past (219). Under the regimes of both Mayan kingship and Spanish imperialism, Mesoamerican women were societal inferiors but societally crucial. Unequal with men, they were nonetheless mothers of the divine, keepers of the home, and managers of the domestic economy. This sociopolitical correspondence explains in part the indigenous ability to confront colonial subjugation. It also factored into the emergence of revolutionary women in Central America in the late twentieth century.

Evidenced by Menchú's *testimonio* and organizations like CoMadres, traditional maternal roles remained traditional. But the very characteristics of that tradition nursing and nurture, forbearance and fortitude, patience and resolve became sources of modern power. They led women to assert themselves in the political process, demand a seat at the table of decision-making, and press for governmental accountability. As Menchu believes, women need to be useful to the community (218). Menchú's mother, for example, joined the revolutionary Committee for Peasant Unity (*Comité de Unidad Campesina*, CUC), we are told, after she got to know the guerillas in the mountains while tending their sick and assisting women in child birth (218). Maternal service translated into revolutionary service. Menchú's participation in rebel activity similarly grew out of a gendered sensibility, but she developed an understanding of women's sociopolitical clout much more akin to modern feminism than to Marian or traditional maternalism. Although fighting alongside *compañeros*, she was a *compañera* who still had to confront their *machismo* (222). Revolutionary female leadership as embodied in Menchú, therefore, could not ignore the influence of gender, but it did seek to overcome it. Femaleness, like maleness, could not be obliterated, but it should be redefined; it needed to be politicized in a new way: In the new revolutionary construct, women and men should accord each other equal political weight. Women would not wield influence solely as concerned mothers, daughters, and sisters. Instead, they would also, and simply, be valued in two other ways: as individuals in their own right and as members of the community whose *human* capabilities, talent, and productivity contributed to the life of the whole.

And so, as Menchú has affirmed, the fight for dignity and life in Guatemala led her to discover her own consciousness. Forced into an adult world of responsibility and terror while yet a child, she forged a multivalent, activist sense of self, gender, and people. Her *testimonio* makes clear as well that both the process and product were purposeful but not always consistent. Her story, therefore, illustrates the majesty and the messiness of establishing and refining human identity.

"Identity," Menchú remarked in 1998, "is not just nostalgia for eating *tamales*. It is holistic, and comprises all the integral aspects of a culture."[19] Fittingly, her 1983 narrative describes the construction of her self-awareness out of her respect for her traditional past and her need for a politicized present, out of her terrible confrontations with violence and her enduring hope in the future, out of her encounters with the legacy of conquest and her anti-colonialist impulsion. Born in conflict, her identity was dialectical. It was held together under and by pressure. It was sometimes contradictory. She combined traditional spirituality and Catholic beliefs. She used the legacy of conquest in her fight against neo-colonial oppression. She was both female and feminist, communitarian and individualist. To dismiss her story on this basis, as some critics do, is to miss the point of the narrative and the humanity of its author.

Equally important for understanding Menchú and others like her, *concientización* impelled her to act. Reflecting on her youth in *Crossing Borders*, she recalled that in "the Committee for Peasant Unity, we used to say, 'Clear head, caring heart, and fighting fist of rural workers,' and the words were said with conviction. We wanted justice, and we wanted human dignity to be respected. We wanted the equal distribution of land to be a basic right. Each time we wanted something good for our people, it became a conviction. These in turn became part of a deep belief, that of aspiring to a better world. We believed that it was necessary and possible to change society" (214). Menchú has indeed changed society, but not because she and her compatriots merely wished it; they made it happen, Menchú with her activism, the members of CoMadres with their persistence, Bemberg with her films.

In the end, "what *I, Rigoberta Menchú* forces us to confront is the subaltern not only as a represented subject but also as the agent of a transformative project."[20] It is a project that claims for its author and her companions historical and social agency. It is testimony that challenges its audience to take seriously the voice of the marginalized and then to accord that voice central status. It is, therefore, a portrayal that intends, first, to create within us discomfort with our "relative privilege and authority in the global system" and, second, to ground us in the logic of the Guatemalan majority, thus making us all the more human.

NOTES

1. *I, Rigoberta Menchú: An Indian Woman in Guatemala*, ed. Elisabeth Burgos-Debray, trans. Ann Wright (London: Verso, 1984), 1.

2. *Illiberal Education: The Politics of Race and Sex on Campus* (New York: Random House, 1991), 72.

3. The key argument here continues to be Spivak's article "Can the Subaltern Speak" in *Marxism and the Interpretation of Culture*, ed. Cary Nelson and Lawrence Grossberg (Urbana: University of Illinois Press, 1988), 271-313.

4. Alice A. Britten, "Close Encounters of the Third World Kind: Rigoberta Menchú and Elisabeth Burgos's *Me llamo Rigoberta Menchú,*" *Latin American Perspectives* 22 (1995): 101.

5. My own research on Indian-European relations in eighteenth-century Spanish America demonstrates that Indians, while nominally inferior in terms of imperial power relationships, in fact utilized institutions of imperialism in the defense of their own societal and cultural autonomy. The Guajiros, who have inhabited the northeastern Colombian province of Riohacha for centuries, for example, managed their incorporation into the Atlantic economy in such an astute way as to adopt a pastoral economy and then trade those horses, mules, and cattle to English and Dutch merchants in return for guns with which they fought Spanish forces and other merchandise which they smuggled into Spanish consumer markets. Significantly, the Guajiros' materialist adaptation to European commerce and geopolitics did not undercut their cosmology or their political philosophy. Instead, they folded a new economy into their traditional world-view. Much the same can be said of Cuban baseball. Initially a North American import that was supposed to Anglicize Cuban culture, baseball in Cuba is now Cuban by definition. Cubans appropriated the sport and made it their own, and for much of the twentieth century they have used it as a tool against United States domination.

6. (San Francisco: Institute for Food and Development Policy, 1987).

7. See Gordon Spykman, et al., *Let My People Live: Faith and Struggle in Central America* (Grand Rapids: Eerdmans, 1988).

8. Quoted in *Let My People Live*, 9.

9. "The Nobel Peace Prize for 1992," 18 June 1998, Norwegian Nobel Committee, 21 March 2000 < http://www.nobel.se/laureates/peace-1992-press.html>.

10. Marc Zimmerman, "*Testimonio* in Guatemala: Payeras, Rigoberta, and Beyond," *Latin American Perspectives* 18 (1991): 22-23.

11. *Bitita's Diary: The Childhood Memoirs of Carolina Maria de Jesus*, ed. Robert M. Levine, trans. Emanuelle Oliveira and Beth Joan Vinkler (Armonk, NewYork: M. E. Sharpe, 1998); *I'm Going to Have a Little House: The Second Diary of Carolina Maria de Jesus*, trans. Melvin S. Arrington Jr. and Robert M. Levine (Lincoln: University of Nebraska Press, 1997); *The Unedited Diaries of Carolina Maria de Jesus*, ed. Robert M. Levine and José Carlos Sebe Bom Meihy, trans. Nancy P.S. Naro and Cristina Mehrtens (New Brunswick, N.J.: Rutgers University Press, 1999).

12. Quoted in *Let My People Live*, 233.

13. See, for example, Freire's *Pedagogy of the Oppressed* (New York: Herder &

Herder, 1970), *Education for Social Consciousness* (New York: Continuum, 1973), *The Politics of Education: Culture, Power, and Liberation* (South Hadley, MA: Bergin & Garvey, 1985), and *Learning to Question: A Pedagogy of Liberation* (New York: Continuum, 1989).

14. See, for example, Valerie Miller, *Between Struggle and Hope: The Nicaraguan Literacy Crusade* (Boulder, CO: Westview, 1985); and John L. Hammond, *Fighting to Learn: Popular Education and Guerilla Warfare in El Salvador* (New Brunswick, N.J.: Rutgers U P, 1998).

15. The films are *Los Olvidados* (1951), *Pixote* (1982), and *Rodrigo D: No Futuro* (1988).

16. Alonzo Salazar, "Young Assassins of the Drug Trade," *NACLA Report on the Americas* 27 (1994), 26.

17. Salazar, "Young Assassins of the Drug Trade," 26.

18. *La Historia Oficial*, 21 March 2000, <http://us.imdb.com/Title?008927>.

19. *Crossing Borders*, 223.

20. John Beverley, "The Real Thing (Our Rigoberta)," *Modern Language Quarterly* 57 (1996): 138.

5

Standpoint Epistemology and Women of Color

Jorge Valadez

In the latter part of the twentieth century several new developments in epistemology have emerged that challenge traditional conceptions of the nature of human knowledge. Epistemologists have traditionally been concerned with such foundational issues as the reliability of sense perception, the existence of other minds, the definition of knowledge, and the nature of truth. These issues are regarded as foundational because, depending on the position one takes with regard to them, one's understanding of many other areas of human knowledge will be deeply affected. Thus if one decides that the senses are untrustworthy as a means of acquiring knowledge of the external world, one will be compelled to seek alternative ways of acquiring reliable information about the world. Traditional epistemological issues were also perceived as foundational because any empirical knowledge claim would necessarily presuppose a position regarding these issues. A claim concerning the prevalence of gender-based social roles, for example, makes a host of assumptions concerning the existence of the external world and the reliability of memory and sense perception.

The philosopher most responsible for determining the course of epistemology during the last three centuries is René Descartes. He was primarily concerned with the foundationalist project of developing a theory of knowledge grounded on an indubitable foundation. Recently, however, philosophers have questioned both the necessity and the possibility of an indubitable foundation for human knowledge. There is wide acknowledgment among contemporary philosophers that the search for an indubitable epistemological foundation has been a failure.[1] In questioning the necessity for such a foundation, some philosophers have pointed to the progress of the natural and social sciences to indicate that human knowledge can expand without the need for an absolute proof of the validity of human cognition. The foundationalist project may be important for those interested in developing an intellectually complete picture of how our knowledge of the world hangs together, but it is surely not necessary for progress and development in the various branches of human knowledge. Indeed, if we took seriously the idea that we do not know whether the external world really exists or if memory is reliable we would be incapable of functioning in the world. If we maintained that a foundation for human knowledge is indispensable, it is unlikely that we would ever get around to addressing the important problems of human oppression and suffering.

With the waning of the foundationalist project, a number of alternative ways of conceptualizing the nature of epistemology have emerged in recent years. Here I will discuss and defend only one of them, feminist standpoint epistemology, and identify the special contributions that women of color have made and can continue to make to epistemology. As we shall see, the experiences and insights of women of color are of great importance for realizing the strengths of these episte-mological perspectives.

The core idea of feminist standpoint epistemology is that knowledge is so-cially situated, and is influenced by "noncognitive" factors as one's gender, cultural perspective, and socio-economic status. According to this perspective, the gender and social position of knowers are relevant to understanding how claims are formu-lated, understood, and legitimized. Standpoint epistemologists also maintain that knowledge claims influenced by noncognitive factors include not merely normative and sociopolitical beliefs, but also the "objective" claims of the social and natural sciences. For the standpoint epistemologist there is no such thing as value-free, neutral science because knowledge is invariably affected by social factors. Since conventional wisdom maintains that we should think of scientific theories as the paradigm of legitimate knowledge, standpoint epistemology presents an important challenge to orthodox views on truth and knowledge.

Several considerations can be adduced in support of standpoint epistemol-ogy. First, empirical evidence always under determines theories in the social and natural sciences.[2] In other words, scientific theories transcend available empirical evidence in that the scientific investigator has a conceptual space within which to formulate different, and incompatible, theories which are all consistent with the empirical evidence. It is within this conceptual space that values and sociopolitical factors, including material factors, can play a crucial role in the formulation of theories in the social and natural sciences. According to this argument, theory formation involves not an objective description of a ready-made world, but rather a conceptual structuring of experience in accordance with empirical, theoretical, and noncognitive factors.

Second, the acquisition of scientific knowledge is a collective enterprise in which investigators exchange scientific information and collaborate on joint research projects. Those investigators who are not part of a research team never-theless rely on the current and past research of others in formulating their research projects. Because a great deal of social and natural scientific research presupposes a prior body of theory and data, the scientific investigator does not begin her research from ground zero, but rather works against a background of a historically and socially situated scientific tradition. Disciplinary conventions, prevailing scientific schools of thought, economic funding interests, and other sociopolitical factors all affect the collective decisions of scientific communities. As Thomas

Kuhn shows in his landmark work, *The Structure of Scientific Revolutions*, and as other philosophers of science have corroborated, the acceptance or rejection of a scientific theory is not always, or even typically, based on purely cognitive or evidential factors, but rather is deeply influenced by noncognitive considerations.[3]

Third, there are cognitive values[4] of a very general nature that guide the formulation of scientific hypotheses and the structure of scientific method. These cognitive ideals, predictive power, quantitative formalizability, algorithmic uniformity, experimental replicability, and the technological capacity for manipulating nature, function as fundamental guiding principles for the general cognitive framework within which specific scientific theories are articulated and evaluated. Though these cognitive ideals of instrumental rationality are generally regarded as neutral and objective, they in fact represent a particular orientation to knowledge acquisition and a particular vision of what constitutes legitimate and valuable human knowledge. The capacity to predict and control events in the natural world, for example, is granted pride of place in the conventional scientific perspective. What is usually not recognized by most scientists, however, is that the conceptual scheme of orthodox science delegitimizes those forms of human knowledge that are not articulated and understood in terms of these cognitive values. Ways of knowing that seek to unite mind and body into an integrated whole, for instance, and kinds of knowledge that are embodied and implicit are not recognized as legitimate. Thus a whole realm of human experience and wisdom is excluded from the category of the epistemically legitimate.

Standpoint epistemologists accept the influence of values and sociopolitical factors in knowledge acquisition and legitimation but, in contrast to orthodox epistemological perspectives, they believe that this influence is a positive factor that can enhance and deepen our understanding of epistemology. Standpoint epistemologists maintain that an explicit awareness of the influence of both cognitive values and sociopolitical factors increases theoretical rigor because it clarifies the processes through which our theories of the world are formed, and because it allows us to hold in check possible distortions and biases in theory formation and selection. And, more importantly, such awareness makes possible the development of an epistemology guided by clearly specified and consciously chosen values and theoretical ideals. Standpoint epistemologists reason that since noncognitive factors cannot be excluded from the processes of claim formation and adjudication and that because they are an integral part of these processes, an adequate epistemology is one that systematically integrate these factors into its account of human knowledge. Instead of seeing noncognitive factors such as gender and social position as distorting knowledge acquisition, standpoint epistemologists articulate a theory of knowledge that thematizes the function of epistemology within the broad context of human thought and action. The goal of this thematization is to use gender and social position as positive influences and to enhance the objectivity of knowledge claims.

But what is the proper role of epistemology within the larger scheme of things? It is clear that our conceptions of valid knowledge greatly affect the way we view the social and natural world, relate to others, and form our self-identity.

Since we all have a proprietary interest in conceptions of knowledge regarded as legitimate, epistemology should be conceived as an egalitarian process in which everyone has an opportunity to participate in the creation, elaboration, and clarification of bodies of knowledge to which we will collectively assent. Otherwise, the systematic exclusion of the experiences of particular groups will likely lead to partial and distorted theories of knowledge. Such theories will neglect or devalue the points of view of the excluded groups.

Sandra Harding has argued for an epistemology which starts from women's lives. Such an epistemology would begin with women's experiences, perceptions, needs, and interests, and use such materials for formulating research questions, setting knowledge-seeking priorities, and specifying the general criteria of adequacy for knowledge formation and legitimation. Harding identifies several epistemological advantages to focusing on women's lives. She argues that in a gender-stratified society the activities and experiences of women are different from those of men, and that women's lives could be used as grounds to critically examine the accepted structures of knowledge which are based primarily on the perceptions and experiences of men in the dominant classes in society. Women bring an "outsider" perspective on epistemological issues that provides insights not readily accessible to men, who benefit from the status quo and who therefore have less incentive to question it. The social distance created by women's outsider status facilitates observations and challenges to the prevailing social order.

In addition, the struggles that women have waged to fight oppression and attain dignity and self-respect have sensitized them to the "hidden aspects of social relations between the genders and the institutions that support these relations."[5] This knowledge, born of struggle and pain, is valuable in critiquing taken-for-granted ideologies and forms of social organization that sustain the marginalized status of women. A great deal can be learned about the nature of oppression by examining how those in positions of power in society respond to challenges to their power. Finally, women's often unappreciated methods of coping with problems of survival in everyday life constitute valuable strategies of political resistance to oppression. As Harding says:

In labor struggles, the family and community networks that women have forged in their daily lives have sometimes proved more important than the unions in securing better conditions for workers. Women's resistance on behalf of their children to poverty, to social agencies of the dominant culture, to slavery and concentration camps, to molesting and abusive husbands and fathers have made survival possible for people who, in poet Audrey Lorde's phrase, were "never meant to survive."[6]

By recognizing women's responses to different forms of domination, we gain important knowledge, namely the practical wisdom of marginalized groups which they have used to cope with their exclusion and oppression. This knowledge can transform our perception of the members of these groups from passive victims to proactive agents of social change who have made valuable contributions to countering structures of oppression.

According to Harding, by incorporating aspects of women's lives into our epistemology greater objectivity is possible than with theories that do not include gender and social position. By being conscious of the ways in which women's lives and experiences can broaden and deepen our critical perspectives, we attain a more comprehensive and accurate understanding of the ways in which theory formation and adjudication function. Standpoint epistemology thus emerges as a perspective that is particularly well suited for pluralistic, stratified societies that contain diverse groups with different experiences and interests. Rather than degenerating into a trivial relativism, this more inclusive epistemological perspective sharpens the criteria for what qualifies as adequate and objective knowledge. It affords a better understanding of the reasons for accepting particular knowledge claims by helping us to identify the various social factors that play a role in their conceptualization, formulation, and validation.

Standpoint epistemology also provides the theoretical framework within which to conceptualize the epistemic advantages and unique contributions of women of color. The lives of women of color are at the intersection of multiple forms of oppression, and their experiences and insights can illuminate the interconnections between these different forms of oppression.[7] This is extremely important because forms of domination tend to reinforce one another and often times a particular form cannot be eradicated without eliminating the other forms. For example, a class-based form of oppression, such as the denial of equal educational opportunities for African-Americans and Latinas at the primary and secondary levels, can result in lower levels of educational achievement for these groups and thus reinforce negative racial stereotypes about their academic ability.[8] But when we realize that it is not lower academic potential that accounts for their lower levels of educational achievement, but rather fewer economic resources invested in their education, the interconnection between class disadvantage and the perpetuation of racist perceptions becomes clearer. The difficulty of trying to change perceptions concerning the capacities of these minority groups without eradicating class inequalities also becomes apparent.

Another advantage of adopting the epistemic standpoint of women of color is that it facilitates the recognition of how a person may both perpetrate and are subject to oppression. Black feminist Patricia Hill Collins describes the matrix of domination within which different forms of oppression coexist. Even though her comments focus on African-American women, they can be readily generalized to other women of color, many of whom also occupy a position at the intersection of different forms of oppression:

The significance of seeing race, class, and gender as interlocking systems of oppression is that such an approach fosters a paradigmatic shift of thinking inclusively about other oppressions, such as age, sexual orientation, religion, and ethnicity. Race, class, and gender represent the three systems of oppression that most heavily affect African-American women. But these systems and the economic, political, and ideological conditions that support them may not be the most fundamental oppressions, and they certainly affect many more groups than Black women. Placing African-American women and other excluded groups in the center of analysis opens up possibilities for a both/and conceptual stance, one in which all groups possess varying amounts of penalty and privilege in one historically created system.

In this system, for example, white women are penalized by their gender but privileged by their race. Depending on the context, an individual may be an oppressor, a member of an oppressed group, or simultaneously oppressor and oppressed.[9]

Realizing that a human being may suffers from oppression and yet benefit from the oppression of others can help create the kind of social solidarity necessary for developing inclusive social movements to fight racism, sexism, classism, and other forms of oppression. Such a comprehensive social vision undermines the potential fragmentation that can result from the struggles of different groups to fight their own oppression, while clarifying the specific ways in which some groups are affected by multiple forms of oppression.

Hill Collins also maintains that within the African-American community the ethical dimension in epistemology is emphasized. That is, an individual's character, values, and ethical behavior are considered as relevant for evaluating her or his knowledge claims. From this epistemological perspective, knowledge claims made by individuals who exemplify high moral integrity carry more weight than claims made by those who exhibit unethical behavior or whose conduct contradicts their avowed ethical commitments. Hill Collins describes an incident in which she assigned an all-female class the task of critiquing an analysis of Black feminism advanced by well-known Black male scholars. The women in the class demanded to know such concrete details as the authors' relationships with women and their social class backgrounds before assessing the significance and relevance of their claims. The students refused to evaluate the scholars' ideas without some information about their credibility as ethical human beings. By highlighting the importance of personal responsibility and accountability in epistemology, underscores the idea that knowledge acquisition and dissemination are not purely cerebral activities without ethical implications. Rather, they carry moral responsibilities to others.[10]

The standpoint of women of color can also alter the ways in which mainstream feminism, dominated by white, middle-class women, perceives and relates to men. Both women of color and men of color have experienced the effects of racism and class oppression. Women of color thus know the injustices and suffering experienced by men who have been discriminated against because of their color and limited economic resources. They know all too well that the real positions of power in society are not held by all men, but primarily by wealthy white men, and that the most dangerous expressions of male power are instigated by white males. As Ana Castillo points out in response to the claim that the machismo of Latino males is much worse than that of white males: "...machismo is an exaggerated demonstration of male virility that is inherent in most cultures, but is exemplified most in the United States by their own Anglo leaders, who in the past decade maintained an olympic trillion-dollar defense budget."[11] The shared experience of racism and class oppression creates a common understanding of the mechanisms of oppression and underscores the urgency of simultaneously fighting sexism, racism, and classism. Because of the daily impact of racism and class oppression in their lives, women of color cannot afford to focus exclusively on fighting one form of oppression.[12]

The common experience of racism and class oppression also makes it less likely (though not impossible) that women of color will adopt a separatist "us vs. them" orientation in relation to men. Assuming that an ultimately successful feminist challenge to dominant power structures will have to include the participation of a significant number of men, especially men who have suffered multiple forms of oppression, the gender inclusive perspective of women of color is of particular relevance for a feminism interested in developing the solidarity between men and women that is needed to develop a broad-based movement against the dominant structures of oppression. The empathy that women of color feel for men of color is important for white women to understand because it demonstrates in a concrete way how important affective bonds can persist between an oppressed and an oppressing group despite an awareness of intergroup relations of subordination between them. Feminist women of color realize that strong empathy for suffering men does not preclude adopting a strong critical stance against the oppression of women and the gender privileges men enjoy.

Women of color have a long legacy of struggling beside men in opposing oppression, and this historical memory of mutual struggle makes them keenly aware of the role that men can play in fighting sexism. bell hooks puts the point well:

Separatist ideology encourages us to believe that women alone can make feminist revolution; we cannot. Since men are the primary agents maintaining and supporting sexism and sexist oppression, they can only be successfully eradicated if men are compelled to assume responsibility for transforming their consciousness and the consciousness of society as a whole. After hundreds of years of anti-racist struggle, more than ever before nonwhite people are currently calling attention to the primary role white people must play in anti-racist struggle. The same is true for the struggle to eradicate sexism, men have a primary role to play. This does not mean that they are better equipped to lead feminist movement; it does mean they should share equally in resistance struggle. In particular, men have a tremendous contribution to make to feminist struggle in the area of exposing, confronting, opposing, and transforming the sexism of their male peers. When men show a willingness to assume equal responsibility in feminist struggle, performing whatever tasks are necessary, women should affirm their revolutionary work by acknowledging them as comrades in struggle.[13]

At the most fundamental theoretical level there are also important contributions that women of color, particularly those from indigenous cultures and from Third World countries, have made. By drawing from the epistemic resources of their cultural traditions, women of color help feminists and other theorists stage a revolutionary challenge to the dominant Western conceptions of knowledge. According to the prevailing Cartesian conception of knowledge in technologically advanced Western countries, legitimate knowledge is instrumental, impersonal, decomposable, replicable, and universal. This system of knowledge, which following Stephen Marglin we can call *episteme*,[14] is theoretical and taught in formal settings. Its primary purpose is to provide a cognitive, analytical account of reality based on principles with universal applicability. *Episteme* is the theoretical base for Western scientific and technological knowledge, and is a kind of knowledge that is unattached to social or ecological contexts and can be applied anywhere. The belief that *episteme* has universal applicability finds its clearest manifestation in the efforts of Western societies to export their systems of knowledge and technology to Third World countries, particularly in the areas of agriculture and industrial and technological development.

In contrast to *episteme*, many traditional nonwestern cultures employ systems of knowledge that are implicit, embodied, practical, and grounded in local contexts. These localized systems of knowledge, which we will call *techne,* are intrinsically connected to the cultural practices of the people who employ them. *Techne* is thus culturally meaningful and a part of the daily lives of the members of such groups. In addition, *techne* is implicit knowledge and often not capable of being explicitly articulated by its practitioners. *Techne* involves knowing how to weave or farm or heal, but not knowing how to write an instructional manual or provide a theoretical account of these skills. Thus, with *techne* "one knows with and through one's hands and eyes and heart as well as with one's head."[15]

In many nonwestern traditional societies women of color perform the bulk of the daily work and are the primary bearers of *techne*. They are often responsible (though not exclusively) for the maintenance and transmission of the accumulated wisdom of their people. Women of color can play a central role in challenging the hegemonic control that Western technocrats and specialists currently exercise over economic and social development in technologically advanced and developing countries alike. The importance of challenging this epistemological hegemony becomes clear when we consider that Western conceptions of economic and social development are having devastating ecological, cultural, and economic consequences around the world.[16] By relying on their familiarity with *techne* and the ways in which it reinforces and sustains community and economic self-reliance, women of color can help expose the numerous detrimental consequences that result when *episteme* is imposed on local communities and local systems of knowledge are delegitimized.

While it must be acknowledged that white feminist epistemologists often critique Western, Cartesian conceptions of knowledge and contrast them with the contextual, embodied forms of knowing characteristic of women, white feminists do not possess extensive nonwestern knowledge on the alternative concrete experiences of women of color from other cultures. It is one thing to theorize in academic settings about developing comprehensive, alternative ways of dealing with the world, but it is quite another to live one's life in a cultural context with a radically different epistemological orientation. In short, the special knowledge and standpoint of women of color is crucial for critically juxtaposing *episteme* and *techne* and fighting the global epistemic colonization currently perpetrated by Western societies.[17]

The perspectives of women of color are crucial not only for challenging the theoretical hegemony of prevailing Western systems of knowledge, but also for developing alternative self-governing, sustainable communities that can determine their own economic, political, and cultural futures. After all, the ultimate goal of overthrowing the prevailing oppressive socioeconomic systems is to replace them with egalitarian social structures that answer to the needs of all women and men in society. An essential feature of such egalitarian social structures is that they be viable over time, i.e., that they have an ecologically sustainable material base. Ecological degradation and the depletion of natural resources tend to destabilize a society and undermine its sociopolitical institutions. Limitations of space do not permit a thorough discussion of the necessity of ecological sustainability; it will have to suffice to note that there is increasing agreement on the need for societies to satisfy their material needs without jeopardizing the ability of future generations to satisfy their needs.

Traditional communities in the Third World, particularly indigenous communities, provide us with the only existing models of sustainable living, and women of color, as major bearers of traditional knowledge in these communities, have a special role to play in the articulation of the radically different worldview needed to create a truly ecological society. As Native-American activist Winona LaDuke states:

Reciprocity or reciprocal relations define the responsibilities and ways of relating between humans and the ecosystem. Simply stated, "the resources" of the ecosystem whether corn, rocks, or deer, are viewed as "animate" and, as such gifts from the Creator. Thus, one could not take life without reciprocal offering, usually tobacco or *saymah*, as it is called in our language. Within this act of reciprocity is also an understanding that "you take only what you need and leave the rest." Implicit in the understanding of Natural Law is also the understanding that most of what is natural is cyclical: whether our bodies, the moon, the tides, seasons, or life itself. With this natural cycling is also a clear sense of birth and rebirth, a knowledge that what one does today will affect us in the future, on the return. These tenets, imply a continuous inhabiting of place, an intimate understanding of the relationship between humans and the ecosystem, and the need to maintain the balance. For the most part, social and economic systems based on these values are decentralized, communal, self-reliant, and very closely based on the land of that ecosystem. This way of living has enabled indigenous communities to live for thousands of years upon their land as, quite frankly, the only examples of continuous sustainability which exist on Turtle Island (North America). We hope there will be more.[18]

Even though ecofeminists like Karen Warren and Carolyne Merchant have emphasized the importance of adopting an ecocentric worldview, their perspective, while of major importance, arises primarily from theoretical reflection and not from lived experience in a community with an ecological worldview.[19] By contrast, the ecological perspective of women of color in some Third World and indigenous communities is grounded on embodied knowledge and concrete experience, and is comprehensively integrated with the cultural beliefs, values, practices, and sentiments of their communities. While academic ecofeminists have an invaluable role to play in challenging the technocratic, male-centered worldview that predominates in academia, women of color have made and continue to make unique and irreplaceable contributions in bringing about revolutionary social change. Activists like Mayan feminist Rigoberta Menchú, Brazilian organizer Evelina Dagnino, Indian feminist Vandana Shiva and many other women of color have used their knowledge of the ecological values of their cultures to mobilize their communities for political and social change.[20] Their effective use of the human and cultural resources of their communities for grassroots praxis illustrates the need for a more comprehensive approach for political mobilization, an approach that incorporates not only feminist concerns but the broader concerns of the community.

In short, it is not enough to provide a theoretical articulation and defense of the transformations needed to bring about ecologically sound sociopolitical structures. It is also necessary to devise feasible strategies for mobilizing and transforming communities for social change. Women of color have particularly valuable contributions to make here, because of their embodied knowledge and experience in integrating the political, affective, and material dimensions of ecological transformative praxis. Failure to recognize the special knowledge of women of color and to encourage their participation and integration into feminist praxis is not only unjust, it also diminishes the realization of our collective human potential.[21]

NOTES

My thanks to Michael Wreen for a number of useful editorial comments on an earlier draft of this essay.

1. See, for example, Hilary Kornblith, *Naturalizing Epistemology,* 2nd ed., (Cambridge: MIT Press, 1994), 1-14.

2. For an exposition of the notion of the underdetermination of scientific theories, see W.V.O.Quine, *Ontological Relativity* (New York: Columbia UP, 1969).

3. See Thomas Kuhn, *The Structure of Scientific Revolutions*, 2nd ed. (Chicago: U of Chicago P, 1970). For an account of how theory formation and validation in scientific communities is often guided by sociopolitical, idiosyncratic, and other interests, see Miriam Solomon, *A More Social Epistemology*, ed. Fredrich Schmitt (Lanham, MD.: Rowman and Littlefield).

4. These cognitive values are themselves products of cultural traditions. Cognitive values such as predictive power and control usually evolve gradually and as a result of diverse sociopolitical and material influences within a culture.

5. Sandra Harding, *Whose Science? Whose Knowledge?: Thinking from Women's Lives* (Ithaca, N.Y.: Cornell UP, 1991), 128.

6. Ibid.,130. The quotation is from Audre Lorde, "A Litany for Survival," in *The Black Unicorn* (New York: Norton, 1978).

7. For a very thorough and eloquent discussion of this point, see Zillah Eisenstein, *The Color of Gender* (Berkley U of California P, 1964).

8. For an excellent account of educational inequalities between minority groups and mainstream society, see Jonathan Kozol, *Savage Inequalities: Children in America's Schools* (New York: Crown, 1991).

9. Patricia Hill Collins, *Black Feminist Thought: Knowledge, Consciousness, and the Politics of Empowerment* (Boston: Unwin Hyman), 225.

10. Patricia Hill Collins, "The Social Construction of Black Feminist Thought" in *Signs* 14 (1989).

11. Ana Castillo, *The Massacre of the Dreamers* (Albuquerque: University of New Mexico Press, 1994), 14. Gloria Anzaldúa also addresses the issue of the discrimination of men of color in *Borderlands/La Frontera: The New Mestiza* (San Francisco: Spinsters/Aunt Lute Press, 1987).

12. Of course, poor white women and poor white men also share the experience

of class oppression. However, the degree of race consciousness in most contemporary societies is so high that race is generally a more important factor than class in the formation of one's self-identity and in group identification. Further, while one can change one's class membership, it is much more difficult, and in many cases impossible, to change membership of one's racial or ethnic group. These considerations make it reasonable to maintain that, on the whole, race-based experiences of oppression are likely to be more pervasive and deeply rooted than those based on class.

13. bell hooks, *Feminist Theory: From Margin to Center* (Boston: South End Press, 1984), 81. hooks' analysis is heavily influenced by the Combahee River Collective Statement.

14. For a summary of Marglin's distinction between *episteme* and *techne*, see Stephen Marglin "Farmers, Seedsmen, and Scientists: Systems of Agriculture and Systems of Knowledge," in *Decolonizing Knowledge: From Development to Dialogue* (Oxford: Clarendon Press, 1996), 226-233. Even though Marglin's account of *episteme* is not entirely accurate, his distinction between these two kinds of knowledge is generally sound and is useful for our purposes here. In this section I will basically use the two terms as he does.

15. Ibid., 230.

16. For an account of some of these effects, see Herman E. Daly and John B. Cobb, *For the Common Good: Redirecting the Economy toward Community, the Environment, and a Sustainable Future* (Boston: Beacon Press, 1989).

17. "Western societies" here refers specifically to white male-dominated society, not all societies, cultures, or subcultures that may be found in the West.

18. Winona La Duke, "In Honor of Women Warriors," *Off Our Backs*, February, 1981.

19. See Karen J. Warren, ed., *Ecofeminism: Women, Culture, Nature* (Bloomington: Indiana U P, 1996) and Carolyn Merchant *Death of Nature* (San Francisco: Harper, 1990).

20. For example, *Alive: Women, Ecology, and Development* (Atlantic Highlands, N.J.: Zed Books, 1989).

21. See, for instance, Rigoberta Menchú *I, Rigoberta Menchú: An Indian Women in Guatemala* ed. Elizabeth Burgos-Debray, trans. Ann Wright and Evelina Dagnino (London: Verso, 1984); "An Alternative World Order and the Meaning of Democracy," in *Global Visions: Beyond the New World Order* (Boston: South End Press, 1993), 239-245; and Vandana Shiva, *Staying Alive: Women, Ecology, and Development* (Atlantic Highlands, NJ: Zed Books, 1989).

PART II

RAISING AND LISTENING TO OUR VOICES

6

Ethical Authority and Women Writers of Color

Mary Sullivan-Haller

Feminist work in the humanities often inspires ethical reflection upon the topics of women's subjectivity, their relations with others, and textual race relations, that is, racial differences among readers and writers. We need to reflect upon the ethical issues of human subjectivity and agency in order to more fully respond to all the voices we hear in our classrooms, be they authors or students, male or female, of a dominant race or not. Popular culture, too, has an interesting exchange of literary education at work through Oprah Winfrey's televised book club. The popular television talk show host invites her viewers to read a specific novel each month and submit responses in a kind of essay contest. Winners, usually women, are then filmed dining with the intensely empathetic Winfrey and the author, often a woman. She has featured three of Toni Morrison's novels, *Song of Solomon, Paradise* and *The Bluest Eye*, novels frequently found on college syllabi. Winfrey's success is worth mentioning because she has had a powerful impact on the American public's perception of black women's authority on matters of race and female identity. Like Winfrey's work with women's attitudes about race and gender, but not as lucratively, feminist academicians have long used literature in their pedagogical intent to increase understanding and decrease racial tension.

This essay begins out of my observation that many literary theorists have been announcing a desire to rid literary language of racist assumptions and foster more loving relations among women. Toni Morrison's author-function makes her the passionate voice behind *Beloved* and an ethical judge of other American writers. Such a role has provided a number of occasions for the identification of white offenses against black identities. I synthesize some theoretical arguments about how non-white subjectivities are formed. Examples from literary texts, selected from those popular in Women's Studies courses, do the ethical work of making theoretical language more accessible to a reader, as does a personal voice in critical writing. For example, Maria Lugones reminds us of the importance of emotional responses to philosophical thinking. This essay provides evidence that much literary theorizing about women and race reveals a subtext about ethics. Many writers demonstrate a desire to care for those who are different from themselves, a desire for a positive moral identity, and a desire for social justice. Once we have seen what causes harm and hurt, perhaps we can focus on what it takes to move on. As literary criticism of women writers has increasingly turned to the problematics of race and ethnicity, a dominant strand of guilt becomes visible. It takes the form of anxiety over failures to end the legacy of racism, a failure Ann DuCille sees evident in the continued production of African-American women as "other:" I am alternately pleased, puzzled and perturbed, bewitched, bothered and bewildered, by this, by the alterity that is perpetually thrust upon African-American women, by the production of black women as infinitely deconstructable "othered" matter . . . . the last race, the most oppressed, the most marginalized, the most deviant, the quintessential site of difference. [1]

Examples of this guilt include what duCille calls "guilty white conscience rhetoric" and the admission by writers of color of their own internalized racism. We must ask ourselves how helpful talk about race relations can be. If we believe that language has ethical effects on people, capable of harming or empowering their sense of self, for example, then we do not have to dismiss academic talk about race as an evasion of political or moral action. After all, the classroom is one of our culture's most public spaces and it is filled with many occasions for caring relations to develop. Literary study is an important occasion of talk about race. DuCille's address to academics exposes a feminist desire for caring relationships among women. We often discuss women's care and mutual respect for self and one another in familial terms like sisterhood. Women's love offers a number of moral challenges, especially for maternal relations. Maternal ambivalence is a frequent theme in feminist literature. From poetry to philosophy to the social sciences, writers like Adrienne Rich, Simone de Beauvoir and Nancy Chodorow have pondered maternity and the possibility of women's agency apart from their role in reproduction. The presence of a mother with her normative powers inevitably brings up ethical issues of identity and care. A woman's identification with her mother is an ethical issue because a woman often learns that parts of her identity make her an object of a dominant group's scorn. When this is the case, particularly for women of color, it is especially difficult to extend healthy care and love to others who belong to the same outcast group, namely one's own mother and or one's children.

Personal criticism and literature by women writers of color tend to confess the ethical challenges involved in confronting the intertwined forces of racism and sexism. I have come to think of these discursive expressions about right and wrong as a kind of ethical imagination. In order for a writer to articulate her own ethical imagination, she needs some rhetorical authority through which to be heard. Such authority appears to allow her to absolve herself of any failures connected to either racism or love.

This essay explores the importance of race to the ethical authority constructed for women writers through feminist literary studies. I refer to some examples of personal criticism by women of color. Also I analyze several literary texts popular in both American Studies and Women's Studies, including *The Awakening* by Kate Chopin, *Incidents in the Life of a Slave Girl*, by Harriet Jacobs, *The Woman Warrior* by Maxine Hong Kingston and *Beloved* by Toni Morrison. Because *Beloved* encourages readers to say something about the desire to heal and move on, it is a particular touchstone for my work which bridges not only feminist ethics and literary criticism, but nineteenth and twentieth century American textual practices.

Beloved is a Reconstruction era slave novel/ghost story that won a Pulitzer prize in 1988. Sethe is a runaway slave who attempts to murder her four children as slave catchers' approach. One daughter dies and returns years later, seemingly literally, to the household of Sethe, her daughter Denver, and her lover, Paul D. We meet the central characters well settled in their habits of "beating back the past" when Beloved arrives in the flesh just after Sethe's sons leave their haunted home and Sethe's freed mother-in-law, "holy" Baby Suggs, passes away. The central action throughout the narrative is the revelation of a past that inspires strong emotional responses in both the characters and readers.[2]

Many feminist literary scholars have an intense interest in knowledge of race and ethnicity, often leading these writers to complicated meditations on privilege, guilt and moral identity. Guilt may be an especially textual moral emotion because it can function like heritage, passed on to subsequent generations through narrative. Take a literary example. The riddle that ends *Beloved* states, "This was not a story to pass on" (275). To pass on can mean either to transmit or to forgo. I believe *Beloved* invests too much work in the art of "rememory," to ultimately suggest that its readers perpetually "beat back the past."[3] Just as Sethe needs to confront the guilt of infanticide in order to embrace the living, contemporary readers of racial texts are exhorted to explore the ethical consequences of both forgetting history and failing to imagine it. Morrison is taking history beyond the fact of slavery into the psychological texture of the lives of individual slaves. As the girl ghost, Beloved, joins her sister Denver in Sethe's home, and temporarily expels her mother's lover, Paul D., the burdens of history make themselves known through the demands of mother and daughter relations. Although it is primarily Sethe's guilt and pride which fuel the mysteries of the plot, Morrison reveals the workings of the willful agency of other characters to illustrate how individual actions respond to the attitudes held by the community in which they take place. Once Beloved's benign haunting turns ravenous, it is Denver who steps out of the household's isolation to fight for survival, forming social relationships.

The ghost is ultimately exorcised in the forgiving presence of a circle of women who had rejected Sethe, even prior to the murder. The women gather to the left of 124 Bluestone Road. As they pray and speak in tongues, Denver's new employer, white Mr. Bodwin, approaches from the right. This scene parallels the moment of the infant's murder, when Stamp Paid and Baby Suggs are looking one way, and Schoolteacher arrives from the other. In the penultimate scene, Sethe leaves Beloved on the porch, flying after the white man on horseback with an ice pick in her hand. She demonstrates that her murderous intentions were never meant for her children, her "best things." The next thing anyone realizes is that Beloved is gone, Sethe has told her stories of compromise, of rape, escape and murder, and now Paul D wants to "put his story next to hers." Also, Denver has joined the world outside her door. Sethe finally manages to separate her own self from a merged maternal identity. She assents to Paul D's assertion, "You, your own best thing." Beloved may be gone from Sethe's household but she has left no assurance that she won't return. Ever since Morrison introduced her, this resurrected daughter has been haunting American feminist literary criticism with anxieties about the perpetuation of racism and disturbing perceptions of motherhood and daughterhood. Even in critical texts that are not about African-American literature, *Beloved* often appears. For example there may be a reference to the promise of the power and beauty of the future of American Women's writing. This *Beloved* trope, as I am calling it, may also convey guilt over not having taken the time to include an African-American author in one's analysis. One such example is found in Gayle Greene's study of Anglo-American feminist fictions. Because Greene is studying fiction that "rewrites the old plots [of "the Great Tradition"] as a search for women's freedom," she omits Morrison's "metafiction." Yet she remarks: "One can hope that the fiction of minority women may take over from where white women's fiction left off: certainly, Morrison's *Beloved* is remarkable in the eighties for its delving into the past as a means to change and its focus on reconstruction from the nightmare of the past."[4] Not only is the plot of *Beloved* fueled by the guilt of Sethe's act of murder, the critical discourse surrounding the novel confesses a kind of guilt.

Black writers, also, have hesitated to put pen to paper about *Beloved*. The novel was released as a film in 1998. A commercial failure, the project, though well promoted, inspired mostly silence among critics. *New York Times* writer, Margo Jefferson admired the film, but waited until June of 1999 to voice reasons for both black and white avoidance of the film, remarking that "Sometimes writing about race can make you feel you are about to choke on disdain and despair. And turning those feelings into lucid prose? Well, it's always tricky, especially if yoUPride yourself overmuch on your good manners. In this case, the result was a courteous and utterly useless silence."[5]

In a personal essay published in *The Chronicle of Higher Education*, Katherine Mayberry relates a conference anecdote about her thwarted efforts to read a paper on *Beloved* as part of an all white panel on African-American Literature. She confesses "a deep sense of culpability for my failure to have considered the cruel ironies of a middle-class white woman's professing to explain and interpret a powerful slave narrative."[6] After several black attendees refused to hear the panel, the moderator canceled the paper readings and devoted the session to a discussion on white appropriation of black texts. In response to Mayberry's "passive response in the face of black women's anger," a white critic, Malin LaVon Walther, laments the "far too many white feminists latching on to black women writers such as Toni Morrison as the 'great black hope' for feminist literary criticism." She warns of the solipsism of whites reading African-American Literature to learn more about themselves: "African-American Literature is not about me, in fact, much of it couldn't care less about me. But that doesn't mean I can't understand it, analyze it, or teach it."[7]

R.B. Schmerl's letter to the editor praises Mayberry's "marvelous satire."[8] However, most readers believed Mayberry's sincerity. Ann duCille, cited above, could add Mayberry to her long list of critics like Houston Baker, Jane Gallop, John Callahan and Missy Dehn Kubitscheck. They announce honorable intentions, confess an outsider status- by race and/or gender, and ultimately treat black women as "newly discovered foreign bodies, always already Other" (612).[9] DuCille has authored a text trying to "delineate the difference between critical analysis that honors the field [African-American Women's Literature] and guilty conscience rhetoric that demeans it"(618). DuCille's text contains many ethical currents. She admits her proprietary interests in black women's texts as both professional and personal. Like many contemporary critical texts, her article includes the work histories of her peers:

I do not mean to imply that all black women scholars see themselves as what Hurston called 'tragically colored,' but I think that it is safe to say that these testimonies from across the country represent a plaintive cry from black women academics who see themselves and their sisters consumed by exhaustion, depression, loneliness. . . . But it also seems to me that Jane Gallop's anxieties. . . Nancy Miller's fear . . . and Houston Baker's desire . . . also represent plaintive cries. Clearly both white women and men of color experience the pain and disappointment of failed community. . . I have little faith that our generation of scholars . . .will succeed in solving the problems I have taken up in this article. . .too set in our ways, too alternately defensive and offensive, too much the products of the white patriarchal society that has reared us and the white Eurocentric educational system that has trained us (623-4).

DuCille may find a measure of hope in a new generation of scholars, "able to grapple less with each other and more with issues." At the same time, there are significant scholarly and ethical consequences of having turned these anxieties and resentments into such a central issue in the field of literary studies.

We, the current generation of scholars and undergraduates, now face an ethical challenge in our critical tasks. Are we obliged to soothe these anxieties and relieve these fears by resolving the ethics of theoretical issues like "racial appropriations of texts?" Resolution is the work of judges, based on a morality of justice. In a care-based morality of choosing to whom and to what we should attend, resolution is not the only point of talking about "problems." We identify dominant features of textual traditions so that we may choose worthwhile subjects on which to write, building moral identities out of an ability to move on from anxieties, with room in our lives for thoughtfulness and interracial solidarity. Writers of color are calling on white readers to admit the ethical shortcomings of colonizing relationships and avoid reproducing them.

Most women writers of color have had to face what the postcolonial theorist Homi Bhabha calls the invitation of the colonizer.[10] The colonizer can be understood in terms of whiteness. Whiteness is not a blanket condemnation of "white" or Euro-American peoples, but a trope signifying, in Carol Boyce Davies' words, "participation in the domination of others."[11] Its use indicates a critical perspective that seeks to expose the way that the modern language of rights, obligations, consensus, and freedom depends upon the presence of an unentitled, disenfranchised population. Such a critical perspective refuses the practice of enforcing racelessness in discourse. As Homi Bhabha says, it "insists that cultural and political identities are constructed through a process of alterity" (175). The cultural authority of Western academic discourse continues to function on a plain of whiteness, even as an increasing number of theorists of color interrupt that discourse. The colonizer may also be understood as one who maintains and authorizes the conventions of academic discourse. For academic women of color, "the very place of identification, caught in the tension of demand and desire, is a place of splitting. . . .[It is] impossible to accept the colonizer's invitation to identity: 'You're a doctor, a writer, a student, you're different, you're one of us'" (Bhabha 44). Embedded within the hospitality of such an invitation is a dominant group's desire for foreign authenticity. The dominant group is also issuing an imperative of repudiation; the writer must give up her home. The person addressed is 'different' from a larger community (her tribe, her family, or her nation). She then becomes the 'same' as some implicit 'us' (those in power). Yet in spite of an insistence that she repudiate her identity, others still expect her to represent an authentic otherness or exoticism. [12]

In "Third World Diva Girls," Gloria Watkins (bell hooks) explains the difficulty of knowing who you are, as a black woman intellectual. She describes several encounters between black women writers, Third world feminists, and alternately hostile and adoring white academics. hooks is concerned with both black women's reasons for policing one another in professional settings, and the role of "go-between, of mediator" played by Third world nationals who manifest "contempt and disrespect for blackness." [13] She claims that "one of the real danger zones is that space where one encounters black women/ women of color outside home communities in predominantly white space . . . [W]e are like siblings fighting for the approval of 'white parents' whose attention we now have" (92-3). Her comments reinforce the psychological complexity of the desire for otherness because black women have had a particularly maternal authority in American culture.

Black women's literature has often confronted the historical fact of black women's mothering work for whites. This includes care-giving as a wage-earning service, and has often involved some measure of loving. Ann duCille notices Adrienne Rich's failure to do for her fondly remembered "black mother," that which the text, *Of Women Born*, had intended. Rich's book promises a restoration of an independent identity for women who are mothers. [14] It did not occur to Rich that her feminist theories ought to address of women of color. In contrast, writers of color have had to address both the dominant audience of educated whites and other marginalized groups. Their authority comes, in part, from a refusal to be governed by the intentions of others. hooks regrets the price paid for the privileges of exceptionality because not only does it inhibit solidarity among women of color by reinforcing the role of overseer, it leaves benevolent racism on the part of whites unchallenged. For hooks, feminist solidarity can only be maintained by a feminist ethics that engages in self-critique and attends to the effects of the responses given to "Diva Girls" or academic stars.

Because identity has emerged as an important topic within the discourses of postcoloniality and multiculturalism, and because, as hooks indicates, a feminist ethics involves a measure of self-criticism, it is not surprising that so much academic writing by women is self-referential. Becoming a member of the intellectual class involves the unconscious taking on of privileges as well as some conscious accommodations, refusals and denials of certain attitudes. Drucilla Cornell points out that professional women who repudiate femininity to escape identity with the "second sex" are actually reinforcing stereotypes of femininity "as the truth of Woman." For Cornell, the work of an "ethical feminism" is to "come to terms with the damaging effects of the unconscious fantasies that give body to gender hierarchy." An ethical feminism will also,indicate the aspiration to a nonviolent relationship to the other and to otherness in the widest possible sense. This assumes responsibility to struggle against the appropriation of the Other into any system of meaning that would deny her difference and singularity.... {This definition} demands that we pay attention to what kind of person we must become in order to aspire to a positive, affirmative relationality.[15]

By speaking of "unconscious fantasies," Cornell highlights the limited concepts of femininity in our culture. The more privileges a woman has, identifiable in terms of education, class, race, age, health and sexuality, the easier it is for her not to disrupt the established order of things, "passing" as a "good girl." An ethical feminism can draw insights from the language of psychoanalysis in order to better understand why women become divided from one another. If we heed Cornell's phrase about otherness in the widest possible sense then we should be less likely to reduce otherness to matters of only racial difference.

Recalling Simone de Beauvoir's formulation of Woman as the most basic "Other" in dichotomous, binary, Western thought patterns, Cornell argues that "it is the Other, including the other in ourselves, that calls us to this responsibility" (84). Cornell seems willing to accept Woman's designation as an Other, if only provisionally, in order to exploit it in an effort to undo the damages caused by gender hierarchies. Ann duCille is more ambivalent about her status as Other. With a strong emphasis on the economics of racialized commodities, she renders an account of the damages done to black women in the name of "letting them speak for themselves" in scholarship by black men and whites.

Although women writers of color are frequently figured as the colonized "Other," doubly othered by race and gender, it is important to note Homi Bhabha's third place for otherness. He remarks that otherness is "the tethered shadow of deferral and displacement." It is "not the colonialist Self or the colonized Other, but the disturbing distance in-between" (45). It is simpler and more concrete to locate the concept of otherness only within a person identified as an "Other." For example, Ann duCille describes a white feminist's desire for the approval of a black feminist. It is a desire which fetishizes the black woman as "somewhere between monster and mammy: demanding, demeaning, impossible to please, but at the same time possessing irresistible custodial power and erotic allure as the larger than life (racialized) Other" (609). Otherness may then become an object one possesses, a kind of fixed object existing in a self-contained, history-less, present moment. In order to talk about otherness in a way that can displace racial stereotypes rather than simply judge them as either negative or positive, it is necessary to recognize why stereotypes depend on the construction of an unchanging, repetitive otherness. Bhabha claims that "fixity" belies the process by which those who read otherness are vacillating between fear and desire. He focuses on how racism is produced through the power of representation wielded by the colonizer, the one who renders skin a marker of discrimination.

Having already been described, in effect made, by the discourse of the powerful, those who inherit the position of the colonized need a language with which to break the fantasies of those in power and restore history to their dehistoricized memories. It is certainly debatable whether or not literary language can accomplish such a revolution, but feminist perspectives on patriarchal power have been effectively conveyed through a variety of literary genres, particularly the autobiographical.

Another literary woman in contemporary American literature who, like Sethe, confronts the ghosts of women's history is Maxine Hong Kingston's *The Woman Warrior: Memoirs of a Girlhood Among Ghosts*. The narrator of this memoir/folktale/coming of age Chinese-American narrative is constantly negotiating between "Chinese feminine" and "American feminine" behavior. There is no easily summarized plot for this text, a sequence of folktales and incidents in the life of a Chinese-American girl growing up in mid-twentieth century California. She is trying to understand and love her powerful mother. She reveals that the Chinese character for "girl" is the same as that for "slave" and begins the text sounding the notes of guilt.[16]

Her first story elaborates upon her mother's brief cautionary tale about the burdens of female sexuality and maternity. The narrator's paternal aunt (No-name woman) drowned herself and her newborn in the family well. The narrator displays bad manners by imagining the conditions surrounding the shameful pregnancy. She also exposes herself to the ghost's wrath by making the tale and her speculations public. Brave Orchid, her mother, forbids questions and subsequent references to No-name woman. After the narrator imagines a love story for her aunt, she reconsiders: "Adultery is extravagance. . . To be a woman, to have a daughter in starvation time was waste enough. My aunt could not have been the lone romantic. . . Some man had commanded her to lie with him and be his secret evil. . . I wonder whether he masked himself when he joined the raid on her family" (6). Narrative suicides are especially haunting because they promise a dialogue that remains unfinished. In a general sense, Kingston's text can be understood as a signifier of the guilt of being American born in an immigrant family: "After the one carnival ride each, we paid in guilt; our tired father counted his change on the dark walk home" (6). Her account of female identity also explores the consequences of keeping silent. One may keep the law and keep the peace but suffer internal pangs of dishonesty.

The narrator declares that her storytelling resembles the intricate designs tangled by the outlaw knot makers of China. Though she is now an assimilated knot-making teller of tales, she recalls three years of shameful childhood silence, during which time, "I liked the Negro students (black ghosts) best because they talked the loudest and talked to me as if I were a daring talker too" (166). After she adapts to the American style of classroom instruction, she directs her rage at her own impotence toward another Chinese girl afflicted with silence. She envied the Mexican and Filipino girls, their chance each Saturday to tell even thoughts that were sinful. If only I could let my mother know the list, (of over 200 things that I had to tell my mother so that she would know the true things about me and to stop the pain in my throat) she -- and the world -- would become more like me, and I would never be alone again (197-8). The narrator wants to heal and move on, but only if she can make everyone over in her own image, a girl willing to tell all. Regardless of her ethnic identity, every woman writer has to face her culture's attitudes and admonitions about women's silence.

Feminist literary studies has been fascinated by the trope of silence. Consider Joanna Russ connecting female silence to the challenge of literary production:

An alternative to denying female agency in art is to pollute the agency--that is, to promulgate the idea that women make themselves ridiculous by creating art, or that writing or painting is immodest.... Literary history is, I think, familiar with the Catch 22 by which women who were virtuous could not know enough about life to write well, while those who knew enough about life to write well could not be virtuous.... What remains unacceptable is clearly marked not by 'impropriety (the nineteenth century term) but by the modern 'confessional.' [not art and shameful and too personal] [17] (25-29)

Beloved and *The Woman Warrior*, two texts representing the work of women finding the words to speak their identities, are twentieth-century fictions informed by feminist and historical knowledge. As many Women's Studies courses do, we can also look to the nineteenth-century for other codes of silence, at a time when the subject of virtue was more explicit.

With political urgency, yet personal reluctance, Harriet Jacobs narrates her journeys out of slavery as Linda Brent in an 1861 autobiography published by white abolitionist, Lydia Maria Child, *Incidents in a Life of a Slave Girl*. Jacobs deliberately engages the moral discourse of feminine virtue. She pleads for her (mostly white and female) audience's pardon for her decision to bear the children of a white bachelor, not her master. She hopes to obtain freedom for herself and her children, and to avoid being moved to an isolated cottage, where she would be subject to all Master Flint's "will and whims":

Pity me and pardon me, O virtuous reader! You never knew what it is to be a slave; to be entirely unprotected by law or custom; to have the laws reduce you to the condition of a chattel, entirely subject to the will of another. You never exhausted your ingenuity in avoiding the snares, and eluding the power of a hated tyrant. . . I know I did wrong.[18]

The life she documents follows a conventional seduction plot; an older gentleman torments a virtuous maiden. The plot is complicated by the idea that a slave girl could have been trained to honor what historians call the cult of True

Womanhood, defined by Elizabeth Ammons as, "an ideal stressing domesticity, moral and sexual purity, submissiveness to authority and removal from public affairs."[19] With her light skin, her literacy and her pious grandmother's counsel, Linda has many privileges, including Dr. Flint's flattery, which can account for her ability to perceive herself as virtuous.[20] Through her pleas for her reader's understanding, Jacobs is introducing the possibility of a different ending to the usually fatal one designated for both the tragic mulatto and the seduced heroine. Even as Jacobs assures her readers "that this is no fiction," she is distancing her text only partially from the work of the sentimental genre. She triumphs over her master and ends the text announcing a dream for her own home because her family are still living under the benevolent roof of a white benefactor: "Reader, my story ends with freedom; not in the usual way, with marriage" (201). Throughout their youth, Jacobs shields her children from the truth of their paternity. Daughters, especially, ought to remain pure.

In contradistinction to nineteenth-century visions of family affirmed by Jacobs, Nancy Armstrong offers an interpretation of *Beloved* as an overturning of a particularly American sentimental impulse to gather pure daughters at one's hearthstone. She emphasizes the way that through Denver's decisive agency, the "assimilated" daughter replaces the "pure" daughter.[21] Armstrong notes the centrality of the daughter in the need for an English family to remain tied to its country of origin: "Such a [patrilineal] culture abhors a mixture. It prefers a dead daughter to an ethnically impure one" (12). In American tales of social reproduction and ethnic assimilation, from the colonial era through the present day, daughters transmit both biological and cultural identities. Comparing the slave narratives of Jacobs and Morrison, Armstrong writes that:

To reproduce herself- indeed to have a self-Jacobs has to keep her daughter pure. Upon taking possession of her children depends her power to write a happy ending. Toni Morrison decided it was time to reverse this equation . . . She exploits the gap between household and family, first of all, in order to grant priority to the home. . . . defin[ing] the mother and not the father as the origin of the family. (18)

Armstrong is articulating in literary terms the dreams of many women writing in the discourse of feminist ethics who insist on the use of narratives in formulating an ethics. To redefine the patrilineal family in terms of chosen relationships within a given historical context also allows for a redefinition of the self. Armstrong remarks of Morrison's "great" literary accomplishment that she " portray[s] racial identity as a process, or textual production, rather than a state of being, or condition of the body; who you are depends not upon who your father was or where you came from but on how you reproduce yourself in others and on how you tell your story" (19). Harriet Jacobs's text, with its multiple layers of rhetorical conventions, has been used to make similar arguments about the relation of voice and storytelling to racial identity, defining that identity as one in process. It remains tempting to want to fix a decisive interpretation on Jacobs's story, believing that Linda's primary triumph, like that of sentimental heroines, was to resist Dr. Flint's seduction.

Such a definitive reading, although it respects Jacobs's assertions of truth-fulness, may, as P. Gabrielle Foreman contends, silence the equally important elements of triumph having to do with her "undertold" constructions of female agency. In "Manifest in Signs," Foremen identifies "undertell" as Jacobs's "ac-knowledged tension between the 'strict truth,' which nonetheless 'falls far short of the facts and a mistrust for an audience she feels will not accept the 'facts'" (77-8). Foreman also observes a redefinition of sexuality in light of Linda's choice to have relations with Mr. Sands. She suggests that Linda did so to complicate paternity. Perhaps already pregnant by Flint, the protagonist's 'doom' consists not of sexual relations themselves; rather it is the threat of being sold and separated from her children (82). Though she does not wish to be sold herself, Linda actually hopes that Flint will sell the children to Sands, with whom they would receive care. Because Flint usually sells the children he has fathered by slaves, Linda hopes that he will claim fatherhood and therefore sell them. Foreman points out that Linda's strategy fails because Flint refuses to contest the paternity. Such an interpretation suggests that Flint has indeed raped Linda. Although Jacobs asserts her honesty repeatedly, there are numerous gaps and indirect passages, making the text an ongoing puzzle about the truths of slavery. For contemporary readers grasping for racial knowledge, the important puzzles surround interracial relations, not only sexual ones between slave and master, but textual ones between a black writer and her white editor/publisher and audience. My point is that the ethical issues arising from the study of Incidents complicate our assumptions about nineteenth century perspectives on sexual virtue and the truthfulness of autobiography.

Consider how another widely read nineteenth-century American text probes the truth of female identity and virtue. Kate Chopin's *The Awakening* employs a different kind of "undertell" from *Incidents*.[22] Jacobs inhabited a world wherein breaking codes of silence, such as naming your children's paternity, could cost you your life or your family. Chopin's white heroine Edna Pontellier lives among a free speaking, sensual Louisiana Creole community, more French than American in manners. Her silences and gaps in speech indicate the emotional struggle it takes to articulate one's desire for freedom from conventional female subject positions.

The Awakening has undergone a feminist revival since Annette Kolodney famously argued for its inclusion in the canon of American literature.[23] Readings that celebrate Edna's resistance to the conventions of bourgeois marriage proudly note the response of censure and disapproval received by the novel originally.[24] This text joins the Americanness of women-authored texts by engaging the assimi-lation/purity divide identified by Armstrong above. As Edna's Presbyterian reserve encounters her husband's French speaking Catholic peers assembled on holiday at Grand Isle, she begins a series of emotional awakenings that culminate in adultery and finally suicide. Interestingly, Edna feels very little guilt over the adultery; in fact, aside from her moments falling in love with young Robert, learning to swim, and painting in the companionship of Mademoiselle Reisz, she is scarcely awake. Hence her suicide becomes her only deliberate act. Romantic fantasies and assimi-lation into this "non-American" world kill her.

Although Chopin's short stories and reputation as a local colorist provide many avenues into studies of racial and ethnic identities, scholars have chiefly related *The Awakening* to traditional literary subjects. These include contemporaneous canonical French novels, influential modern thinkers like Darwin and Freud, turn-of-the-century feminism, and mythical parallels to Edna like Aphrodite, Thanatos and Eros. More recent readings of the novel focus on race and ethnicity; such essays constitute the most significant change in the widely used Norton Critical edition of the novel twice-edited by Margo Culley (1976-1994). Therein Anna Elfenbein focuses on sexual desire and racism, Helen Taylor traces Chopin's use of the slavery metaphor for women's oppression, and Elizabeth Ammons analyzes the labor done by the women characters of color. Critics who use a novel centered on white women to contemplate race relations repeat a gesture many creative authors have made.

In *Playing in the Dark: Whiteness and the Literary Imagination*, Toni Morrison refers to one of Willa Cather's novels as, "a means for the author to meditate on the moral equivalence of free white women and enslaved black women."[25] Her remark applies to the meditations composed by some contemporary critics as well. *Playing* is a collection of lectures investigating the construction of American identities through literature by Poe, Cather, Melville and Hemingway and their dependence upon images of whiteness and darkness for metaphors of freedom and terror. Some of the power of Morrison's readings arises from her knowledge of the composition process and her own success as a novelist capable of deliberately obscuring the racial identities of her characters.[26]

From a feminist perspective, Morrison's most fascinating analysis concerns a little-known novel by Willa Cather, *Sapphira and the Slave Girl*, The plot tells of a desperate invalid mistress jealous of her husband's affection for Nancy, her slave and nurse. Sapphira arranges a visit from her lecherous nephew, expecting a rape to foil her husband's seduction of Nancy, but Nancy escapes with the help of Rachel, Sapphira's abolitionist daughter. Sapphira's villainy is as obvious as her daughter's heroism. In this novel the daughters differentiate themselves from their mothers in the name of freedom. The ultimate reunion of Nancy with her still enslaved mother takes place before the white narrator, a five-year-old girl, rendering this novel autobiographically significant for Cather.

Elizabeth Ammons attributes the critical failure of Cather's novel to her "racism and ethnocentricity." She notes that, "appearing to celebrate black and white women's shared struggle, and particularly the heroism of a black woman, the novel in fact steals the black woman's story to give it to white women. At the center of the book is not Nancy Till as an agent in her own drama but Sapphira, Rachel and vicariously Willa Cather as Nancy's manipulators." [27] Rather than dismiss the novel for its racism, Morrison, reading with the sympathy of a fellow novel writer, takes the trouble to examine how race happens to trigger a breakdown in "the logic and machinery of plot construction" for Cather. For example, consider Morrison's observation that since "[g]iven the novel's own terms, there can be no grounds for Sapphira's thinking that Nancy can be 'ruined' in the conventional sense" (25).[28] If we believe that Nancy is capable of being ruined, or at least harmed, by an act of sexual violence then we grant her more human dignity than the ideology of slavery did. Of course contemporary readers can see the immorality of a historical ideology more clearly than those who lived through it. Historical fictions told from a woman's point of view often allow for a feminist critique of particular ideologies.

Jane Smiley tries to imagine the perspectives on marriage and abolition held by well-meaning white folks of the nineteenth century in her 1998 novel, the *All True Travels and Adventures of Lidie Newton*.[29] She creates an independent-minded orphan of Quincy IL, who has "cultivated a pitch of uselessness" in the domestic arts (28). Lidie marries an abolitionist, learns what it means to become one, falls in love with her husband, attempts to avenge his murder, avoids marrying a plantation master and fails at aiding a slave woman's attempt to escape.

At the start of the story, Lidie boldly accompanies Thomas Newton to nineteenth-century Kansas territory. He is a "d___ abolitionist" according to her brother-in-law. She studies Miss Catherine Beecher's *A Treatise on Domestic Economy* as she confronts the demands of running a household in a territory fraught with ideological conflict and violence. As she learns what it means to become abolitionist, while having no contact with actual slaves, she confronts the challenges made to one's sense of self by the habits of marriage. After anti-abolitionists murder her husband, she disguises herself as a young man and seeks revenge, experiencing a male dimension of white privilege and freedom for three weeks. Ultimately, after miscarrying and collapsing upon the lawn of Day's End plantation in Missouri, she receives an opportunity to compare her anti-racist ideology with direct experience of a relationship with a black woman.

The concluding adventure for Lidie begins when a marriage proposal from the widowed master of Day's End goads her into action. As she plans for departure, delaying her response to the proposal, Lorna, a family slave, claims Lidie as her savior. After making it as far as Kansas City, the pair is captured while trying to gain ship passage North and Lidie is recognized. Lidie reports on the melee, "All I remember is how frenzied it made me to know that it was through me that Lorna had been betrayed" (435). Smiley comments in the novel's appendix, "A Reader's Guide," that she had wanted Lorna to have the last word. Although Lorna is sold down South, her declaration about ownership vs. freedom triumphs. Smiley's constructions of slavery try to trump the benevolence of even kindly individual slave owners like Papa and his daughter Helen.

Smiley, Morrison, Jacobs and Cather each feature white women who are "exception(s) to the meanness of whites" (*Beloved*, 82). Sethe's kind mistress, Mrs. Garner sanctions her slave girl's "marriage" to Halle, and Linda learns to read and write as a child. In Morrison's novel, Miss Amy Denver, a runaway indentured servant appears out of the woods to aid the escaping Sethe in the labor and delivery of her fourth-born. The infant is a daughter who inherits Amy's name and longing for autonomy. Amy, "with good hands and "no meanness around the mouth," is united to Sethe, "two throwaway people, two lawless outlaws"(84). Amy's presence inspires some of Stanley Crouch's sarcasm. He calls Denver's birth scene: "the obligatory moment of transcendent female solidarity, featuring a runaway white girl . . . Woman to woman, out in nature, freed of patriarchal domination and economic exploitation, they deliver baby Denver. Amy is also good for homilies."[30] Although Crouch dismisses Morrison's fiction as didactic, I believe he is accurate in locating a feminist desire for interracial solidarity, a search for a kind of love, in Morrison's historical imagination.

Beloved's importance is profoundly tied to its moral relation to history. We see this through the many ways to interpret the ghost. The surface text assures us that Beloved is the murdered "crawling already" baby girl who is hungry for every scrap of story Sethe can feed her. There are other signals to indicate her identity with the "60 Million and more" slaves lost to slavery, many between Africa and the Americas during the slave trade.[31] We learn, too, that Sethe's mother had borne babies by slave traders and thrown them overboard, keeping only Sethe, offspring of a desired union. In a puzzling, multi-voiced Faulknerian section of the text, "unspeakable thoughts unspoken," Denver, Sethe and Beloved each narrate a chapter about longing for one another's company. After we have been told that the three women are alone in the house, there is a time of speaking in tongues. Desires are admitted, and apologies offered and refused. Morrison's themes of love and merging with the beloved echo the Eros expressed in the biblical Song of Songs, especially through her numerous images of the nursing breast. However, the novel's epigraph is from Romans 9:25: "I will call them my people, which were not my people; and her beloved, which was not beloved." Whoever she is, Beloved wants to be claimed. From her speech, the text reads: "my face is coming I have to have it I am looking for the join. . . . I want to be the two of us; You are my face; I am you. Why did you leave me who am you?. . . You are mine" (210-217). Aside from this longing for the mother, she has maternal desires of her own. She has also lain with Paul D., commanding him to "touch her on the inside part" and she conceives . Her ghostly influence moves him, literally, out of Sethe's bed and home, giving him no rest and no control over his own actions. In spite of, and in part because of Beloved's power to deliver pain to those who are hungry for love, and worn out from suffering, she also moves the community of former slaves closer to hope for their futures.

To say that Morrison's novel ends with hope is not to obscure the jarring, dangerous and violent path it takes to get there. I emphasize such dispositions because they link us back to the work readers expect literary texts to do: provide aesthetic pleasure. As Hilde Hein points out, "We are capable of deriving intense aesthetic pleasure from things we know to be horrible, sometimes finding this very enjoyment a cause for ethical anguish- a state which in its own turn, can yield a redoubled, doubly disturbing second-order aesthetic gratification."[32] There are subtexts in *Beloved*, *The Woman Warrior* and *Incidents in the Life of a Slave Girl*, which reflect on the mix of pleasure and pain caused by storytelling.

Many of the narrators in women-authored texts offer textual asides to their audiences about the nature of narrative. For example, Jacobs tries to assure her readers that her story is true, emphasizing the agony of telling it, and both Kingston and Beloved beg their mothers to tell them stories that are painful to the older women. As the younger women work through their identities, their desire for narrative illustrates how personal the exchange of stories can be. Yet these authors also speak to a general audience; readers are called to be witnesses to grief made public. From the pain revealed in the experiences of others' suffering, readers take pleasure imagining positive changes in a wider framework, meaning a turn to the future. For some, that wider framework consists of theory, and for others a turn to the future requires attention to present day, "real world" conditions of suffering. A theorist's work often translates expectations for the future with reference to literature.

Both Homi Bhabha and Drucilla Cornell find expression for the ultimate, albeit cautionary, optimism in the verb tense known as the future anterior, that "which will have been." And significantly, each cites *Beloved* to clarify the functions of this tense in the transformation of "our sense of what it means to live, to be, in other times and different spaces, both human and historical" (Bhabha, 256). Because of their power to imagine changes in social organizations, and transformed human relations, literary texts are charged by meliorating theories, like feminism and postcoloniality, with the work of representing communities in the process of healing. The mysteries of healing and progress are complicated by the linear habits of Western time. Bhabha explains the postcolonial temporality in terms of a 'time-lag' and a 'projective past.' This temporality can explore "forms of social antagonism and contradiction that are not yet properly represented, political identities in the process of being formed, cultural enunciation in the act of hybridity" (252). The projective past interrupts the linearity of modernity. It is a kind of contramodernity, but it is neither an assertion of timelessness nor an oppositional argument against modernity. Bhabha writes that Beloved, the murdered daughter of African-American slavery, is the "furious emergence of the projective past which Morrison sees as the stressed, dislocatory absence that is crucial for the rememoration of the narrative of slavery" (254). Until slavery is articulated, it does not actually have a past. In other words, it has not been remembered. Yet. The future perfect allows Morrison to know that hers is a story that will have been "passed on," once it has been written and read.

The future anterior is a way of restoring history to discussions of agency that tend to fall into vague hopes for the future, or abstractions. Cornell's project seeks to explain sexual difference outside of the masculine symbolic, the dominant fantasies of Woman, in order to free up women's autonomy. If women's autonomy can be articulated outside of a masculine symbolic on a psychoanalytic level, then it may also become more clear how and why women have acted, and failed to act, within history. Cornell cites the historian Joan Scott approvingly, because Scott "understands that there is an inconclusive futurity of what will always already have been: a 'time' which can never be entirely remembered, because even if read as already constituted, the past is being constituted even as it is read." [33]

To comprehend such an alternative time frame, we can think about the ways that self-conscious writing works, calling attention to the constructed nature of texts. The narrator of *The Woman Warrior* knows that she cannot write about her family's identity in the simple past and present tenses. She remarks that her brother's version of certain events, "may be better than mine because of its bareness, not twisted into designs, the hearer can carry it tucked away without it taking up much room" (163). When we twist our narratives into designs, we recognize that we have deliberately shaped a perception on the past locked into the concerns of the present. Cornell explains that women writing within an alternative sense of time, the future anterior, can take us out of the fixed time of the present that lends itself to the denial of the "otherness and exteriority of actual women."[34] The present tense can be a selfish time of individuated selves who understand themselves to be self-constituting, free standing egos. Cornell concludes that an ethical feminism must always refuse the temptation to reduce the exteriority of the Other, such as what happens when women interiorize their mothers as part of their own identities, but ignore their mothers' autonomy. In the important, loosely punctuated litany contained within Morrison's novel, explicated above, Cornell identifies Beloved as an Other whose subjectivity belongs to the time of the future anterior.

Homi Bhabha quotes similar passages from *Beloved*, and like Cornell, he invokes the "ethical love" of Emmanuel Levinas which can "see inwardness from the outside" (15-17). Since a high percentage of women's texts reproduce love stories, they are especially useful for philosophers dealing with abstractions like 'ethical love,' a transformative exchange of care and respect which does not deny differences, which does not insist that the other be exactly like me (the self). Such love stories are not necessarily heterosexual romances, but can include maternal love and even love of God (Morrison's theme in her most recent novel *Paradise*).[35] Combining study of the ethical dimension of the subject/other relation with Morrison's representation of slavery's female subjectivity is symptomatic of critical theory's ambivalent desire for black women. Racialized language, a means of establishing a system of difference between peoples and assigning characteristics to them, differs from the concept of racism; it is rarely exclusively negative. It often turns on affection or even idealization. What can account for the desire of influential critical theorists to fix what I am calling an ethical imagination upon the figure of a Black woman writing?

I am not implying that Bhabha should be taken to stand for (male) postcolonial theory at large, nor Cornell for (white) feminist theory, although each attempts to generalize on behalf of larger critical projects. The significant point is that they both turn to the female subjectivity of a fictional slave, a ghost actually, in order to posit a hope-filled future (anterior) for their theories. Also, in turning their ears to the woman of color behind the slaves (Morrison), they produce an "ethical" gesture toward an other. Cornell and Bhabha are speaking out of their own disciplinary authority, opening additional space for this expression of black female subjectivity. Fiction moves into theory and ethical discourse moves into literary studies. Because literary language can articulate the specific conditions that construct gendered subjectivities through mechanisms of plot, voice, genre and character development, literary criticism depends upon narrative genres to illustrate how ethical love translates into actions. Philosophy, too, can depend upon narratives to call forth the sentiments that motivate an argument.

Feminist authority, or at least influence, dependent as it is upon the ethical insistence that social conditions for women improve, is necessarily established through some uses of sentimental genres. Yet feminist discourse is often embarrassed by the sentimental; it can seem like an exclusively middle class and white luxury, dominated by images of motherhood and purity. Sentimental authority can be judged unsophisticated, but has been politically effective occasionally, as in Harriet Jacobs's autobiography. Assume for a moment that women do not wish to banish sympathy and sensibility from their habits of perception. What use can we make of the sentimentality that positions white women, filled with pity, longing and anxiety, gazing upon women of color, even when women of color author their own stories?

Maria Lugones has little patience for that blank gaze, that sibstance depriving "ghost making gaze" that she has labeled a form of "arrogant" or "boomerang" perception. As a child in Argentina, she was taught to train this gaze upon her mother, to take her for granted and to believe that love was consistent with enslavement of another. She struggled with a longing for an identification with her mother that she could not reconcile with this arrogant perception. She realizes that her failure to learn this lesson in supposed love is actually a good thing.[36] Failures to love motivate many of Lugones' texts. Whether she is considering the inability of white women in the United States to love across color lines, horizontal hostility within races, or her own mother's independent subjectivity, she proposes a practice of loving perception. With love as one of her most frequently used concepts, as it is for Morrison, she writes within sentimental boundaries. Lugones's definition of love does not include the collapse of the self into the other; it is neither a merging nor a surrender.

Elizabeth Spelman, a white philosopher who has collaborated with Lugones, coined he concept of "boomerang perception." Spelman describes well-meaning white adults telling their children that "'black people are just like us'-- never, however, that we were just like blacks."[37] The good intentions of whiteness are clear; race provides a way into a meditation on morality. Boomerang perception names an arrogant practice that masquerades as a benevolent one. Such perception renders the seer the original, making the object of the gaze a distorted copy. Perception is Lugones' key to the formation of a counter ethical imagination, an imagination which enables not just survival for people of color, but coalition building. She asserts that a willful and playful use of consciously loving perception can increase trust. She tries to transform a compulsory act for racialized others, inhabiting worlds that do not feel like home, into a site of power.

Such a transformation requires the maintenance of a "double vision that combines an understanding of the oppressor's powerful imagery with the active exercise of one's home-grown prophetic sense of self."[38] One consequence of this acrobatic vision is that those who appear culturally homeless become subject to tests of racial authenticity, not only by Others, but by themselves. Perception, then, must escape the logic of a white imagination whose blankness can only invent two categories, the original and the imitation.

During the past seven years of writing in the United States, Lugones has often meditated on boomerang perception. Initially she focused her energy on explaining herself to white feminists. Like Morrison, she wants to understand the mentality of racism, not just the effects of racism on its victims. The logic behind this focus assumes that if we hope to eradicate racism, we have to understand how racist attitudes and beliefs get formed. In both "On the Logic of Pluralist Feminism" and " Playfulness, 'World'-Traveling and Loving Perception" Lugones generously considers the possibility that even those "at ease in the mainstream" can also practice loving perception. However, she does use an insistent "you" to conjecture reasons why white women refuse to "notice" women of color. Lugones claims that recognizing the problem of difference and worrying about how feminist theories might be harmed by charges of racism are not the same as addressing the harm a theory might do to people of color. In her argument for "the logic of pluralist feminism," she pinpoints white women's reliance on their self-perception as constructors of a well-meaning, ethical discourse:

What we [women of color] reveal to you is that you [white women] are many. . .. [W]e are also more than one and not all the selves we are make you important. . .. Your sense of responsibility and decision making are tied to being able to say exactly who it is that did what, and that person must be one and have a will in good working order. And you are very keen on seeing yourself as a decision maker, a responsible being. It gives you substance . . .. Plurality speaks to you of a world . . . inhabited by beings who cannot be understood given your ordinary notions of responsibility, intentionality, voluntariness (42-3).

Writing in the discourse of philosophy places her within some of those white, singular notions of intentionality. Yet she questions those ideas about responsible agency which are considered ordinary. Also, she exposes the assumptions on which a white ethical identity is built. She describes white self-perception and white apprehensions in order to halt the guilty conscience, good-intention rhetoric that so often fills the awkward silences of feminist discussions of race. Whiteness has no choice but to pause in the light of Lugones' authority, fragile as it may be. It is fragile because the plurality of her own subjectivity endows her with too little (she's an outsider, lesbian, Argentine) and too much (she's a trained philosopher, a grassroots activist, bilingual, authentic) authority simultaneously. The kind of authority Lugones represents can either be dismissed or idolized. Yet by constructing an ethos of multiple positions she providing her readers with an example of self-construction.

When I suggest that a white audience pause in recognition of a writer of color's authority, I repeat a gesture many find unethical because it denies my own power. If I perceive myself as "letting" Lugones or Morrison speak, here in this essay or in the classroom, then I am arrogantly appropriating their authority to reinforce my own self-perception as well-intentioned. However, I refuse to take the breast-beating path exposed in the guilty confessions of many of contemporary critics. Since the language of feminist ethics encourages such responsive attitudes like loving perception and care, I see scholarly work as potentially humble. While it takes a courageous agency to speak out, it also takes an act of ethical agency to simply listen. Unfortunately, listening may sometimes involve the ethically questionable act of eavesdropping.

For example, Lugones's more recent essays announce her wish to address people of color. However, she knows that "because public spaces are not sufficiently occupied by this conversation," her intentions will be hard to sustain ("Ginger," 1). Like the intention to separate an egg, a central metaphor in "Purity, Impurity and Separation," writing philosophical argument has often been an exercise in purity that turns messy. She makes concessions to the white logic governing the reading process. Her comparison of mayonnaise and eggs guides the reader into an argument about identity formation and thinking processes. She favors a curdled, multiplicity/*mestiza* over the binary logic of unity and fragmentation. She suggests that "as I investigate the conceptual world of purity, you will keep the world of *mestiza* of curdled beings, constantly superimposed onto it, even when that is made difficult by the writing's focus on the logic of purity" ("Purity," 462-3). Her participation in the genre of personal criticism disrupts the governing logic of her discipline. She has begun to include more Spanish language terms in her essays, affiliating herself with Latina fiction and poetry, and she also provides explicit examples of cross-racial encounters. While not ignoring the whiteness in her audience, she refuses to let white people's concerns take center stage.

Like Lugones, Homi Bhabha wants to find new ways of conceptualizing theories that are ethical. Hopeful that postcolonial writing will help people think more justly about freedom, he is especially attuned to how white audiences depend on the dominant theories of modernity to be a locus for ethical gestures. He suggests that those discourses often tell compelling stories that occlude the political situations of "unfreedom" that they depend upon. For example, he characterizes influential postmodern perspectives as exhibiting an "increasing narrativization of the question of social ethics and subject formation. . . . [W]hat we encounter in all these accounts [by Lyotard, Habermas, MacIntyre and Rorty] are proposals for what is considered to be the essential gesture of Western modernity, an 'ethics of self-construction'" (239-40). Writing about ourselves then, even in a postmodern moment, may be ethically ineffectual. Yet he wants postcolonial perspectives, such as those offered by Morrison and Lugones to interrupt these Western discourses of modernity, enacting a new ethics of self-construction.

Although Bhabha's examples of interruptive, hybrid enunciations in fiction by women indicate his appreciation for women's articulations of postcolonial agency, he does not theorize the specificity of gender in relation to postcolonial discourse, apart from his use of Lacan and Kristeva. Feminists have accused postcolonial theorists of erasing gender and material understandings of race. Carol Boyce Davies documents some objections to postcolonial discourse's abstractions, including the way in which it forces people to respond, once again, to the centrality of European discourses. Women writers of color had a frustrating relation to the master discourse of postcoloniality. Davies asserts, "[Although] many current formulations of race/class/gender/sexuality discourses, and the whole understanding of the need to complicate unitary subjectivities come out of the critical speech of a number of subordinated groups, the authority to speak on these matters is still hierarchically assigned" (*Migrations*, 41).[39] Davies's complaint makes an ethical appeal to fairness, and rightful ownership of ideas on behalf of subordinated women writers of color.

She also believes that the "articulation of feminisms in non-Western contexts is the submerged discourse" of postcoloniality (88). This discourse is submerged because postcoloniality and feminism are dependent upon Western formulations even when critical of them. Davies develops her notion of "migratory subjectivities" for black women writers from the starting point of women "already positioned, represented, spoken for or constructed as absent or silent or not listened to" (*Migrations*, 21). She wonders about the particular dilemma of audience for theoretical scholarship by Black women; neither those schooled exclusively in critical theory, nor those schooled only in life experiences of racism can function as their ideal readers. She adds that we must also consider the popular reception given to writing which is in fact a critique of dominance but received in the spirit of multicultural celebration.[40] Davies's framework for a discussion of subjectivity emphasizes space and movement, and, like many other texts about race and writing, "border crossings." Also, it is extremely difficult, as feminists have repeatedly pointed out, for black women writers to refuse to engage the concerns of the other groups with whom they interact.

That engagement is often adversarial. In "Speaking in Tongues," Mae Gwendolyn Henderson explains that when talking about black women's relationships to other groups, one should keep in mind their uses of both "testimonial" and "contestorial" dialogues. Competitive discourse articulates the conflicts and, Henderson suggests, is legal in its effects. Like a judge at trial, or an ethical theorist at work, it "adjudicate(s) competing claims" and focuses on the "differences between Self and Other" (22). She also characterizes a "dialectic of identity" through which black women participate in an "I-Thou" conversation which speaks to the "same within, "seeking resolution.[41] Henderson claims that it is the complexity of black women's participation in both a "dialogic of difference and a dialectic of identity" that "enables these women writers authoritatively to speak to and engage both hegemonic and ambiguously (non)hegemonic discourse" (21).Yet a supposed authenticity of racial identity may seem more legible than the authority of scholarship.

This heterglossic ability has proved a mixed blessing for writers of color, as they describe a double consciousness that may never be resolved, but instead appropriated by some form of "whiteness."[42] Morrison understands this well as she builds an intellectual reputation out of a willingness to engage a number of hegemonic discourses. In particular, she addresses both the political and the aesthetic dimensions of writing. An editor, a scholar, and a novelist, she emphasizes her experience as a writer in order to authorize her insights into the imaginations of white fiction writers. Morrison insists that an Africanist presence inhabits what she calls the "white imagination," by which she means white writers writing for white readers, imagining what it means to be "American." Morrison's earliest responses to Black characters in fiction by white authors assumed that their marginal presence reflected their minor influence on the imagination of the writer. Black characters provided only "some touch of verisimilitude" or a "needed moral gesture, humor, or bit of pathos" (*Playing*, 15). However, once she began reading as a novelist, she saw this "fabrication of an Africanist persona [as] an extraordinary meditation on the self; a powerful exploration of the fears and desires that reside in the writerly consciousness . . . [a] revelation of longing, of terror, of perplexity, of shame, of magnanimity" (17). Africanism, then, is a white invention, all about a white self. The whiteness of an "authentic" (northern) American self stands out in relief against characters of color, the maleness of this self against markers of heterosexual difference. The Africanist presence has been carefully and unavoidably constructed while its significance has been evaded.

Morrison's brand of literary criticism dissuades us from reading as sociologists or even as literary critics. Literary criticism, as she describes it, either ignores race out of "polite repression" or focuses on only the victims of racism and not the dynamics of racist mentalities.[43] She insists that we think about a writerly consciousness, and implies that it is also possible to consider the workings of a writerly conscience. The act of writing may expose the psychological dynamics of the first, and betray the best intentions of the second. Morrison stresses the play between conscious and unconscious beliefs, emotions and desires that shape representations of race. However, she also indicates that consciousness is linked to a kind of ethical intentionality. Specifically, this intention includes a writer's plan to convey admirable virtues in an American identity. Morrison analyzes the gaps in plots, the contradictions in characters, the shifts in perspectives, and the linguistic contortions that make up both literary "failures" and "masterpieces" composed by writers imagining a free American self mirrored by a bound Africanist other. She encourages us through her example, to read as writers, as people aware of the linguistic struggles and surprises that happen as we write.

Even those of us who write without inventing fictional characters and situations must arrange our words within the inheritance of racial divisions. Our "characters," be they authorities, colleagues or other anecdotal personae, are always already racialized, that is, identified as members of particular racial groups. Perhaps, the self-conscious announcement of one's racial identity is entirely in keeping with a modern desire to govern other people's perceptions with assertions of one's good intentions and pursuit of truthfulness. Nevertheless, Morrison's exposure of Africanism indicates that it is ever present in American texts. Once exposed in the 'white imagination,' Africanism then becomes impossible not to see.

Morrison, however, is careful to use 'racialism,' not 'racism' when explaining the features of Africanism. She avoids the polarities of ad hominem accusations of an author's racism, leaving room for the occasional places where Africanism signifies a more complicated response than either a clear resistance to, or reinforcement of, racism. The consequences of Africanism may indeed contribute to racist behavior, but literary analysis can remain distinct from both psychological analyses of behaviors and moral judgments by focusing on the textual and grammatical effects of racism. If writers of any race wish to extinguish racist thought patterns from their cognitive habits, they can act upon Morrison's implication that their language patterns often reveal failures to imagine agency on the part of racialized others.

Suppose there are many language acts in our culture, beyond the discursive field of literary texts, whose assumptions are in fact white. These discourses then identify people of color with the negativity of "darkness," "evil," and the "unfree." When people of color internalize these discourses, they will experience dissonance, producing the kind of split subjectivity that informs many self-conscious texts. To illustrate a white imagination outside of literature, Morrison comments on our national discourses -- arguing that:

Freedom (to move to earn, to learn, to be allied with a powerful center, to narrate the world) can be relished more deeply in a cheek by jowl existence with the bound and unfree. The ideological dependence on racialism is intact, and like its metaphysical existence, offers in historical, political and literary discourse a safe route into meditations on morality and ethics, a way of examining the mind-body dichotomy; a way of thinking about justice; a way of contemplating the modern world. . .[the reference to black people] exists in every one of this nation's mightiest struggles. (64-5)

Although Morrison staunchly defends the aesthetic qualities that delimit the literary, she does not deny the presence of politics and ethics in fiction writing. The first part of the passage above indicates some similarities between national discourses and the language of academic criticism. She suggests that the ability to construct oneself as a rhetorical authority ("to narrate the world"), particularly in United States culture, depends upon a referent to a racially marked "other" population.

Authority is nearly always understood as authority over a particular domain. "Women of color" exists as a category of authors because whitnessblackness functions as an opposing designation. But whiteness is always already in the position of authority. What, then, is the domain over which women of color can write and speak, and be heard? It seems that the literature classroom has claimed their voices most insistently. Many issues arise out of the circulation of women's texts in the institutional context of English departments and Women's Studies, disciplines responsible for the creation and maintenance of women's rhetorical authority.

As women assert an ethical authority in their writing, academicians have been investing much time and energy on the subject of racial difference. Because a number of women writers of color resent having their stories used as moral meditations by whites, we must shift our focus from personal anxieties to the very mentality of racist thought. If we can change the ways we think and write about race, we can perhaps better avoid the self-centeredness of whites and the suppression of female power.

NOTES

1. Ann duCille, "The Occult of True Black Womanhood: Critical Demeanor and Black Feminist Studies" *Signs* 19 (1994), 591-2.

2. Toni Morrison, *Beloved* (New York: Penguin), 1988.

3.   "Rememory" is Sethe's word and has lead to analysis of the re-membered slave woman's body in a number of feminist critical texts. See Mae G. Henderson, "Toni Morrison's *Beloved: Re-Membering the Body as Historical Text*," in *Comparative American Identities: Race, Sex and Nationality in the Modern Text*, ed. Hortense Spillers (New York:

Routledge, 1991), 62-85.

4. Gayle Greene *Changing the Story: Feminist Fiction and The Tradition* (Bloomington, Indiana UP, 1991), 212.

5. Margo Jefferson, "Writing About Race, Walking on Eggshells," (*New York Times*; June 10, 1999; E1. E2).

6. Katherine Mayberry "White Feminists Who Study Black Writers," in *Chronicle of Higher Education* (October 12, 1994, A48).

7. Malin LaVon Walther, Letter in *Chronicle of Higher Education* (26 November, 1994. B3).

8. R.B. Schmerl, Letter in *Chronicle of Higher Education* (26 November, 1994, B3).

9. Also, in "Black Feminist Theory and the Representation of the 'Other,'" Valerie Smith echoes this theme when she writes: "it is striking that at precisely the moment when Anglo-American feminists and male Afro-Americanists begin to reconsider the material ground of their enterprise, they demonstrate their return to earth, as it were, by invoking the specific experiences of black women, and the writings of black women." In *Changing Our Own Words: Essays on Criticism, Theory, and Writing by Black Women*, ed. Cheryl Wall New Brunswick: Rutgers UP, 1989), 45.

10. Homi K. Bhabha, *The Location of Culture* (London: Routledge, 1994).

11. Carol Boyce Davies, *Black Women, Writing and Identity: Migrations of the Subject* (London: Routledge, 1994), 6.

12. "Home" is a much problematized concept in the discourses of identity, ethnicity, immigration, slavery and colonialism. Feminists have been especially tuned to the anxieties generated when the (private) subject of home is made public because home, or the domestic, as the subject of women's literary productions, has often been dismissed as an unsuitable subject for art.

13. hooks reclaims a number of words loaded with stereotypes and insults, an African-American strategy known as "signifying." "Third World Diva Girls" is a label expressing "intense womanist affection" and "a reminder of how easy it is to imagine we are superior to others and therefore deserve special treatment or have the right to dominate" in *Yearning: Race, Gender and Cultural Politics* (Boston, MA: South End Press, 1990), 100.

14 . Rich fails to recall her black nanny's name, an especially offensive oversight to duCille, given the feminist intentions of *Of Women Born: Motherhood as an Institution* (New York: Norton, 1976; rpt. 1986).

15. Drucilla Cornell, "Rethinking the Time of Feminism" in *Feminist Contentions: A Philosophical Exchange*, ed. Seyla Benhabib Judith Butler, Drucilla Cornell, Nancy Fraser (New York: Routledge, 1995), 78-84.

16. Maxine Hong Kingston, *The Woman Warrior: Memoir of a Girlhood Among Ghosts* (New York: Vintage Random, rpt. 1989).

17. Joanna Russ, *How to Suppress Women's Writing* (Austin: University of Texas Press, 1983), 25-29.

18. Harriet Jacobs, *Incidents in the Life of a Slave Girl*. ed. Jean Fagan Yelllin (Cambridge: Harvard UP, 1987), 55.

19. Southern literary historians have identified the ideals of feminine virtue at work in the nineteenth-century American South. See Elizabeth Ammons, *Conflicting Stories: American Women Writers at the Turn into the Twentieth Century* (New York: Oxford UP, 1992). Linda's grandmother personifies "True Womanhood" in *Incidents*.

20. P. Gabrielle Foreman notes that Jacobs's photo, as an elderly woman, on the popular current edition of the text, "balances Child's editorial decision to close with 'tender memories of my good old grandmother ' instead of ending with John Brown as Jacobs

wished (201). Rather than bolster Jacobs's condemnation and revision of true womanhood, the photo offers its iconographic triumph" "Manifest in Signs: The Politics of Sex and Representation in Incidents in the Life of a Slave Girl" in *Harriet Jacobs and Incidents in the Life of a Slave Girl,* ed. Garfield and Zafir (New York: Cambridge UP, 1996), 91.

21. Nancy Armstrong, "Why Daughters Die: The Racial Logic of American Sentimentalism," Why Daughters Die: The Racial Logic of American Sentimentalism," *Yale Journal of Criticism* 7 (1994), 19.

22. Patricia. Yeager's 1987 article, "Language and Female Emancipation" analyzes Edna's world of "limited linguistic possibilities, of limited possibilities for interpreting and re-organizing her feelings, and therefore of limited possibilities for action" in Margo Culley, ed., Kate Chopin, *The Awakening* (1899) in *The Norton Critical Edition of The Awakening,* 2nd ed. (New York: Norton, 1994), 285.

23. Annette Kolodney, "Dancing Through the Minefields: Some Observations on the Theory, Practice and Politics of Feminist Literary Criticism" in Warhol and Herndl, eds., *Feminisms: An Anthology of Literary Theory and Criticism* (New Brunswick, N.J.: Rutgers U P, 1991), 102. Originally published in *Feminist Studies* 6 (1980).

24. "[*The Awakening*] is not a healthy book; if it points to any moral or teaches any lesson, the fact is not apparent." *St. Louis Daily Globe-Democrat* 13 May, 1899:5 (quoted in Culley), 163.

25. Toni Morrison, *Playing in the Dark: Whiteness and the Literary Imagination* (Cambridge: Harvard UP, 1992), 27.

26. Morrison's "Recitatif" depicts a friendship between two girls who meet as children in foster care, and reunite briefly as young adults in the 1960s. One is black and the other white but the codes of racial identity are interchanged. In J.J. Phillips, ed., *The Before Columbus Anthology of Short Stories* (New York: Norton, 1992).

27. Ammons, 135.

28. In an interesting contrast, Harriet Jacobs, through the sincerity implied in the genre of autobiography and the depiction of the grandmother's high moral standards, constructs a Linda Brent capable of being ruined.

29. Jane Smiley. *The All-True Travels and Adventures of Lidie Newton* (New York: Fawcett, 1998).

30. Stanley Crouch, "Aunt Medea," *The New Republic*, October 19, 1987, 42.

31. The inscription on the frontispiece of *Beloved* is dedicated to "Sixty Million and more."

32. Hilde Hein, "Refining Feminist Theory: Lessons from Aesthetics," in Hein and Korsmeyer, eds., *Aesthetics in Feminist Perspective* (Bloomington: Indiana UP, 1993), p. 10.

33. Drucilla Cornell, "What is Ethical Feminism?" in *Feminist Contentions: A Philosophical Exchange: Seyla Benhabib, Judith Butler, Drucilla Cornell, and Nancy Fraser* (New York: Routledge, 1995), 152.

34. Cornell, "Time," 154.

35. The most recent publication by bell hooks shifts away from her usual cultural criticism to study love in all its dimensions. She believes it is the most important story of each person's life. See her *All About Love: New Visions* (New York: William Morrow, 2000).

36. Maria Lugones, "Playfulness, World-Traveling and Loving Perception," *Hypatia* 2 (1987), 161.

37. Elizabeth Spelman, *Inessential Woman: Problems of Exclusion in Feminist Thought* (Boston: Beacon Press, 1988), 12.

38. Maria Lugones, "Boomerang Perception and the Colonizing Gaze: Ginger

Reflections on Horizontal Hostility." *Ms. Humanities Institute*, SUNY, Stony Brook, New York, April, 1995, 10.

39. Davies also writes: "One can test this "politics of citation by attempting to produce a professional paper and citing only Black women/women of color critical thinkers" (*Migrations* 2).

40. For example, she mentions Maya Angelou's 1993 Presidential inaugural poem and its success as participating in the "discourse of the prize" (*Migrations*, 21).

41. "I-thou" is an expression found in Martin Buber, but in "Speaking in Tongues," Mae G. Henderson uses Hans-Georg Gadamer's formulation of 'I-thou' as a reconciliation with otherness. In *Changing Our Own Words: Essays on Criticism, Theory, and Writing by Black Women*, ed. Wall (New Brunswick, Rutgers UP, 1989), 20.

42. See Denise Heinze, *The Dilemma of Double-Consciousness: Toni Morrison's Novels* (Athens: University of Georgia Press, 1993). Also, Homi Bhabha describes resolution in unfavorable terms, recognizing the emptiness of cultural relativism brought about by a well-meaning politics of identity. "The power of the postcolonial translation of modernity . . . does not simply revalue the contents of a cultural tradition or transpose values 'cross-culturally'. The cultural inheritance of slavery or colonialism is brought before modernity not to resolve its historic difference into a new totality, nor to forego its traditions. It is to introduce another locus of inscription and intervention, another hybrid, 'inappropriate' enunciative site, through that temporal split, or time lag, that I have opened up for the signification of postcolonial agency" (242).

43. There is much scholarship which celebrates Morrison herself for having portrayed so many "victims" of racism, colorism, poverty, incest and sexism. See Susan Parr, *The Moral of the Story* (New York: Teacher's College Press, 1982); and *Mark Ledbetter, Victims and the Postmodern Narrative, or Doing Violence to the Body* (London: MacMillan, 1996).

7

Postcolonial *Daughters*: Nairobi, Beijing and Paule Marshall

Laura H. Roskos

In her essay "Finishing the Agenda," Angela Davis ridicules Maureen Reagan's inept leadership of the United States delegation to the U.N. End of the Decade Conference in Nairobi. She writes:

When Maureen Reagan delivered her opening address at the official UN conference, she proclaimed that women in the United States are well on their way to emancipation. In fact, she said that "all barriers to political equality have long since been eliminated." The four main issues relating to the sexist oppression of women in our country, she said, are "women refugees, women in development, literacy, and domestic violence." Certainly these issues have their place on women's agenda, but when they are presented as the only truly important questions defining women's oppression in the United States, they fundamentally distort our situation. What about racism? What about unemployment and economic inequalities? And, indeed, what about militarization?[1]

Reagan, Davis claims, is propagating a kind of blindness that would negate Davis's own experience of the Nairobi conference and NGO forum, as well as the experiences of the over 1,000 other African-American women present there. She sees herself, along with her African-American cohorts, as both privileged to partake of the exchanges available at Nairobi and as emissaries representing a disenfranchised and discriminated against population within the United States: "As an Afro-American woman, I sensed that the more than 1,000 of us present in Nairobi were breaking new ground for our sisters and brothers at home. We were exploring the global sociohistorical conditions of our own oppression, and we were building new bridges linking us to the defiant women, the militant workers, the struggling peoples and the progressive, peace-loving nations of the world" (111).

Participation in the "militant and celebratory dance rhythms and chants" of the forum, rebalanced the doubled perspective that Davis lives and writes from by emphasizing the positive and the possible:

time in the history of international women's conferences that the majority
s were women of color. For those of us who have grown accustomed to
"minorities" because we are people of color living in Europe and North
robi experience reaffirmed a basic historical reality: If indeed we happen
rity on some of the world's continents, globally we constitute the majority
pulation. (110)

While Davis lingers on the promise of an emerging and maturing international women's movement, Reagan attempts to cut United States women, including
women of color, out of the picture. Reagan's announcement that political equality
has already been achieved back home suggests that the roles United States women
play within an international women's movement be limited to those of exemplar and
potential benefactress. In doing so, her rhetoric erases the possibilities of sisterhood,
coalition-building and strategic alliances, relationships which presume reciprocity
and mutuality. Davis is concerned that Reagan's vision of United States women
will disable our transformation of ourselves; therefore, she insists it must be rejected.

Davis's account is just one of many testimonials to illustrate implicitly
how, at the Nairobi conference, the impetus of the international women's movement
seemed to shift from Western feminists to women of the southern hemisphere. Ten
years later, in the process of drafting the Platform for Action adopted at the Fourth
World Conference on Women, held in China in 1995, the interdependencies of
women from developed and developing nations became acknowledged fact. In the
forums and talk-backs following the Beijing conference, the United States women
in attendance recounted their experiences and repeatedly stressed three things that
we in this country can do to increase our usefulness as collaborators in the dynamic
forcefield of a global women's movement: first, we need to develop, in conversation
with women from around the world, a woman-centered analysis of the economic
forces restructuring the relationships among us; second, we must actively resist
fundamentalism in our thinking and in our communities, recognizing that fundamentalism in all its manifestations poses the most immediate threat to the lives of
women and children both here and abroad; and third, we need to devise effective
strategies for improving the practice of democracy within the United States. For
those of us grounded in the humanities, Paule Marshall's fiction provides an excellent crash course illuminating the international significance of these priorities.

Marshall's novel *Daughters* is post-colonial in that it invites the reader to
rethink the real politics of international relations from a perspective centered around
the multiple experiences of women of color. Women returning from Nairobi, and
now Beijing, are typically energized by what they describe as an "ah-ha" moment
of consciousness shattering, or raising, that drastically reorders their perceptions of
the world and of the women in it. So far, our accepted ways of reading contemporary women's political fiction imperfectly reflect this emerging consciousness.
Marshall herself has described the female characters in *Daughters* as forming a
constellation gravitating around a single male polestar. The reading offered here
instead places the female characters at the center of the stage, and takes their
interpretations of their experience seriously.

When we first meet Ursa MacKenzie, the protagonist of *Daughters*, she is "temporarily" unemployed, uneasily awaiting approval of an applied research grant that will allow her to return to Midland City, New Jersey, to evaluate a project she began several years ago. A few months before the story begins, she quit a high-paying job in marketing to finish an abandoned master's thesis, but now her savings are depleted and she is doubting the wisdom of the decisions she has made. The question of values, and by extension of literary value, is at heart a question about what is really important. Feminist theory insists that what we choose to value as knowledge has ethical implications. These implications come into play when we attempt to situate contemporary texts in their social and historical contexts. Just as many commentators have been careful to characterize Beijing as a process rather than as an event, the years between Nairobi and Beijing have become, in common expression, "a road." Because Angela Davis was at Nairobi and because her experience of that trip noticeably changed some of her ways of talking about reality, it seems appropriate to locate Ursa, and *Daughters*, which was published in 1991 between the two conferences, on the road from Nairobi to Beijing.

In *Women and Peace*, Betty Reardon uses the interconnections between Equality, Development and Peace articulated in the "Nairobi Forward Looking Strategies" as a starting point for generating a thick description of peace as the matrix of political and environmental conditions conducive to the meeting of human needs.[2] Specifically, she asks us to give up the dream of "negative peace," peace envisioned as idyllic stasis, in favor of participation in a myriad of local actions that could begin to remake structures of violence into the dynamics of positive peaceful living. Regardless of the strategies that might be employed in a specific situation (i.e., negotiation, infiltration, legislation, subversion, disruption), Reardon correctly realizes that all change requires conflict. Careful to distinguish non-violence from pacifism, she restores a positive value to conflict and, in the course of so doing, struggles to differentiate static, reiterative, sedimented conflicts, the type that are more likely to turn violent, from conflicts that are fluid, mobile, and quite possibly productive. These latter become the cornerstone of Reardon's theory of non-violent practice and peace. In this regard, the series and patterns of conflict played out in the international women's conferences held under the auspices of the United Nations and the NGO Forums which accompany them serve as a practical demonstration of the synergy that is possible in linking feminist and postcolonial political concerns.

In the United States press coverage of the 1985 Nairobi conference, three loci of conflict stood out: a conflict between national foreign policy and the conventions adopted by the UN official bodies, a conflict between the agenda of the official UN bodies and those of the non-governmental organizations seeking to address similar concerns, and a conflict between western and third world women. Of these, the last was also the most fluid, the concepts of western and third world as identity markers are, then as now, vague and inaccurate at best. Depending upon the issue at stake, the split might more accurately be described as occurring between north and south, or as taking shape along racial lines, or as one of class or perceived class, or of developed vs. developing economies. In the negotiations among participants, positional identities proved unstable and had a tendency to multiply so that the preposition "between," and dualistic modes of description, were soon abandoned by participants and sympathetic observers in favor of the preposition "among," resulting in a more nuanced, pluralistic rendering of areas of disagreement.[3] The outcome of this splintering was paradoxically the claim that "global sisterhood is a reality," an assessment shared by numerous commentators including Reardon, and based at least in part on the observation that during the UN decade for women, women of color asserted themselves as key players in the international equation. The sisterhood realized at Nairobi, and "forged in struggle," refers to a consciously chosen "politics of solidarity."[4] Solidarity in this instance differs from claims of identity based on shared biology to refer to a considered commitment to a process that is being improvised, and negotiated, even as it is being enacted. At Nairobi, 15,000 women from around the world enjoyed the possibilities of face-to-face interaction. Nevertheless, the common ground established there, Angela Davis has written, was only a "foundation" of things that might yet come to pass, and was in this way both prescient and provisional.[5]

Peace activist Barbara Deming once wrote that "if the complicated truth is that many of the oppressed are also oppressors, and many of the oppressors are also oppressed nonviolent confrontation is the only form of confrontation that allows us to respond realistically to such complexity. In this kind of struggle we address ourselves always both to that which we refuse to accept from others and to that which we can respect in them, have in common with them—however much or little that may be."[6] Employing the image of "two hands," Deming speaks of the increased power that results from two non-congruent pressures applied simultaneously. This dual movement, I think, is also what Toni Morrison refers to when she talks and writes about loving her reader: confronting her audience with their culpability in perpetuating horrors while reaffirming and even training in them the humane sensibilities that would enable the perception of the horror and inherent excess of pain and suffering.[7] In *Daughters*, Paule Marshall's literary embrace serves both to frame a devastating social critique even while locating among the debris potential sites for social reconstruction.

The themes that Marshall cultivates in this novel include the distinctions between fixation and attentiveness, between slow revolution and slow retrogression, between indulgence and love, between sensations of pain and pleasure, and most importantly perhaps between lineage and legacy. In each case, her method is to take terms that seem to be ambiguously close and gently massage them apart, filling out the space thus created with detailed examples. Michelle Wallace has characterized this technique of making available new discursive terrain by improvising "variations on negation" as one distinctive to the cultural practices of black women, insofar as they create from a position of the other (black) of the other (white women) within our society.[8] Far from creating a monolithic self-portrait of ideal black womanhood, the cast of *Daughters* reveals some overlap but much heterogeneity as well. Furthermore, these differences, such as those separating the characters Estelle and Astral, spark curiosity and occasional sympathy but never empathetic merger on either's part. Because the story is staged at the intersection of three societies, no single marker, age, lineage, color, gender or class, overdetermines a character's social standing. In these ways, *Daughters* confirms Rhonda Cobhan's observations that postcolonial feminist texts refuse a "founding myth of wholeness" and the quixodian quest for a pure identity to embrace, instead of racial, ethnic and class ambiguities.[9] As Marshall herself points out, in this novel even more than in her other works, she was able to call out this multiplicity through the textualization of accents, syntax, and idioms expressive of each character.[10]

These expanded discursive continuums yield tropes that convey a vision of positive peace as dynamic process; this is another way of saying that here aesthetic vision and technique exceed simple considerations of pleasing form and begin to make an ethical contribution. The concept of "usefulness" emerges as a key designation in *Daughters*. For example, Lowell Carruthers, a character in that novel, is deemed useless not so much because he cannot extricate himself from a demeaning, and racist, work environment, but because he cannot tell pleasure from pain even in the facial expression and gestures of his lover of seven years. Ursa muses that he can no longer even see her across the dinner table, seeing instead only his white nemesis Davison, mesmerized by his obsessive wonder over, "how could he do this to me?" until it becomes a ritual of self-indulgence, cutting him off from all connection with the people in his life.

In an earlier novel, *The Chosen Place, The Timeless People*, Marshall probed some of the "whys" predicating the animosity and distrust between colonial peoples and agents of imperialism, with a rigor that suggested that it might be possible to discover just how many and what kinds of ceremonies of reconciliation would serve to put the parties back on an equal footing. In her brilliant reading of that novel as a meditation on nuclear destruction, Eugenia DeLamotte discusses Marshall's rendering of the return of the repressed as an experience of visual overflow.[11] Several of the characters in *The Chosen Place, The Timeless People* undergo moments in which the visual field becomes flooded in a kind of perceptual double exposure, during which they confront historical and economic connections usually relegated to their unconscious. These eruptions of memory are, for the white characters, traumatic and the action of the plot is predicated on how each deals with what they must now admit at least to themselves that they know. On the other hand, Merle, the most fully developed black character in the novel, experiences this overwhelming awareness virtually all the time. She vents her perceptions in a perpetual stream of harangue, and her project, within the novel, is to extricate herself from this web of heightened consciousness just long enough to make productive use of what she knows she knows all too well. While *The Chosen Place, The Timeless People* is a drama of stark contrasts, *Daughters*, written 25 years later, holds onto the phenomenon of perceptual overload but explores its potential usefulness as a tool for social change in more subtle ways. Tracing the violent manifestations at the interface of materialist and humanist values, *Daughters* veers away from critique and the search for root causes, to explore potential avenues of generative action available to differently positioned women of color. Here, Marshall's mimetic mode of theme and variation destabilizes oppositions, creating a rich, unsettled text. It is perhaps because the protagonist, Ursa, displays both the capacity for sustaining long-term relationships and a knack for successful risk-taking, that *Daughters* inhibits readerly responses of cynicism or despair.

"Over twenty wars in two centuries!" the wide-eyed Estelle Harrison coyly exclaimed upon meeting Primus Mackenzie (27).[12] Having boned up at the local library, Estelle went on "And you hold the record, I guess you know. That's the most wars of any of the islands." "We were quite a prize back then," Primus replies, lingering over the ambiguity of her pronoun, eager to position himself as someone worth fighting over. Thus in the convergence of one woman's fascination with the spectacle of war and one man's uncritical identification with his country of origin, begins the chain of events eventually giving birth to Ursa-Bea. But while the central plot of *Daughters* begins with this encounter staged on the back lawn of an estate built with robber baron money and belonging to a prominent philanthropist, and in an atmosphere of romantic thralldom that confuses eroticism with the desire to dominate, this is not where it ends. The epigraph to the novel provides a clue when it assures us that Ursa, the "little girl of all the daughters," "ain' no more a slave" but is a woman now.

The role Estelle, who comes from a long line of teachers and social workers, envisions for herself and sees reflected in Primus's face is that of co-conspirator, modeled on the egalitarian partnership she imagines is represented by the monument to Congo Jane and Willie Cudjoe, co-leaders of a slave revolt in Triunion, the island from which Primus hails. And as far as Estelle can see, with her state-side understanding of politics and the public sphere, this model seems to hold for the early years of her marriage to Primus. But by the time Ursa finally lets herself be born after a series of miscarriages it has become clear to Estelle, and the reader, that the conjugal couple is not the basic unit of Island society. Recognition of the way things are done there leads Estelle to reconsider issues of personal pride and autonomy, but not to abandon the frustrating work of building a sustainable local economy that might be able to provide for Triunion's growing population *and* preserve its lush biodiversity.

In identifying himself with his birth island, Primus positions himself as the booty, or spoils, fought over in twenty-two successive wars waged among Spanish, French and British colonizers. This mix reasserts itself in the women who surround him: Astral, his keep-miss who hails from Spanish Bay and who manages Mile Trees Colony Hotel for him; his childhood nurse, Celestine, who is French Creole and who has remained to manage his housekeeping and help raise his daughter; and Estelle, the English-speaking wife he "went and found in the United States," who comes in handy at diplomatic events and who oversees his law practice. Certainly it is the combined shadowwork of all three of these women that sustains the public figure of the P.M., but in turn, each of these women enjoys social and economic security as part of a relatively stable group. Through Primus's sexual vitality, each of these women gains access to the "free zone" of uncensored personal exchange where dreams intimately voiced might just gain the charge they need to become material. But at significant points, for each woman, Primus's physical presence, his body, literally blocks out her vision of the world beyond, a view of the trees, the stars, the beaches all around. At these moments, Primus looms larger than life as he acts to shade out the complex interdependencies that make up island society and ecology. Just as Primus blocks out the comprehensive vision of the women, his friend Roy reveals that something happened to obstruct Primus's own vision of a socialist transformation in Triunion during his Carnegie-sponsored tour of the United States, where he first met and fell in love with Estelle. Marshall's recurrent imagery suggests that a common phenomenological experience consistently undermines the material translation of the dreams articulated in the "free zone" of heterosexual lovemaking.

On the other hand, when Ursa breaks off her relationship with Lowell and stops looking at him looking, her perception of the world becomes subject to double and even triple exposure: Midland City, New Jersey overlaid not just with the photographic image gleaned from the morning daily but with the memory of the barrios on Triunion's Armory Hill:

Dresden, she said to herself and then immediately changed it to Beirut. On her way to rent the car this morning she passed a newstand on Broadway and saw a picture on the front of the *Times* of a bombed-out section in Beirut. So that when she entered the South Ward she found herself thinking 'Beirut.' Beirut as she drove past the run-down or burned-out frame and shingle houses and the walk-ups leaning and sinking in on themselves, past the boarded-up stores and the idle men holding up the sagging walls...There seemed to be more decayed and gutted houses and stores this time, more waiting men and boys, women and girls, more broken glass and debris, garbage and straydogs everywhere, and more children playing amid it all under the glare-filled sky that trailed her from New York trying to warn her. Beirut. And Armory Hill along the old abandoned section of the main road. Driving over to Howard Street an hour ago, there was no separating the landscapes that filled her mind. (296-7)

Amidst these streets littered with the fallout from ongoing class warfare, the kind of charismatic virility exemplified by the P.M. and envied by Lowell seems incidental if not dysfunctional. Marshall's evocation of a "free zone" of exchange between men and women invites the reader to reconsider the idea of "free" trade between structurally unequal partners; and it is Primus's obsessive involvement with a public/private development scheme that ultimately destroys even the last remaining "free zone," that between he and Astral. When it is revealed that the public assets to be invested in this scheme include land in which each of the women holds a stake, Primus's public career is abruptly derailed. As Ursa recalls it, Government Lands beach, which Primus is about to help turn into a convention center for foreign guests, currently serves as the hub of an indigenous fishing industry central to the subsistence economy of the Morelands district that he is supposed to represent. While it is Estelle who asks Ursa to intervene, Ursa acts upon her own principles, and in so doing ensures the continued viability of the family-owned Mile Trees and Astral's position as its manager. In this win/win scenario, *Daughters* articulates a cultural praxis of collaboration among different classes and generations of women of color.

In contrast to the vivid texture of the landscapes Marshall frequently evokes, her representations of violence and bodily suffering in *Daughters* are low-keyed and restrained. Aside from Grady, a peripheral figure whose injury is inflicted off stage, only two characters in this novel experience literal physical pain. Astral Forde is brutally raped and beaten by a football player she meets at a dance, and later, as a result of his assault, procures for herself a clumsily performed abortion that renders her sterile. The novel begins with Ursa's anti-climactic visit to a midtown clinic where she has an abortion that, she thinks, hurts too little, but the pain deferred reenters her body months later as a traveling abdominal pain following a fall. In each instance, the pain associated with the abortion is played off against the emotional and financial uncertainties of carrying a pregnancy to term and thus made to carry a metaphysical, rather than merely medical, charge. Judith Wilt has observed that abortion in contemporary fiction often signals the existential anguish that living in an inhospitable world, a world where not all children are wanted or valued, brings.[13] However, the analytic and political skills affirmed in Nairobi have led, since then, to the collection and dissemination of data indicating that such a world is not just an imaginary chimera. From this research it follows that the conflict between what is and what might be is *ethical* rather than *existential*, that there is in fact a material and social basis for the "utopian fantasy" of a hospitable and abundant world.

Within *Daughters*, the women who do bring children to term, Ursa's mother Estelle, Ursa's friend Viney, even, to the extent we can register, Astral's friend Malvern, take good care of them, investing in them not only all the comforts their money can buy, but a dream of human perfectability as well. In part this means raising them against gender stereotype: Estelle raises Ursa to take her place "on the barricades" in the struggle against racist imperialism; Viney raises her son Robeson to be trusting and open, a sensitive communicator.

Traditional gender roles have a negative effect on the male characters in *Daughters*. Lowell is limited and undermined by his employer, but he is not the only one. Sandy Lawson, the African-American mayor of Midland City who Ursa helped elect, has been fêted and diverted from his campaign agenda by the white power structure of that town; and, Ursa's father, "the PM," was robbed long ago of his opportunity to become Prime Minister of tiny Triunion by the threat of US military intervention. In the argument Lowell and Ursa have preceding their break-up, Ursa is most stung by Lowell's accusation that she is controlled by her identification with an introjected ideal of her father. But within the novel, Marshall pairs alternative identifications at both the private and public levels: the patriarchal family is juxtaposed to the matrifocal community, the nation-state to a transnational affinity with women beyond the state's borders. Reardon has linked the dynamics of the "traditional" family to that of the nation in that both make claims to inviolability that "impede social intervention to rectify gross injustices and both are cloaked in secrecy that [can be] invoked to 'protect the family honor' and 'preserve national security'"(74). When Ursa chooses to ally herself with a constellation of maternal figures by gently obstructing her father's destructive plans, there is no way that her feminist impulse can be construed as racial disloyalty. In fact, Marshall's plot has dissolved the conundrum of paternal allegiance into multiple pragmatic questions of efficacy and relevance: does the other candidate stand a chance?, can he be trusted?, how can the information be leaked?, how can we mitigate the damage?

To return then to the monument of Congo Jane and Willie Cudjoe: "you couldn't call one's name without at least thinking of the other, they were that close," Ursa remembers her mother saying. Yet at college, it was the girlfriends, Viney and Ursa also known as "the long and the short of it," who are so closely associated in the minds of the campus community that no one could call one's name "without at least thinking of the other." And it is not the heterosexual couple which marks the utopian horizon of this novel, but rather the possibility of a whole galaxy of women working together in mutually supportive ways. It is Estelle's statement to Celestine regarding the successful outcome their dual parenting of Ursa,"I've always believed in sharing the wealth" (388),which sets into motion the resonating waves of hope that carry through to the novel's ending.

Responding to an interviewer's question, Marshall once said that she believes Ursa eventually does complete her previously abandoned senior thesis, which she hopes to base in part on Angela Davis's research into the domestic lives of slaves.[14] In the summer of 1985, Angela Davis returned from Nairobi renewed and refreshed by the experience of recognizing herself, as a member of the majority women within a majority, people of color, of the world's population, talking all about "women of color" as the emerging force in the historical struggle against "capitalist exploitation, racist oppression, and nuclear militarization."[15] Although Ursa might succeed in demonstrating her thesis in an historical context, her findings may no longer be directly relevant to her ongoing political involvements. In her life, as depicted by Marshall, there are only "empty spaces" where a male partner might be, and there is very little in the text itself to indicate that a reciprocal, egalitarian heterosexual relationship is possible for the immediate future. And while Viney keeps insisting that sexual intercourse is beneficial because it clears the tubes, elsewhere the novel implicitly asks if in the distorted afterglow of lovemaking women might not tend to misapprehend the material basis of their best dreams for transforming the world by giving credence to the wrong progenitor.

Daughters is a complex novel open to a variety of contestatory interpretations. This brief sketch reveals that the transnational work of women in the interests of equality, development and peace can provide a useful experiential context for this novel, and by inference for a number of contemporary novels, particularly political novels, by women, particularly women of color. At a time when racist media images continue to demonize African-American women as welfare queens, it is particularly necessary to remind ourselves that there are historical and material contexts other than impoverishment in which to ground their contemporary literary achievements. Global feminism as it evolved and continues to coalesce in regional conventions and international conferences provides a context in which women of color can be seen to speak from positions of realized power in the world co-equal to the power of their creativity to alter the expectations of their audiences. To neglect this possibility implicitly suggests that the domain of cultural production is co-extensive with political and economic disenfranchisement and this, I would argue, is not the case. Through the processes and events associated with the NGO forum and the 4th International Conference on Women, thousands of women like the women portrayed in *Daughters*, are tenaciously maintaining relationships with other women, often taking considerable risks to implement projects and strategies that cut across borders of religious affiliation, national loyalty and racial identity.

NOTES

1. Angela Davis, "Finishing the Agenda: Reflections on Forum '85" in *Women, Culture and Politics* (New York: Vintage Books, 1990), 112-13.

2. Betty A. Reardon, *Women and Peace: Feminist Visions of Global Security.* (Albany: SUNY Press, 1993). 3. Contrast, for example, coverage of the Nairobi conference in *Time* and *Newsweek*, which emphasized the "posturing" by third world women protesting United States actions in South Africa and Central America, with the analysis provided in *Ebony, Essence, Working Woman* and *Ms. Black Enterprise, Essence* and *Ms.* each ran stories in anticipation of the conference, and disseminated information to their readers on avenues of participation. As Angela Davis points out the tension between the haves and have nots was endemic even among the United States women present (*Jet* 68, July 29, 1985, p. 10). Demographics prove important here, because while African American women made up more than half the United States women participating in the NGO forum, they represented only five out an official delegation of thirty-five. (Story by Dorothy Butler Gilliam in *Ebony* 40, Oct. 1985, pp. 156-8)

4. Phrases marked in quotations are borrowed from bell hooks's discussion of the struggle for "black liberation and self-determination." However, on the basis of arguments she makes elsewhere in the same book, I imagine that she would characterize emergent international feminism in a similar way. From *Outlaw Culture: Resisting Representations* (New York: Routledge, 1994), 47.

5. Angela Davis, "Finishing the Agenda: Reflections on Forum '85," 110. The attendance figures for Beijing, estimated at between 40 and 50,000, seem to bear out Davis's predictions of increased participation and activity.

6. Cited in Pam McAllister, *You Can't Kill the Spirit* (Philadelphia: New Society Publishers, 1988), 6.

7. Television interview with A.S. Byatt.

8. Michelle Wallace, "Variations on Negation and the Heresy of Black Feminist Creativity" in *Reading Black, Reading Feminist: A Critical Anthology*, ed. Henry Louis Gates, Jr. (New York: Meridian, 1990), 52-67.

9. Rhonda Cohban quotes Haraway in "Revisioning Our Kumblas: Transforming Feminist and Nationalist Agendas in Three Caribbean Women's Texts" *Callaloo* 16 (1993), 45.

10. Marshall credits her encounter, "quite late in [my] life," with the work of Zora Neale Hurston as the catalyst enabling the fine-tuning of voices in *Daughters*. See "Meditations on Language and the Self: A Conversation with Paule Marshall" by Melody Graulich and Lisa Sisco in *NWSA Journal* 4 (1992), 294. The interpretation of *Daughters* Marshall offers in that interview differs substantially from my own. Marshall's attentiveness to speech is well documented; see, for example, her essay, "The Making of a Writer: From the Poets in the Kitchen," in *Reena and Other Stories* (Old Westbury, NY: The Feminist Press, 1983), 3-12.

11. Eugenia DeLamotte, "Women, Silence, and History in *The Chosen Place, The Timeless People*" in *Callaloo* 16 (1993), 227-42.

12. Paule Marshall, *Daughters* (New York: Plume/Penguin, 1991).

13. Judith Wilt, *Abortion, Choice and Contemporary Fiction: The Armegeddon of the Maternal Instinct* (Chicago: U of Chicago P, 1990).

14. Marshall actually cites this "real" article which was published in *Black Scholar*.

15. Angela Davis speaking in Prahitba Parmar's film, *A Place of Rage* (1992). See also "Finishing the Agenda: Reflections on Forum '85," *op. cit.*

8

Like Words for Pain/ *Like Water for Chocolate*: Mouths, Wombs, and the Mexican Woman's Novel

Diane Long Hoeveler

One of the most hotly debated issues on the cultural studies scene today concerns the critique of ethnocentrism and colonialism as discourse systems that have functioned virtually unchallenged within the poststructuralist framework. Most recently, however, theorists like Gayatri Spivak and Homi Bhabha have questioned the "subaltern instance" of Euro-deconstruction, pointing out the presence of ethnocentrist assumptions in virtually all aspects of the Western metaphysical project.[1] In partial response, Bhabha's important work, *The Location of Culture* (1994), presents his theory of what he calls "hybridity," with its potential for subversive mimicry, as the unique effect of colonialist power and its representations. Bhabha argues that, rather than consisting of an hegemonic command of authority or the silent repression of native traditions, colonial power operates through cultivating the very hybridity, the mixing of cultures, it purports to condemn:

Hybridity reverses the *formal* process of disavowal so that the violent dislocation of the act of colonialization becomes the conditionality of colonial discourse. The presence of colonialist authority is no longer immediately visible; its discriminatory identifications no longer have their authoritative reference to this culture's cannibalism or that people's perfidy. As an articulation of displacement and dislocation, it is now possible to identify 'the cultural' as a disposal of power, a negative transparency that comes to be agonistically constructed *on the boundary* between frame of reference/frame of mind. (114)

What Bhabha's work charts in much more sophisticated detail than I can examine here is the creation of what he calls the "effects of power," the inscriptions of strategies of domination in cultural practices that construct the colonial space.[2] I begin with Bhabha's theories because I believe they shed light on how one particular Mexican woman's novel embodies the very concept of hybridity that Bhabha defines as central to the results of the colonialist project. How exactly does

Bhabha's work elucidate issues raised in a "hybrid" work like Laura Esquivel's *Like Water for Chocolate*? How exactly does the novel position itself as a hybrid text, embodying both Western metaphysical notions and native, indigenous traditions? And, finally, how does this very hybridity ensure the popularity of this particular text, the first "Tejano" or border text to successfully make the crossover to widespread popularity in both Mexico and the United States?

It is surely no coincidence that Esquivel began her career as a script writer and that she was married to Alfonso Arau, the man who adapted her book (1989) to the screen (1993). As many critics have noted, the film's popularity insured the runaway success of the book. But Esquivel's achievement looks less original when one examines Rosario Castellanos' short story "Culinary Lesson," published almost 20 years earlier than Esquivel's novel. Castellano's fiction uses the extended metaphor of a young woman cooking a piece of meat while at the same time she is attempting to adjust to her new marriage. Although much shorter than Esquivel's work, "Culinary Lesson" uncannily condenses much of the imagery and themes of the later novel: "Your momma forgot to tell you that you were a piece of meat and should behave as such. It curls up like a piece of brushwood. Besides I don't know where all that smoke is coming from, since I turned off the oven ages ago. Of course, Dr. Heart. What one should do now is open the window, turn on the air purifier and the odor will disappear when my husband arrives."[3] Whether Esquivel was working, as some critics have claimed, in the tradition of "folletin," sentimental romances that were serialized for the lower-classes in Mexico during the first half of the twentieth century, or whether she is writing as a contemporary "magical realist," is less significant than the fact that her novel was the first to garner international attention for the field of Mexican women's literature.[4]

This essay will explore the novel's popularity and international appeal by juxtaposing mouths and wombs, the spirit or logos and the flesh, in a way that suggests finally that Esquivel's novel is about mothers who eat their daughters and daughters who eat to convince themselves that they live in a world presided over by beneficent rather than cannibalistic mothers. These contradictory equations lie at the heart of *Like Water for Chocolate*, and they explain why the novel has touched such a deep response in both this country and Mexico. The reviews of the novel, by both Chicano/a and Anglo critics, are divided as to the tone and intention of the work. In brief, critics like Antonio Marquet have claimed that the novel is "simplistic, and Manichean," "plagued with banal conventionalisms, bereft of any clear stylistic intention," and without "any aspiration other than novelty." In contrast, feminist critics like Niebylski tend to see the novel as a parody of a love story, the attempt by Esquivel to "romance women's historically forgotten or disparaged occupations (cooking, sewing, knitting, homeopathy), even as she works her ironic deconstruction on the conventions of the popular discourses that celebrate these occupations." The final apotheosis of the text occurs in critiques that attempt to transform the novel into a quasi-theological tract. As Rosa Fernandez-Levin notes, the "kitchen becomes a mystical abode in which the protagonist is empowered and permitted to re-create reality in order to avoid social and spiritual annihilation." Further, she claims that the cookbook in the novel "is more than a legacy to posterity; it is an act whose significance is two-fold: it validates a feminine task and brings about the creation of a feminine logos."[5]

Let me begin with the novel's title, however, and see if it allows us to attempt to take hold of this ambiguous tale of love lost and found, of food eaten and rejected, of pain so intense that we can find no words to describe it. When the narrator of Laura Esquivel's novel, the nameless great-niece of Tita De La Garza, explains the significance of the title of her narrative she states that "like water for chocolate" suggests the point at which water can convert chocolate from a solid to a liquid, or within the vernacular of the text, the point at which emotions at the boiling point cause an event to occur (151). That central image, the transformation of physical substances into something liquid and consumable brought about by time, heat and pressure, recurs throughout the novel, but most dramatically in the portraits of the major female characters: Tita, who is described as a fertility goddess in the tradition of Ceres (76), Mama Ellena, who is depicted as the castrating Medusa-threat (68) and an extremely "Western" force, and Nacha and Morning Light, both of whom are presented as Demeter-figures, maternal guides who lead Tita not to the promised land, but ironically to the kingdom of death (244). These latter two female characters are initially presented as indigenous Mexican folk heroines (72), but their subscription to Western metaphysics throughout the text fatally compromises them as well. All of the mother-figures in the novel, then, are hybrid creatures, tainted by their allegiance to the very colonial and patriarchal powers they should be subverting.

My initial contention would be that for all of its superficial affinity with the Latin American tradition out of which it arose, that is, its often amusing use of a sort of hyperbolic magical realism, the bedspread, for instance, that Tita crochets throughout the novel to keep warm and ends up covering the entire ranch and feeding the fire that eventually destroys the place, this contemporary Mexican woman's novel is more consistently informed by ancient Greek mythology and Western metaphysical and platonic archetypes than by any traditions that we would recognize as emerging from an indigenous Mexican culture.[6] And that is one of the points Esquivel is trying to make in this novel. Like a recipe made up of disparate ingredients that cohere only when heat is applied, so is the modern Mexican woman's novel constructed of many traditions, many mutually contradictory religions, cohering only when the heat of pain and love are applied in fairly equal proportions.[7] And so the novel initially asks, what happens when you mix one part Plato with one part Native-American traditions, one part Christian metaphysics with one part pagan mythology? You get a Mexican woman's novel, a text that proclaims in its very confusion of sources Mexico's mixed and ambivalent heritage. This is a novel that in its use of recipes combining disparate ingredients presents a template for how contemporary Mexican culture came to be. The result is a strange novel that straddles both old-world traditions, both paganism and Christianity, and suggests that a new world for Mexican women will be born only under great pressure and over long periods of time. The ultimate formula given in *Like Water for Chocolate* is the recipe for being a contemporary Mexican woman, and this recipe is a very complicated and explosive one.

Tita De La Garza, the heroine and ghostly subject of the novel, is literally born in a flood of tears that produces so much salt that the family larder is stocked with its residue for years (6). That initial image, a birth producing tears producing salt, a necessary product that is used and consumed over many years of cooking in the family kitchen, stands as the first of many such images in a text that mediates continually between the products of women's bodies, their wombs, tears, blood, or milk, and the words, pain, and food that magically emerge like surrogate or spiritual children out of those bodies. [8] In a style we would recognize as a species of postmodern magical realism, Esquivel's novel evokes the smells, sounds, and tastes of life for Mexican women, but in doing so the novel also undercovers the connections between words or codes of behavior and the pain and heartbreak they cause, just as the recipes and home remedies that run throughout the novel are more prosaic examples of cause and effect phenomena. When the author gives us a recipe for matches we know that an explosion will eventually occur in the text (106). The conflagration that consumes the De La Garza family ranch, supposedly producing the most fertile soil in all of Mexico, occurs because memory was mixed with desire, the past was mixed with the present, Plato was mixed with Native-American beliefs and the result was, quite simply, a hybrid combustion.

The major conflict in this work, however, is the struggle between the physical body and the spiritual essence that inhabits the body, while this dualism has much more in common with Plato than it does with any indigenous Mexican notions about the connections between the body and the spirit.[9] The penultimate recipe given in this novel is how to die for and through love, and this is a recipe given by Morning Light, the Native-American herbalist who, although dead, nurses Tita back to life after her break from Mama Ellena. When Dr. John initially gave this recipe to Tita he little realized that twenty years later she would use it to commit suicide with her erstwhile lover Pedro.[10] But listen to its metaphysical intensity and you will understand the lure of the fantasy that motivates Tita throughout the text:

My grandmother had a very interesting theory; she said that each of us is born with a box of matches inside us but we can't strike them all by ourselves; just as in the experiment, we need oxygen and a candle to help. In this case, the oxygen, for example, would come from the breath of the person you love; the candle could be any kind of food, music, caress, word, or sound that engenders the explosion that lights one of the matches. For a moment we are dazzled by an intense emotion. A pleasant warmth grows within us, fading slowly as time goes by, until a new explosion comes along to revive it. Each person has to discover what will set off those explosions in order to live, since the combustion that occurs when one of them is ignited is what nourishes the soul. The fire, in short, is its food. If one doesn't find out in time what will set off these explosions, the box of matches dampens, and not a single match will ever be lighted. If that happens, the soul flees from the body and goes to wander among the deepest shades, trying in vain to find food to nourish itself, unaware that only the body it left behind, cold and defenseless, is capable of providing the food. (116-17)

This vignette is a strangely platonic interlude in a novel set very firmly on Mexican soil. In its curious transmutation of platonic, pagan, and Christian elements, *Like Water for Chocolate* presents its readers with only one certain recipe: how a mother can destroy her family and the lives of her three daughters. In a novel that attempts to reify family, the mother ironically can only destroy every family with whom she comes into contact. In a novel that memorializes mothers and the power of the matrilineal line, the heroine can only hate and curse her mother, sending her finally into a strange shadowland from which she can never return to haunt her daughter. And in a novel that valorizes love as a divine power, a fate from which one can never escape, the heroine finally chooses to self-combust, dying in a blaze that is ignited when she eats candles at the same time she revives in her memory her sexual encounters with her beloved Pedro.

But Dr. John gives even more details from his grandmother's recipe, and these are the crucial ones for understanding the work: he advises Tita that it is vital to avoid people who have what he calls "frigid breath" because "just their presence can put out the most intense fire." Tita, of course, recognizes that admonition as warning her to stay away from her mother, who has had the power to blast her dreams of love as effectively as the Medusa's head killed with a glance. The final piece of advice he gives Tita, however, proves to be the fatal one. He tells her that she must be careful to light the matches one at a time because if they are all lit by a sudden or strong passion, "'then a brilliant tunnel would appear before our eyes, revealing the path we forgot the moment we were born, and summoning us to regain the divine origin we had lost. The soul ever longs to return to the place from which it came, leaving the body lifeless'" (116-17). The platonic conception of the soul, the ultimate colonialist conspiracy, is the animating power and substance throughout this work. It is the soul as engine that enables Tita to cook so magically and powerfully. It is the soul that speaks in a voice that is so clear that it determines our fate. And it is the soul that decides finally who will live and who will die. The body, the material, the physical, all of these would appear to be afterthoughts in this novelistic universe, and suspect ones at that.

The frustrated love of Tita and Pedro, ostensibly the subject of the novel, actually serves as a distraction from the real concern of this text, and that is with the connection between women and culture, the often deadly and ambivalent connection between women's bodies and the spirit, the words, the belief systems, the ideologies of their society. All of the recipes that women pass on to each other, from one generation to the next in this novelistic universe, are recipes ultimately born of the pain of separation from the idealized and fantasized great mother's body. The great powerful and biological mother who dominates the lives of her three daughter, Maria Ellena is a strange failure in everything but her destructive influence over her family. But there are other ghostly maternal presences felt throughout this novel, glimpsed in the mother surrogates who raise and influence Tita throughout her life: Nacha, the family cook, and Morning Light, John's grandmother, the Kikapu Indian and miracle healer rejected by his Anglo family. Women imbued with secret spiritual wisdom speak another language in this novel, and that language is best listened to by focusing on three key ideas that the author reiterates over and over again in the work.

The first item on what I would call the ideological agenda of this novel, the recipe it gives for the construction of femininity, is the notion that women need to be the nurturers of both their culture and their families. The second issue that emerges in the portraits of all mothers and daughters in this work is the belief that the physical body is suspect and that children born of the body are compelled to reject their biological mothers in favor of allegiance to a more powerful spiritual mother. The final point to emerge in this text is the importance of women as storytellers and mythographers of their own self-created and ultimately spiritual worlds. At one point or another Tita plays all three of these roles, suggesting the infinite demands that will be placed on women who attempt to live in both the old world and the new. The novel, albeit unknowingly, actually presents an irresolvable conflict for women; it suggests that women cannot live equally within their bodies and spirits in this life. The novel holds out the lure of a sort of platonic metaphysics, suggesting that an escape through death, a *liebestod* of the type that consumed Tristan and Isolde, is the best solution for physical beings trapped in mortal bodies with immortal spiritual longings. This novel presents, in short, an old platonic story mediated by down-home recipes and Mexican kitsch. It is a hybridized commodity, a text that attempts to mediate and thereby obviate the insoluble dilemmas that both Western and Mexican patriarchies have constructed for women. But it is ultimately a depressing saga of women defeated by their bodies, and as such I think that *Like Water for Chocolate* is, at best, problematic as feminist fiction.

But I want to focus now on how women are presented as nurturers of their families and by extension, the larger culture. This idea is reinforced in the very structure of the novel, with each chapter beginning with a recipe that Tita cooks as she attempts to live her life amid alien and alienating forces designed to metaphorically starve her. The novel centers on the conceit of a matriarchy more vicious than anything the patriarchy could construct to inhibit and enslave women within its confines. The De La Garza family tradition states that the youngest daughter must renounce marriage and spend her life caring for her mother until that mother's death. Despite her adherence to this tyrannical injunction, Tita manages to express her emotions, her pain, resentment, and repressed sexuality, through the food she cooks for others. Interesting and amusing incidents occur, of course, when Tita's elaborately involved recipes are infused with her passion of the moment. When she prepares the wedding banquet for her sister and Pedro's marriage the guests are nauseated and wholesale vomiting breaks out throughout the city (39). Later when she prepares the wedding feast for Esperanza, her spiritual daughter, and Alex, Dr. John's son, the food causes the wedding guests to be overcome with sexual passion. Hundreds of children were conceived, we are told, on that day (242). Tita as cook, like Nacha as cook or Morning Light as herbalist, is here seen as nourishing the spirit through the medium of the body. "I eat therefore I am" would appear to be the logic operating here. Women are in this capacity the nurturers of human bodies, as well as of the animal and plant worlds that surround this culture, and as such numerous mythological references occur signaling the ancient association between women and animals, particularly birds (93).

It is no coincidence that Tita's selfish sister Rosaura cannot breast-feed either of her children. The text suggests that this is because she is not the rightful or spiritual mother of them, being only their biological mother. Tita is able to breastfeed Roberto (67) and it is Tita who is compared to Ceres, the ancient fertility goddess (76). Finally, it is Tita who is the spiritual or true mother of Roberto and Esperanza or Hope, the daughter whose future life is so imperilled by the demanding and suffocating Rosaura that Tita has no choice but to kill her sister, as she killed her mother, with her venomous cooking. It would appear that there are two types of mothers in this text, mothers of the womb, the body, who are corrupt and fail their children, and mothers of the word, the spirit, who provide their children with ideas and love and true nourishment. As we will see, posing the dichotomy in these terms can only lead to disaster for all of the characters in this novel.

The second ideology dominating the work is an extension of the first and involves what I would call an elaborate ambivalence toward the maternal body and its conflict with the spiritual impulse within human beings. Mama Ellena, depicted by Tita as the ultimate castrater, the Medusa's head with the power to kill others with merely a look, was herself a victim of unrequited love for a mulatto whom her family forbade her to marry (137). The only daughter of Mama Ellena to find any happiness at all was the daughter born of this illicit passion between Ellena and Trevino, her mulatto lover who was mysteriously ambushed and killed before her very eyes while she was pregnant with Gertrudis. The mulatto as a human hybrid, a very literal mixing of two disparate races and two antithetical cultures, has always been presented in Western literary traditions as a threat. Consider the observations of Hortense Spillers on the subject:

Created to provide a middle ground of latitude between 'black' and 'white,' the customary and permissible binary agencies of the national adventure, mulatto being, as a neither/nor proposition, inscribed no historic focus, or materiality, that was other than evasive and shadowy on the national landscape. To that extent, the mulatto/a embodied an alibi, an excuse for 'other/otherness' that the dominant culture could not (cannot now either) appropriate, or wish away. An accretion of signs that embody the 'unspeakable' of the Everything that the dominant culture would forget, the mulatto/a, as term, designates a disguise, covers up, in the century of Emancipation and beyond, the social and political reality of the dreaded African presence.[11]

Trevino as mulatto, existing on the margins of a stratified Mexican society hopelessly attempting to ape European notions of class and status, can only remind Mama Ellena's parents of their own mixed heritage, mixed of about equal parts: Indian and Spanish. Gertrudis as the product of this hybridized union, however, almost loses her husband when many years later she gives birth to a mulatto and her husband, the revolutionary Juan, suspects her of infidelity (180). Gertrudis carries within her own body her mother's long-buried sin of the flesh. The body, like an elaborate and unforgiving machine, never forgets, and it is Tita, in possession of her mother's long-lost love letters, who is able to save Gertrudis' marriage and establish the son's rightful paternity.

The third ideology that the novel proffers, however, contradicts the second. This third position suggests that women have the power to magically recover and reanimate themselves through the ability to give birth, both literally and metaphorically. A powerful talismanic presence clings to the bodies of all of the women in this text, whether they have given birth to children or not. The dead Nacha, who lived all 85 years of her life as a servant on the ranch and never married, has the power to reappear to Tita at key moments in her life, aiding and guiding her to make the correct choices, cook the proper foods. It is Nacha who appears with instructions when Tita is forced to deliver her sister's baby alone. It is Morning Light who, also dead many years, comes back to offer Tita soup and nudge her back to the land of the living after Roberto's death. Tita herself experiences a sort of phantom pregnancy after she begins her illicit affair with Pedro. Bloated and swollen in her belly, she is confronted by her dead mother, who denounces her as a whore and homewrecker only to be denounced in turn by Tita, who repels her mother's ghost with the words, "I hate you" (199). Only those words have the power to send Mama Ellena away once and for all, and at the same time they end Tita's phantom pregnancy. She was, it would appear, surfeit with her mother's ghost, not with a child, and only the act of ridding herself of her mother allowed her to carry on her own life with Pedro and Esperanza.

In short, the connection of women's potential fertility to their immortality suggests that within this culture you simply cannot kill a woman because the living residue of her life walks all around you in the very physical forms of her children or her ideas or her recipes. *Like Water for Chocolate* reveals the powerful tie between the body and the mind, between nature and culture, that finally only women can control and appreciate. In a novelistic world where most of the men are off swashbuckling as revolutionaries, spreading death and destruction in their wake, the women are instead conducting what we would recognize as real life; they are making ox-tail soup and trying to coax each other to speak. What exactly does this book offer its readers? The novel actually explores the most primitive fear that has animated much of Western culture for as long as that culture has been recorded, the fear of woman, the fear of the mother's body.[12] The novel suggests that biological mothers will metaphorically devour their children if given the opportunity. Families, and by extension societies, need to protect children who are most at jeopardy from the encroaching power and selfish desires of mothers to dominate and consume the energies of their young. Intense fear of the castrating mother is specifically recalled in this text, while both Medusa, the mother who kills her children, and Kali, the mother who wears her sons' decapitated heads as ornaments around her waist, are mentioned more than once in conjunction with Mama Ellena.

In using such imagery the novelist suggests that the tie with the body, the purely biological, has no claim on the superior form of life, the spiritual or metaphysical forces. But reifying the spiritual over the physical places the novel in an ambiguous position, just as placing chocolate in water creates something that can be sweet or sour depending on both the proportions and the heat. In an interesting conversation between Gertrudis and Tita, Gertrudis advises Tita to confess her love for Pedro and live openly with him. When Tita protests that she could never do such a shocking act, Gertrudis asks her what is the truth? Does she love Pedro or not? When Tita equivocates and expresses her allegiance to her mother's point of view, that she as the youngest daughter does not deserve any other fate than to care for her mother until her mother's death, Gertrudis states the central position of the text, and indeed of most postmodern fiction. She says, "Truth does not exist; it all depends on a person's point of view" (190). Not a particularly profound idea, but one that animates most of the recipes for pain and suffering throughout the novel. Words that attempt to express what someone recognizes as truth are ultimately born of pain, and pain, or various types of woundings, constitute the core of most literary works as well as cultural productions. "I write because I hurt" would appear to be the impetus of this text as clearly as I cook because I am hungry, or, once again: "I eat therefore I am."

Trying to claim that *Like Water for Chocolate* is typical of contemporary Mexican women's fiction or that it reveals any characteristics of the contemporary Mexican woman's novel may not, of course, be fair because of the novel's immense crossover popularity, its incredibly profitable filmic version and the success of its glossy Madison Avenue sell. All of these factors cause the novel to stand in clear juxtaposition to other, lesser-known Mexican women writing and publishing today in Spanish only. We could more legitimately ask, why was this particular novel able to make the crossover to a large Western audience? The answer is complex, but I would suggest that the novel reads like what we have come to call "comfort food," mashed potatoes, rice pudding, high carbohydrate goodies that assure us that a warm maternal presence is somewhere close by, hovering and protecting us against the harsh demands of life.

All literature, to some extent, is born out of pain, while it would seem increasingly obvious that authors are not compelled to write unless they are working out of or through a trauma that they then project onto their characters. When Tita crochets her immense bedspread she reveals to her reader that her inner chill, the wounding she has received from her mother, is as large and as deep as the land on which the ranch sits. Crocheting the bedspread as therapy is analogous to writing the book of recipes is analogous to writing the novel. Personal pain of infinite varieties is universal, as is the child's fear and ambivalence toward the mother and her body, her womb. Esquivel's novel succeeds because, ironically, it transcends her Mexican ambience by tapping into the universal child's memory of cowering before the mother's powerfully sexual and horrific body. When Tita bathes her mother or when she comes upon her mother's love letters to her mulatto lover she expresses for her readers a guaranteed and universal recipe for sexual nausea, the horror experienced in contemplating the mother's body as a site of desire rather than nourishment.

In finally cooking to death her mother and her avatar, the evil sister, Tita stands as a self-created cultural heroine, the woman who frees herself from the power of the past and the matriarchy with one deadly dish. But she also feeds her readers the ultimate fantasy: that they can destroy the maternal body and their link to the material world and live in some spiritual realm, some land of pure mind and even purer love, free from the taint of children, blood, sweat, tears and milk. In her renunciation and rejection of every biological mother in this text in favor of spiritual mothers like Nacha, Morning Light, and, ultimately Tita herself, this novel expresses a rejection of the womb, the essential female body, as intense as any.

According to Julia Kristeva, "No language can sing unless it confronts the Phallic Mother," and this Tita does in her battle to the death with Mama Ellena. For Kristeva, the mother's split (or what Bhabha has called "hybrid") identity originated for Western culture in the cult of the Lady, a hieroglyphic semiotic practice that inscribes "a conjunctive disjunction of the two sexes as irreducibly differentiated and, at the same time, alike." Further, the increasing dominance of the sign (non-disjunction) over the symbol (conjunction) produced for Western culture a "centered system (Other, Woman) whose center is there only so as to permit those making up the Same (Man, Author) to identify with it." The reduction of Woman to a sign signifies the culture's need to erase disjunction (sexual difference) by either excluding her as the Other or by dissolving her into a series of images (from the angel to the Virgin) that can be opposed to or assimilated by the Same. But in such a culture Woman can only be a "blind center," possessing no value in herself; that is, she can exist only as an object of exchange among members of the Same. Kristeva labels this complex of gestures "devalorizing valorization," a mode of explicit devaluation of women that first systematically appeared in fourteenth-century bourgeois literature (in *fabliaux*, soties, farces).[13]

Esquivel as a Mexican woman writer has styled her heroine Tita as the Same (male-identified) within this text, an embodiment of the cook as artist who has been empowered by swallowing and introjecting the power of her (M)Other. According to Kristeva,

What we take for a mother, and all the sexuality that the maternal image commands, is nothing but the place where rhythm stops and identity is constituted....[The author's] oracular discourse, split (signifier/signified) and multiplied (in its sentential and lyrical concatenations), carries the scar of not merely the *trauma* but also the *triumph* of his [*sic*] battle with the Phallic Mother....The war, however, is never over and the poet shall continue indefinitely to measure himself [*sic*] against the mother, against his mirror-image, a partially reassuring and regenerative experience, a partially castrating, legislating and socializing ordeal.[14]

It is not for nothing that Kristeva reminds us that "Fear of the archaic mother turns out to be essentially fear of her generative power. It is this power, a dreaded one, that patrilineal filiation has the burden of subduing" (*Powers* 77). Patriarchal religion as well as Western Culture as a whole has had a role in separating the "masculine" and "rational" from the fertile and fertilizable feminine body, with its unpleasant and unsettling association with menstrual blood, a particularly unclean object worthy of abjection. The phantasmatic mother of the unconscious, the psychic abyss that the child struggles valiantly to escape, stands, then, as a residual reminder of the Mother Goddess who was only partially displaced by those patriarchal religions that posited instead as objects of worship (read: cleanliness) an absent father and a son-figure in the grip of, what else, the mother. As uncomfortable as it may be to admit, *Like Water for Chocolate* ultimately conforms to patriarchal/colonial and highly hybridized notions of value, and as such, I would claim that it is a recipe for disaster for women.

NOTES

1. For a succinct overview of the issues involved in colonialist critique, see Donna Landry and Gerald MacLean, *Materialist Feminism* (Oxford: Blackwell, 1993), 70-71. On the same subject, see Gayatri Spivak, "Can the Subaltern Speak?" in *Marxism and the Interpretation of Culture,* ed. Cary Nelson and Lawrence Grossberg, (Urbana: U of Illinois P, 1988), 271-313.

2. Homi K. Bhabha, *The Location of Culture* (London: Routledge, 1994), 112-15. Bhabha's writing is notoriously dense, but its importance in charting the emerging field of cultural studies is undisputed.

3. See Rosario Castellanos, "Culinary Lesson," trans. Julian Palley, in *Short Stories by Latin American Women: The Magic and the Real,* ed. Celia Correas de Zapata (Houston: Arte Publico Press, 1990), 43-51. Originally published in 1960, the story also contains the statement: "With good reason Saint Theresa said that God may be found in stew pots. Or, that matter is energy" (50).

4. Clara Roman-Odio defines the *folletín* as "a type of sentimental narrative avidly consumed in Latin America which emphasizes romantic bliss, sexual arousal, and the melodrama of an illegitimate passion" (see her "From Writer to Producer: Conflicting Voices in *Like Water for Chocolate*," in *Cine-Lit, III: Essays on Hispanic Film and Fiction,* ed. George Cabelo-Castellet et al. (Corvallis: Oregon State UP, 1998), 84-89. A lengthier discussion of the *folletin* can be found in Jean Franco, "The Incorporation of Women: A Comparison of North American and Mexican Popular Narrative," in *Studies in Entertainment: Critical Approaches to Mass Culture,* ed. Tania Modeleski (Bloomington: Indiana UP, 1986), 199-239.

5. Antonio Marquet, "How to Write a Best-Seller: The Recipe of Laura Esquivel," *Plural* 237 (1991), 58; Dianna C. Niebylski, "Heartburn, Humor and Hyperbole in *Like Water for Chocolate,*" in *Performing Gender and Comedy: Theories, Texts and Contexts,* ed. Shannon Hengen (Amsterdam: Gordon and Breach, 1998), 180; Rosa Fernandez-Levin, "Ritual and 'Sacred Space' in Laura Esquivel's *Like Water for Chocolate, Confluencia* 12 (1996), 106-07. Another interesting approach to the novel is taken by Monica Zapata, who examines how the "free circulation of cliches constitutes one of the keys to its success" (205). See her "*Like Water for Chocolate* and the Free Circulation of Cliches," in *Latin American Postmodernisms,* ed. Richard A. Young (Netherlands: Rodopi, 1997).

6. Esquivel admits to "really liking" the magical realist works of Garcia Marquez: "Fantasy forms a part of our everyday lives [in Mexico]. It's in the architecture, in painting. What we call magic realism is pre-Hispanic. Our tradition tells us of serpents that fly" [(qtd. in Soledad Alameda, "Laura Esquivel, el sueno y la vida," *El pais semanal* 247 (12 Nov, 1995), 40-46.] The tradition of Latin American "magical realism" is discussed at greater length in Lois Parkinson Zamora and Wendy B. Faris, eds. *Magical Realism: Theory, History, Community* (Durham: Duke U P, 1995); and David Danow, *The Spirit of Carnival: Magical Realism and the Grotesque* (Lexington: U of Kentucky P, 1995). Angel Flores has argued that magical realism is of European origin, and is represented most clearly in the works of Kafka. The phenomenon was imported to Latin America by Borges in his *Historia universal de la infamia.* See Flores' "Magic Realism in Spanish American Fiction," in Luis Sainz de Medrano, *Historia de la literatura hispanoamericana* (Madrid: Taurus, 1992), 336-37.

7. The complex and convoluted history of Mexico's women has been recorded in such works as Anna Macias, *Against All Odds: The Feminist Movement in Mexico to 1940* (Westport, CT: Greenwood, 1987); Ward Morton, *Woman Suffrage in Mexico* (Gainesville: U of Florida P, 1962); and Emile Berbmann, *Women, Culture, and Politics in Latin America* (Berkeley: U of California P, 1990).

8. The best summary of the relationship between women and metaphysical associations with their bodily fluids, tears, blood, and milk, can be found in the work of Julia Kristeva, in particular her "Motherhood According to Giovanni Bellini" in *Desire in Language,* ed. Leon S. Roudiez, trans. Thomas Gora, Alice Jardine, and Leon S. Roudiez (New York: Columbia U P, 1980).

9. Mexican religion and its indigenous beliefs in the union of spirit and matter can be found in Anita Brenner, *Idols Behind Altars* (New York: Harcourt, Brace, 1929); Jacques Lefaye, *Quetzalcoatl and Gaudalupe: The Formation of Mexican National Consciousness, 1531-1813* (Chicago: U of Chicago P, 1976); Andres Guerro, *A Chicano Theology* (New York: Orbis, 1987); and Serge Gruzinski, *Man-Gods in the Mexican Highlands: Indian Power and Colonial Society, 1520-1800* (Stanford: Stanford U P, 1989); and Inga Clendinnen, *Aztecs: An Interpretation* (Cambridge: Cambridge U P, 1991).

10. Laura Esquivel, *Like Water for Chocolate: A Novel in Monthly Installments with Recipes, Romances, and Home Remedies,* trans. Carol Christensen and Thomas Christensen (New York: Doubleday, 1989). All quotations from the text will be taken from this edition, with page numbers in parentheses in the text.

11. Hortense Spillers, "Notes on an Alternative Model-Neither/Nor," in *The Difference Within,* ed. Elizabeth Meese and Alice Parker (Philadelphia: John Benjamins, 1989), 165-66.

12. On the pervasive mythology surrounding the fear of women in Western Culture, see H. R. Hays, *The Dangerous Sex: The Myth of Feminine Evil* (New York: Pocket, 1965); Wolfgang Lederer, *The Fear of Women* (New York: Grune and Stratton, 1968); and Karen Horney, "The Dread of Woman," rpt. in *Feminine Psychology,* ed. Harold Kelman (New York: Norton, 1967), 133-46. Julia Kristeva discusses anthropological reasons for the fear of women in her *Powers of Horror: An Essay on Abjection,* trans. Leon S. Roudiez (New York: Columbia UP, 1982), 77-83; 101. As Kristeva notes, among certain tribes women are viewed as a divisive factor, largely because of male fear of women's generative capacities. While it is recognized that women are essential for reproduction, it is also clear that they threaten the ideal norms of the male-descended clan. While one always knows the mother of a child, paternity is uncomfortably conjectural. Finally, however, the woman's body can only remind man of his own mortality, his own origins in the womb as unclean: "Fear of the uncontrollable generative mother repels me from the body" (79).

13. Julia Kristeva, "The Novel as Polylogue," and "The Bounded Text," in *Desire in Language,* 191; 49-51.

14. *Desire in Language* 193.

9

Intersections of Race, Gender, Sexuality, and Experimentation in the Autobiographical Writings of Cherríe Moraga and Maxine Hong Kingston

Rosetta R. Haynes

This essay addresses the ways in which race, gender, and sexuality converge with textual experimentation within the context of women's autobiographical writing. Focusing on Cherríe Moraga's *Loving in the War Years* and Maxine Hong Kingston's *The Woman Warrior*,[1] I argue that the complex and often conflictual nature of the authors' multifaceted identities motivates their use of hybrid narrative forms. In particular, I address the ways in which race, gender, and sexuality influence their formal choices and the manner in which these texts depart from and challenge traditional conceptions of autobiography.

As the title of Moraga's autobiographical work suggests, there is a war raging, both inside and outside the author's body, that manifests itself in and through the text in both form and content. The four warring factions are her lesbianism, a Mexican cultural heritage which has a deep emotional claim upon her but which places special demands and restrictions upon her as a woman, an Anglo heritage with which she has a problematic relationship, and a white skin which renders her race ambiguous. Similarly, Kingston's title emphasizes a motif of battle that provides some insight into this author's inner struggle to reconcile the Chinese and American cultural heritages that inform her identity, both of which contain elements that are oppressive to women. The conflicts that both writers face converge in the genre of autobiography, bringing to the forefront a current critical issue regarding the problematics of self-representation for racial/ethnic and female autobiographers: finding appropriate forms through which to express a complex, multifaceted self fully.

Feminist critics such as Bella Brodzki and Celeste Schenck have argued that the type of subjectivity that has traditionally been accepted as the norm for autobiographical writing, that of the unified, transcendent self characterized by its universality, representativeness, and authority to speak for the community, has been inadequate for representing the experiences of women.[2] Brodzki and Schenck assert that "[a]t both extremes of subjectivity and publicity, the female autobiographer has lacked the sense of radical individuality, duplicitous but useful, that empowered Augustine and Henry Adams to write their representative lives large."[3]

Though some women have adhered to the linear, totalized stylistic forms that have traditionally marked men's autobiographical writing, many women, conscious of the "multidimensionality of [their] socially conditioned roles,"[4] have chosen to depart from these modes in favor of more diffuse, fragmented styles that more accurately reflect the complex realities of their lives. The ethnic woman writer has been particularly challenged in her attempt to represent a multifaceted identity shaped by the different communities of which she is a part. As bicultural women, both Moraga and Kingston can be said to exhibit what Gloria Anzaldúa calls a "*mestiza* consciousness":

The new *mestiza* copes by developing a tolerance for contradictions, a tolerance for ambiguity...She learns to juggle cultures. She has a plural personality, she operates in a pluralistic mode-nothing is thrust out, the good the bad and the ugly, nothing rejected, nothing abandoned. Not only does she sustain contradictions, she turns the ambivalence into something else.[5]

Anzaldúa highlights the creative as well as the conflictual nature of the *Mestiza*'s coming to terms with the disparate parts of a complex self: "Cradled in one culture, sandwiched between two cultures, straddling three cultures and their value systems, *la mestiza* undergoes a struggle of the flesh, a struggle of borders, an inner war" (78). Both authors are fundamentally "border women," whose internal and external struggles to reconcile multifaceted selves get translated into specific formal choices. In particular, some of their narrative strategies include incorporating a variety of genres in their texts, utilizing fiction, assimilating linguistic elements from each of their cultural heritages, and reinterpreting cultural myths from a feminist perspective. Moreover, both writers insist on claiming and foregrounding the bodies that they have been taught to despise by using the body as an interpretive point of reference for understanding their positions as women of color within American culture.[6] By embodying their texts in such a manner, they symbolically represent the hybridity of their narrative forms in the flesh. Finally, Moraga and Kingston assert the centrality of their relationships with their mothers in helping to shape their identities and their texts. It is the dynamics of mother/daughter interactions which play such a fundamental role in forming their sense of self and the narrative forms through which they represent their life stories.

In reading Moraga's text, one is immediately aware of the diverse array of genres that comprise her work. Not only do we find essays, poems, journal entries, dreams, and sketches, but we also find a blurring of forms *within* genres. For example, there are dreams inscribed in journal entries, journal entries within essays, and poetry contained in essays. Her inclusion of a variety of forms parallels her attempt to acknowledge and validate each aspect of her complex identity. It is as if a single, coherent form is inadequate to express her many selves. Moreover, the blurring of forms within genres seems to suggest the interlocking nature of the various facets of her identity.[7]

By incorporating dreams into her text, Moraga draws upon a deeper level of awareness of her conflicted subjectivity. To acknowledge and act upon the insights that one's dreams provide is to engage in a process of cultivating personal wholeness, which is ultimately what the author seeks to achieve. It is a dream that opens the text, providing a symbolic representation of the great risk that is involved in pronouncing her commitment to loving women. This dream, which describes a frightening scene in which she and her lover are held as prisoners of war, sets the tone for a comprehensive reflection upon the internal and external struggles that mark the author's quest for wholeness.

Like the dreams, the presence of journal entries provides the reader with an added dimension of personal revelation. The entries are interspersed throughout her essays to provide occasions for deeper reflection upon the particular issues being addressed in the essays. For example, within her longest essay, "A Long Line of Vendidas," Moraga explains that because of the Chicano cultural practice of putting men first, Chicana mothers habitually favor their sons over their daughters. Within this discussion the author includes a journal entry describing a painful episode in which her mother abruptly ends a very emotional phone call to Moraga in order to answer another call from her brother (102, 103), thus illustrating this cultural privileging of the male. The journal entry poignantly reflects the interrelatedness of the racial and sexual politics that inform Moraga's struggle to develop her consciousness as a Chicana feminist.

In another critique of traditional autobiographical conventions, Moraga chooses to arrange her text not in chronological order, but according to her emotional and political development. By doing this she proffers an alternative logic for recounting the significant events of her life. These acts of revising received forms are not merely a discursive strategy, but derive from a deep political commitment to transforming social structures that deny certain groups (i.e. women, minorities, homosexuals) dignity and full participation in American life on all levels. An important consideration for Moraga's choice of a creative form and style is to communicate with a broad readership. As a Chicana she is torn between the desire to speak in a manner that is understandable only to those who share her Mexican cultural heritage and the need to reach as many people as possible. This necessity for a broad readership stems from the very real demands of publishing and from her compulsion to escape a frightening feeling of isolation: "I have been translating my experience out of fear of an aloneness too great to bear. I have learned analysis as a mode to communicate what I feel the experience itself already speaks for" (vi). Through her text she helps to build a community of sympathetic readers, including women who may share similar experiences of pain, joy, and self-awareness.

In part what is at issue in Moraga's textual creation is authority, over the production of her own text and over the right to conceive of and promote a new, more just paradigm for human existence (as is advocated by her radical politics). This question of authority points to an issue that often becomes a burden to the racial/ethnic self-writer, which is the pressure to act as a representative for the experiences of his or her particular cultural group. Individuality shown on the part of such a writer may be interpreted as atypical, or even worse, as a betrayal to the larger group. Their authority may be called into question if they are critical of certain aspects of their culture. But ultimately, this author speaks for herself and for the validity of her own reality, thus rejecting the constraints that may be placed upon her by others: "...I refuse to let *anybody's* movement determine for me what is safe and fair to say" (vi).

Like Moraga, Kingston challenges traditional autobiographical conventions by using an innovative style. She strikingly incorporates myth, fantasy, and fiction to articulate the story of a first generation Chinese-American woman trying to come to terms with her identity. Of this unconventional form, Patricia Blinde explains that it "exemplifies what can be described as an all-encompassing response to the complexities of reality and the attendant exploration of several literary forms to represent this response."[8] The presence of fiction may be surprising to the reader who expects a strictly factual rendering of her life story. But to some extent, <u>all</u> autobiography is fictional because the very act of shaping remembered experience into a text requires the use of the imagination.

In her first chapter "No Name Woman," Kingston discloses, against her mother's warnings, the story of an aunt who commits adultery and incurs the violent wrath of a village that depends for its stability on the adherence of its members to prescribed roles. Within the village a woman's identity was defined within an intricate network of relationships among kinsmen. She was not permitted to carve out an independent life for herself. Thus, by becoming pregnant, the aunt must be severely punished for daring to act "as if she could have a private life, secret and apart from them" (13). Worse than the tragic suicide of the disgraced woman and the death of her baby, is the community's injunction to never again speak her name. This tale underscores for the author the central role that language plays in formation of identity. In the traditional Chinese culture of her parents, one's identity was effectively erased through the process of unnaming.

Unwilling to accept her mother's story as a mere warning for her to avoid similar disgraceful behavior, Kingston fashions a new version of the tale which gives agency to the woman who "in the old China did not choose" (6). Her motivation for creating an empowered fictional ancestor is to provide a model for herself that is relevant to her own efforts to construct an identity as a first generation Chinese-American woman: "Unless I see her life branching into mine, she gives me no ancestral help" (8). Throughout the text the author continues this pattern of revising stories and myths for her own use. Critic Sau-ling Cynthia Wong comments:

The narrator's methodology of self-redemption is thus remarkably consistent. Over and over, we find her forgoing the security of ready-made cultural meanings, opting instead to painstakingly mold a new set suited to her condition as a Chinese-American woman.[9]

This strategy of revising, of fictionalizing, thus stems from a focus on her race and gender and the ways that she can establish a meaningful and empowering relationship with these aspects of her identity. The license that she takes with stories and myths is also an assertion of her authority to create her story as she sees fit. As mentioned, the racial/ethnic writer may face critique if she is not perceived as representing the "norm" of a particular group's experience. Kingston did find herself under fire by many Asian-American intellectuals for adapting cultural myths, for allowing *Woman Warrior* to be classified as autobiography instead of fiction, and for her portrayal of male sexism within Chinese culture.[10]

The subjectivity that Kingston tries to create in her text is complex. The many voices which speak throughout the work defy the existence of a traditional "I" that unifies and controls the narrative. The difficulty of constructing a subjectivity is suggested in her final chapter, "Song for a Barbarian Reed Pipe," which includes a scene in which the author has problems pronouncing the English "I" while trying to read out loud in school as a child: "The Chinese 'I' has seven strokes, intricacies. How could the American 'I,' assuredly wearing a hat like the Chinese, have only three strokes, the middle so straight?" (166). Already finding speech difficult, the child lapses into silence whenever she encounters the enigmatic English "I." It is as if she has an early awareness of the letter's inadequacy in representing one's subjectivity with any degree of complexity. In addressing the kind of subjectivity that Kingston creates for herself in this text, Lee Quinby asserts that *Woman Warrior* has been miscategorized as autobiography and should instead be classified as memoirs, as the author's subtitle suggests. One definition of memoirs that Quinby quotes from the OED reads "a record of events, not purporting to be a complete history, but treating of such matters as come within the personal knowledge of the writer, or are obtained from certain particular sources of information."[11] As such, the critic feels that Kingston uses this genre to create a complex "ideographic self" that fundamentally challenges the modern era's power structures that give rise to the totalized "I" of autobiography.

This "ideographic self" negotiates between the Western "I" that "systematically denies its multiplicity and interconnectedness,"[12] and the Chinese "I" that includes a form for women that means "slave." Quinby thus explains, "The ideographic 'I' of Kingston's memoirs valorizes individual freedom while at the same time defining selfhood as an ensemble subjectivity."[13] The concept of the "ideographic self" is insightful and is credibly applied to Kingston's text. However, Quinby's description of the Western totalized and disconnected "I" of autobiography more accurately describes the Western *male* "I" of traditional autobiography. Women were not traditionally defined as independent or disconnected. As I have noted, the subjectivities that women have created in their self-histories have often differed vastly from those of their male counterparts. Looking back at the tradition of women's autobiography, Estelle Jelinek has noticed that it is common for these authors to acknowledge their interconnectedness with family and friends.[14] This does not necessarily diminish their own sense of self, but rather allows women to define themselves in relation to others and to acknowledge the influences that other people have had in shaping who they are.

Moraga's method of critiquing traditional autobiographical forms parallels her critique of dominant ideologies that have historically been damaging to women.

Her radical politics involve exposing cultural constructs that have been destructive to women and showing how they can be reinterpreted from a feminist perspective. An example of this exposure and reinterpretation can be found in her longest essay, "A Long Line of Vendidas," in which she discusses the ways that sexism and heterosexism within Chicano culture have contributed to the belief that women are inherently inclined to treachery. Central to the creation and perpetuation of this myth, Moraga explains, is the female mythical/historical figure of Malintzin Tenepal (Malinche, or "the fucked one"). During the sixteenth-century Spanish conquest of Mexico, this woman had been enslaved and presented as a gift to conqueror Hernando Cortes. Eventually, she acted as his translator and his mistress. The Aztec princess is now recognized as the mother of the Mestizo race and has been blamed for her complicity with the enemy. Her history figures prominently in the collective psyche of Mexican-American people and has done a great deal to instill a suspicion of female betrayal, particularly sexual betrayal.

Moraga, along with other Chicana feminist scholars such as Aleida Del Castillo and Norma Alarcón, has been involved in researching the role of this figure in order to discover more realistic circumstances surrounding her actions, and to foster a more sympathetic understanding of these actions. Moraga notes Del Castillo's assertion, for example, that Malinche's assistance of Cortes stemmed from her deep spiritual belief that Cortes was really the Aztec serpent god, Quetzalcoatl, returned in different form to rescue the inhabitants of Mexico from complete destruction. Alarcón speculates that perhaps Malinche's allegiance to Cortes may in fact have stemmed from the woman's efforts to reconcile herself to an awareness of her utter powerlessness. Alarcón thus refers to Simone Weil's insights on the master-slave relationship:

the thought of being in absolute subjection as somebody's plaything is a thought no human being can sustain: so if a man (I add woman) is left with no means at all of escaping constraint he (she) has no alternative except to persuade himself (herself) that he (she) is doing voluntarily the very things he (she) is forced to do; in other words, he (she) substitutes *devotion* for *obedience*...devotion of this kind rests upon self-deception, because the reasons for it will not bear inspection.[15]

The investigations of Del Castillo, Alarcón, Moraga, and other feminist scholars are in effect helping to recover the voice of a central female historical figure who has been rendered passive and silent through a legacy of interpretation that has been dominated by men. Just as Moraga challenges sexism by revising the cultural myth of Malinche, so Kingston rewrites the Chinese cultural myth of Fa Mu Lan, a woman who attains heroic status as a warrior avenging the wrongs committed against her emperor. This woman, who poses as a man during her ten-year career as a soldier, wages a number of successful battles against her enemies, rising to the rank of general. At the end of the war she is handsomely rewarded by the emperor for her bravery.

Patricia Lin Blinde explains that although the Chinese ballad that recounts this tale is only about sixty lines long, Kingston uses her imagination to weave in parts of other legends, as well as aspects of her own experiences to create a full-fledged narrative of the woman warrior's training and combat experience.[16] As Kingston rewrites the myth of Fa Mu Lan, she counters the damaging stories of female inferiority with which she grew up as part of her Chinese cultural heritage. As a child, she commonly heard sayings such as, " Girls are maggots in the rice," and "It is more profitable to raise geese than daughters." As the author recounts the tale, she places these odious sayings in the mouth of the baron who had drafted the woman warrior's brother in their village. Kingston, who discursively adopts the identity of the woman warrior, represents herself as a "female avenger" and demands that the baron acknowledge the abuses he has committed against women and girls, as well as to confess the specific wrongs he has done to her family. When he refuses, she slays him with her sword. Blinde explains that in so doing, she not only avenges her family, but she also symbolically destroys the misogynistic elements that have plagued all women.[17]

The similarity between the Spanish words for fair-skinned ("la gÿera") and war ("la guerra") suggests that Moraga's skin is a particularly volatile site: "[t]he object of oppression is not only someone *outside* my skin, but the someone *inside* my skin. In fact, to a large degree, the real battle with such oppression, for all of us, begins under the skin" (54). Throughout her life Moraga has had a changing and complex relationship with her skin and with her body in general. Born to a working-class Chicana mother and a white father, she inherited the features of her mother and the white skin of her father. The author explains that light skin was valued in her family because it was seen as an opportunity for increasing success in the dominant society. For a time she "passes" in order to utilize her skin privilege, but later comes to celebrate the brownness within her. However, Moraga's ability to fully embrace her Mexican racial identity comes only after a period of struggle with internalized racism, with the oppressors that lie under her skin. Sidonie Smith asserts that Moraga's text "directs attention to the materiality of skin as the locus of dawning political awareness."[18] This awareness comes haltingly and painfully, yet it is a necessary process in her commitment to understanding the complex nature of oppression. The author's poem, "It Got Her Over," poignantly articulates this connection between skin and growing political awareness, as well as a consciousness of the ways in which her white skin has functioned as a source of safety and privilege. The significance of skin as the signifier of a consciousness born of struggle is one aspect of an "embodied subjectivity" that Moraga creates in and through her text.

Sidonie Smith describes two interdependent histories of subjectivity that were prevalent during the nineteenth century and have implications for autobiographical practices in the twentieth century, universal subjectivity and embodied subjectivity. Universal subjectivity grew out of Enlightenment notions of the self as unitary, rational, and transcendent. This universal self, as disembodied consciousness, could only exist if it rejected the chaotic passions associated with the body. As privileged originator of knowledge, meaning, and truth, the Enlightenment self maintained its universality and exclusivity by establishing normative standards of gender (male), race (white), class (middle), and sexuality (heterosexual). Anyone not meeting these standards was marginalized and perceived as essentially body. Embodied subjectivity therefore makes the existence of universal subjectivity possible. Unlike the universal/male subject, a different type of selfhood is attributed to women, an essential selfhood which is burdened by the body. Woman's destiny is determined by her biology, and she must gain her fulfillment by living for and through others in the assigned social roles of wife, mother, daughter, and sister. She may escape negative associations with the body to the extent that she represses sexual desire and individual identity, subjects herself to man's authority, and serves others selflessly. Because she cannot determine her own destiny, she cannot truly exercise agency.

The discourse of the embodied woman specifically creates the subjectivity of bourgeois white women because just as the universal subject defines himself against those who are not white, male, middle-class, and heterosexual, so the embodied subject creates her identity by excluding women who are not white, middle-class, and heterosexual. Working-class women, lesbians, and women of color are perceived as even more embodied, and as such, possess no possibilities of escaping the stigma of the body, even through repressive and selfless behavior.[19] By refusing to suppress her sexuality and by insisting on the right to "live it out in the body of the poem, in the body of the woman" (v), Moraga embraces a subjectivity that was meant to degrade her. For Moraga, living in the flesh and embodying her text are subversive acts. Smith thus explains that "Moraga brings the autobiographical body out from under the processes of erasure, assuming her body as narrative point of departure. She discovers that the body functions as a lens through which she comes to see her complex positioning as a woman, lesbian, light-skinned Chicana" (139).

It is her lesbian identity in particular that enables Moraga to connect with the suffering of others. As the writer comes to accept her sexuality and to experience the oppression that accompanies it, she gains a greater capacity for comprehending the oppression of others. The centrality of women to her life and work speaks to her political stance of putting women first. But this position not only goes against the grain of Chicano (and Anglo) culture, it risks garnering her the label of "traitor to the race" within that culture. She thus explains, "the woman who defies her role as subservient to her husband, father, brother, or son by taking control of her own sexual destiny is purported to be a 'traitor to her race' by contributing to the 'genocide' of her people, whether or not she has children" (113). It is the lesbian, asserts Moraga, who is most severely denounced as a traitor because it is she who most noticeably exercises independence in her sexual identity and destiny. In particular, it is through the medium of poetry that Moraga uniquely expresses her love and longing for women. Most of the poems in her text were directly inspired by women who have touched her life. Poetry collaborates with her other textual forms, picking up themes articulated elsewhere in the book and speaking the author's reality in ways that evoke the passion, pain, sensuality, and joy that inform Moraga's experience.

Moreover, it is within the medium of poetry that the author is most keenly aware of the significance of her native language in enabling her to express emotions that somehow cannot be fully articulated in the dominant language of English. She comes to this awareness suddenly through a revelation while attending a concert in which Ntosake Shange was reading. Moraga explains:

What Ntosake caught in me is the realization that in my development as a poet, I have in many ways, denied the voice of my own brown mother the brown in me. I have acclimated to the sound of a white language which, as my father represents it, does not speak to the emotions in my poems, emotions which stem from the love of my mother. (55)

The presence of both English and Spanish linguistic traditions in her writing is a testimony to the author's bicultural identity. But her inclusion of Spanish reflects an advanced state of her political consciousness, one that has enabled her to reclaim a language that was not instilled in her during childhood in order to facilitate her assimilation into the dominant culture. Her reclamation of her mother tongue is a kind of symbolic homecoming that represents her embrace of a cultural heritage she had so long denied. Both Moraga and Kingston identify parts of their bodies that signify the extreme difficulty of articulating the truth of their realities to those who are unable or unwilling to hear and accept it. For Moraga, the bodily site of pain and struggle is her back:

The issue of being a "movement writer" is altogether different. Sometimes I feel my back will break from the pressure I feel to speak for others. A friend told me once how no wonder I had called the first book I co-edited (with Gloria Anzaldúa), "This Bridge Called My Back." *You have chronic back trouble*, she says. Funny, I had never considered this most obvious connection, all along my back giving me constant pain. And the spot that hurts the most is the muscle that controls the movement of my fingers and hands while typing. I feel it now straining at my desk. (v)

For Kingston, it is her throat: "Maybe because I was the one with the tongue cut loose, I had grown inside me a list of over two hundred things that I had to tell my mother so that she would know the true things about me and stop the pain in my throat" (197). Back and throat pain become for these two authors the embodiment of the ethnic woman writer's struggle to voice the inarticulable, to insert her experiences into established ways of being and knowing, and in so doing, transforming them. Kingston expresses this belief in the transformative power of self-revelation as she speculates on the results of sharing her list of long-suppressed truths with her mother: "If only I could let my mother know the list, she and the world would become more like me, and I would never be alone again" (198). As autobiographers, Moraga and Kingston have a vested interest in speaking the truth of their experiences, and this not only involves challenging racist, sexist, classist, and homophobic paradigms for living, but it also means challenging received models for autobiographical writing.

In keeping with the imperative to broach the unspeakable, Kingston chooses to address one of the ultimate markers of female embodiment menstruation. It is on the occasion of the author's own menses that her mother relays the cautionary tale of the aunt who commits suicide: "Now that you have started to menstruate, what happened to her could happen to you. Don't humiliate us. You wouldn't like to be forgotten as if you had never been born. The villagers are watchful'" (5). Through the narrative strategy of fictionalizing her connection with the story of Fa Mu Lan, not only does Kingston broach this taboo subject, but she destigmatizes it, treating menstruation in a matter-of-fact manner. When the young warrior-in-training begins to menstruate at age fourteen, she asks the old woman who is helping to raise her if she (the girl) could use her powers to stop the bleeding. But the old woman replies, "'No. You don't stop shitting and pissing...It's the same with blood. Let it run.' ('Let it walk' in Chinese)" (31). Menstruation is thus dealt with openly as a natural part of life that does not diminish the young woman's strength or interrupt her training; it even becomes an occasion for reflection and insight: "I bled and thought about the people to be killed; I bled and thought about the people to be born" (33). Embodying her text in such a manner is a subversive strategy ideologically (by rejecting the belief in female impurity) and textually (by insisting on the validity of a fictional revision of a revered Chinese cultural myth).

Both Moraga and Kingston present their mothers and their relationships with them with complexity, while both mix love, admiration, anger, and compassion when speaking about and representing their mothers, who have had a deep and lasting impact upon their lives and their psyches. Joan Lidoff explains that the "[t]he relation of mother and daughter influences women's ways of imagining not only the self, but also the whole fabric of social relations and the symbolic structures of literature that express and depend on those conceptions" (116). The textual imprint of mother/daughter dynamics most notably emerges through the authors' incorporation of poetry and stories.

Moraga opens her poem, "For the Color of My Mother," with the following declaration: "I am a white girl gone brown to the blood color of my mother/speaking to her through the unnamed part of the mouth /the wide-arched muzzle of brown women" (60). For Moraga, race becomes inseparable from her mother, since it is through this woman that she inherits her Mexican heritage. The racial bond that she shares with her mother is inflected with an intense and complex love stemming from the author's identification with this woman as a kindred sufferer of female oppression within the Chicano culture. Moraga's admiration for her mother stems in large part from the maternal will to survive. It is her mother's stories of being repeatedly taken out of school in order to work in the fields, of lying about her age to gain employment, and of her father's habitual alcoholic dissipation that have resonance for the author: "[T]hese stories my mother told me crept under my "guera" skin. I had no choice but to enter the life of my mother. *I had no choice.* I took her life into my heart, but managed to keep a lid on it as long as I feigned being the happy, upwardly mobile heterosexual" (52). Acknowledging her sexual orientation frees Moraga to return to her mother, to return home.

Whereas Moraga's vulnerability in connection with her sexuality provides the impetus for a more compassionate and understanding view of her mother, it is Kingston's infusion of the maternal voice throughout her text that signals an effort to portray her mother in a more sympathetic light. Lidoff classifies Kingston's work among a group of women's autobiographies that she calls the "forgiving genre," or those in which daughters foreground their parents' stories in order to understand their parents on their own terms. In such autobiographies, the author, rather than placing her own story center stage, articulates her experiences from the interstices. This approach is more compassionate than that of traditional autobiographical writing since blame and anger are tempered as the writer's understanding of the parent grows.[20] Kingston's mother, Brave Orchid, is a woman to be reckoned with. She is a tough-spirited cultural navigator who brings to America the myths and traditions of Old China after being driven from her home by the communist revolution. She realizes that much of her status has been lost in the translation from Chinese to American culture. In China, Brave Orchid was a well-respected doctor who transcended the traditional expectations of woman as wife and mother in order to enter the field of medicine. In America, however, she becomes the co-owner of a laundry.

The relationship that Kingston has with Brave Orchid is notably contentious, as is revealed through the interplay of stories that mother and daughter tell which structure text and subjectivity. Of the significant role that Brave Orchid's "talk-stories" play in helping to shape the author's sense of self, Sidonie Smith explains: "Recognizing the inextricable relationship between an individual's sense of 'self' and the community's stories of selfhood, Kingston self-consciously reads herself into existence through the stories her culture tells about women."[21] The mother herself presents a problematic model for her daughter to follow. On the one hand, she is admirable as she resists traditional expectations to become educated as a doctor. On the other hand, she is someone who passes on damaging cultural myths of female inferiority to Kingston. Just as Moraga's mother enacts the patriarchal values of Chicano culture by putting males first, Kingston's mother relays traditional Chinese patriarchal values by transmitting demeaning images of women.

The motifs of battle that are highlighted in the titles of both Kingston's and Moraga's self-histories underscore the inherently conflictual nature of the process of coming to terms with the disparate parts of a complex self and the circumstances which shaped them. The mode of reconciling often contradictory elements necessarily involves imagination and resolve. The creative discursive forms and styles through which these authors present themselves reflect perhaps more realistically than do the more linear and totalized forms of traditional autobiography, the tentative and exploratory quality of coming to know oneself.

As female writers with bicultural heritages, Moraga and Kingston must negotiate a space that allows them to be true to themselves and to their visions. Asserting their authority to speak in an authentic voice apart from and in concert with others in their cultural communities, these authors reserve the right to revise and reinterpret received cultural forms and ways of knowing and being. Ultimately Moraga and Kingston seem to achieve an acceptance of inner contradiction, to accomplish a dynamic resolution of the internal dialectic that is always taking place among the various facets of their identities.

NOTES

1. Cherríe Moraga, *Loving in the War Years* (Boston: South End Press, 1983), and Maxine Hong Kingston, *The Woman Warrior: Memoirs of a Girlhood Among Ghosts* (New York: Vintage International, 1989). Hereafter, both texts to be cited parenthetically.

2. Bella Brodzki and Celeste Schenck, *Life/Lines: Theorizing Women's Autobiography* (Ithaca: Cornell U P, 1988), 1.

3. Brodzki and Schenck, 1.

4. Estelle C. Jelinek, *Women's Autobiography: Essays in Criticism* (Bloomington: Indiana UP), 17.

5. Gloria Anzaldúa, *Borderlands/La Frontera: The New Mestiza* (San Francisco: Spinsters/Aunt Lute, 1987), 79. Though in speaking of Mestizos Anzaldúa specifically refers to the mixed-race people who emerged from the Spanish conquest of the indigenous Indian population of Mexico in 1519, the characteristics of plural personality that she describes may be extended to Kingston as well.

6. Here I am echoing Michelle Cliff's title: *Claiming an Identity They Taught Me to Despise* (Watertown, MA: Persephone Press, 1980).

7. Lourdes Torres has also written about the strategy that some Latina writers such as Moraga have used of employing multiple genres to represent fragmented, multiple identities. See Torres, "The Construction of Self in United States Latina Autobiographies" *Third World Women and the Politics of Feminism*, ed. Chandra Talpade Mohanty, Ann Russo, and Lourdes Torres (Bloomington: Indiana U P, 1991).

8. Patricia Lin Blinde, "The Icicle in the Desert: Perspective and Form in the Works of Two Chinese-American Women Writers," *MELUS* 6 (1979), 60.

9. Sau-ling Cynthia Wong, "Autobiography as Guided Tour? Maxine Hong Kingston's *The Woman Warrior* and the Chinese-American Autobiographical Controversy," *Multicultural Autobiography*, ed. James Robert Payne (Knoxville: U of Tennessee P, 1992), 271.

10. For an interesting discussion of these criticisms see Wong's essay cited in the previous footnote.

11. Lee Quinby, "The Subject of Memoirs: *The Woman Warrior's* Technology of Ideographic Selfhood," *De/Colonizing the Subject*, ed. Sidonie Smith and Julia Watson (Minneapolis: U of Minnesota P, 1992), 300.

12. Quinby, 305.

13. Quinby, 306.

14. Jelinek, p.

15. Norma Alarcón, "Chicana's Feminist Literature: A Re-vision Through Malintzin/or Malintzin: Putting Flesh Back on the Object," in *This Bridge Called My Back: Writings by Radical Women of Color*, ed. Cherríe Moraga and Gloria Anzaldúa (New York: Kitchen Table Women of Color Press, 1983), 186.

16. Blinde, 67.

17. Blinde, 67.

18. Sidonie Smith, *Subjectivity, Identity, and the Body: Women's Autobiographical Practices in the Twentieth Century* (Bloomington: Indiana U P, 1993), 139.

19. Smith, 5-17.

20. Lidoff, 117.

21. Sidonie Smith, "Maxine Hong Kingston's *Woman Warrior*: Filiality and Woman's Autobiographical Storytelling," in *Feminism: An Anthology of Literary Theory and Criticism*, ed. Robyn R. Warhol and Diane Price Herndl (New Brunswick, NJ: Rutgers U P, 1991), 1058. Also see Barbara Rodriguez, "In One Voice: The Autobiographical Act

in Maxine Hong Kingston's *The Woman Warrior* and Hisaye Yamamoto's *The Legend of Miss Sacagawara*," in *Autobiographical Inscriptions: Form, Personhood, and the American Woman Writer of Color* (New York: Oxford U P, 2000).

10

Growing Up Desperately: The Adolescent "Other" in the Novels of Paule Marshall, Toni Morrison, and Michelle Cliff

Nancy Backes

Theories of difference in the last twenty years often have neglected to address issues of age. Specifically, these theories have ignored what one writer has called the "geologic fault" between childhood and adulthood.[1] How does adolescence intersect with the familiar categories of sexuality, class, and, especially, gender and race? This essay focuses on the convergence of adolescence, gender, and race, with a consideration of class. Through the use of literary examples, I explore how and for what purposes the "Other" is constructed. Governing my assumptions in this paper is the idea that the construction of blackness also is a construction of whiteness, that is, white girls exoticize and romanticize African-Americans. What does that say about the conditions of white girls? Conversely, African-American girls link the Other with forms of destruction. What does this say about what it means to be black?

The creation of the Other shares some features with culturally constructed myths. And what does such a myth explain or show? For black girls, this myth tends to illuminate not only a geologic fault between childhood and adulthood, but also between the races. Moreover, black girls do not freely create this story; it is thrust upon them at their most vulnerable stage of development: adolescence. For white girls, the myth, the exaggerated idealization of the Other, particularly a black Other, encourages rejection of the status quo and highlights the possibility of freedom; in its capacity as an ego ideal, the Other, as the white girl interprets this construction, illuminates the way to a fuller, less restricted life. Also, the girl controls the creation of this ideal, and the creation occurs at the time when the white girl is learning the rigid expectations of class and gender that her imagination helps her transcend. For the black girl, encounters with the Other, specifically, white Others, have the opposite effect: they push her back, keep her "in her place," force her to consider her status as she stands in the shadows of the Other's illumination. Ultimately, both black and white girls chase and reject impossible ideals.

For example, while many critics have interpreted the opening passages of Toni Morrison's *The Bluest Eye*, the Dick and Jane primer passages, as the universalization of the white family, few have recognized that the solid, middle-class family of Father, Mother, Dick, Jane, dog, and cat also is an idealized family, one that doesn't exist for anyone, although white children understand that ideal to be their goal and birthright. Thus the primer tale is alienating to all who read it, black and white. It is a failed myth that nevertheless exaggerates the contours of Otherness, particularly for black readers. (Much later, of course, many white, suburban girls realized that the goals and birthrights represented in the story were oppressive and constricting for them and worthy of rejection.) For black girls, trying to emulate whiteness in all its cultural manifestations, rather than asserting one's own cultural identity as black and female, can only lead to trouble, as virtually every page of *The Bluest Eye* shows. At the novel's opening, the second and third versions of the primer, generally taken by critics to represent the MacTeers and the Breedloves, respectively, demonstrate the senselessness of two things: the deadly folly of emulating an alien ideal and the cruel treachery of promulgating such to be ideal in the first place.[2]

Claude Levi-Strauss noted that the function of a myth is to "provide a logical model capable of overcoming a contradiction (an impossible achievement if, as it happens, the contradiction is real)."[3] Fraught with contradiction though the primer passages are, the white girl through an internal process finally can see herself reflected in the story and accept or reject the construction represented; the black girl, on the other hand, encounters a dissonant, alienating version of herself that individual action cannot overcome. The cultural mirror held up to black girls produces a profound sense of Otherness; what they see and internalize, as Morrison herself put it in her recent Afterward to *The Bluest Eye,* is the "damaging internalization of assumptions of immutable inferiority originating in an outside gaze."[4] White girls own the gaze until adolescence when they are subject to a male gaze; black girls discover that they have never owned the gaze and that it is not theirs to own.

Black women fiction writers vividly describe girls' discovery of this Otherness; it is central to their heroines' coming of age. Simply put, these girls learn about the culture that has named them, and that in this culture they are Other. For example, in Paule Marshall's coming-of-age novel, *Brown Girl, Brownstones*, Selina Boyce's growth to womanhood cannot proceed until she develops racial awareness. This essential encounter with race is, as Marshall sees it, an essential ingredient for female development across the life course. Through her fiction, Marshall determined to create a trilogy "describing in reverse, the slave trade's triangular route to the motherland, the source."[5] The novel reveals that struggles with the source of cultural otherness take place simultaneously with individual struggles of becoming. Thus, the heroines of her first three books move from New York City to the West Indies to Africa, and back to North White Plains, New York, via the Caribbean. Concomitant with this spatial movement, however, are temporal elements. Marshall's fiction portrays the human imperative of moving forward in chronological time while simultaneously moving backward in psychic or spiritual and racial time. Marshall sees such movement as necessary for self-transcendence, and her novels elaborate this struggle. Taken together, her first three books represent a trilogy of black female life as seen in its developmental stages: *Brown Girl, Brownstones*, adolescence; *The Chosen Place, The Timeless People,* middle age; and *Praisesong for the Widow,* early old age. Marshall's portrayal of the black female adolescent struggle is, of course, what concerns me here.

Brown Girl, Brownstones is the lyrical account of the adolescence of a first-generation Barbadian-American girl set in the 1940s. In the beginning, Selina Boyce sees her struggle primarily as one of distinguishing herself--her values, needs, goals--from her mother and her mother's immigrant materialism. She is convinced that the only means to transmute a confining feminine adolescence into a free female adulthood is to replace the narcissistic inertia of her childhood with the differentiation and action associated with adulthood. Selina simply wishes to be free of her mother so that she can live an autonomous life; she wants to be recognized as a distinct and capable being, especially by her mother with whom she shares so many traits. Silla Boyce is larger-than-life and authoritarian; her strength and gift for negotiation with life are traits that she passed onto Selina, making it difficult for her to see her daughter as distinct from herself, a difficulty familiar to mothers and daughters everywhere. Yet Selina longs for her mother to see her as distinct, as a type of Other. The total identification of the mother with her daughter generates resentment on Selina's part, since it creates a relationship with no boundaries, no demarcations, no inside or outside: in short, no accommodation for Selina's growth. To the conclusion, Silla does not see Selina as distinct from herself, but rather views her as "the girl she had once been."[6] Independence and adventure are what Selina craves, and she refuses to let being female stop her from getting outside of her home, in her view, the place of bondage and acquiescence. The house itself--the brownstone--represents boundaries, at first the imagined ones of her body. Then as Selina herself grows, the house also comes to represent the inhibiting barrier that prevents her from completing herself emotionally, intellectually, and spiritually in the world. Race, however, is a noticeably missing ingredient. Her mother protects her by her own example, and she attempts to teach her that hard work and grit, with the help of a strong community of like-minded individuals, can overcome race. Selina simply wants to get free of her mother. But as Selina moves outward in her increasing maturity, she is startled to discover that alienation--eternal banishment to the outside--is the price exacted for her insistence on distinction and freedom.

Selina cannot fight her way out of her mother's tight control because she herself remains in a state of narcissistic omnipotence; rather than hatch from the figurative symbiotic membrane containing mother and daughter, she expands the membrane to suit her re-creation of the world. She remains the center of that world, narcissistically absorbing the environmental elements she fancies on her own terms. Selina cannot grow up, however, until she stops seeing the world in simply her own terms. She will discover that she is the Other in her home, in her Barbadian-American community, and in white society, which can only see her as a stereotypical black. The effect is one of profound alienation. For all her struggles to define herself, the novel's larger message emerges in the last thirty pages when Selina discovers that her culture has always and already defined her. After a college dance recital in which Selina triumphed, the mother of Selina's white friend remarks to Selina that "'it's just wonderful how you've taken your race's natural talent for dancing and music and developed it.'"[7] This observation induces Selina's terrifying epiphany.

Selina develops from a girl of ten who lives in a state of oneness with the world, a state of psychic skinlessness, into a young woman of twenty whose most significant awareness concerns her skin, a membrane that contains her vulnerability and serves as her soft armor. Where brown girl and brownstone were once united and synonymous, where once the membrane of brown skin protected an internal life as the brick of the brownstone held the family romance, now the inviolate structure of racial history holds her energy and attention. Where she was once invisible to her mother, she now knows that she is unseen and unrecognized by a large portion of humankind. Selina's biggest spurt of growth, her largest leap into consciousness, occurs during these final thirty pages; there, Selina makes the change from a child's preference for imagination to an adult's quest for knowledge, from the immature limitations of romance to intimations of reality, a reality that is based in a racial hierarchy that seeks to constrict her. It is not until the end that Selina sees the "lights and shadows"--the black and white--of a painful reality; sharp chiaroscuro has replaced the world's "strong colors" that so thrilled her once upon a time before she knew better. Nevertheless, Selina remains relatively untainted; she stands aloof from power and outside of privilege, cast into a terrible freedom. She is extrasocietal not only in the way that concept is associated with adolescents by bored and compromised adults, but also in the way that the word implies exclusion, this time on the basis of race.

As a child oriented toward the future, Selina imagines a free, unrestricted adulthood, as many children do; as a young adult, however, Selina finds that she must be oriented toward the past (she plans to seek answers in Barbados) in order to reconcile her own created image of freedom with the inherited massive cultural image of racial and sexual bondage. No matter how free-spirited her self-perceptions, she cannot be a woman separate from a cultural context. No matter how much she knows of her inner life, she must negotiate with the world out there. Thus, by the end of the novel Selina also has converted from invulnerability to vulnerability, from sensibility to sensitivity. On the brink of adulthood, she steps backward rather than moving forward. The brownstone once nurtured and imprisoned her, freed her imagination and held harsh realities. Now she is free in the world, free, but contained within the ghostly gossamers of a long, yet undiscovered past.

Selina wants to re-historicize herself, locate herself generationally; she hopes to insert herself into the family picture--the immediate portrait from which she has been excluded, and the larger human one as well. Selina's parents, after all, were immigrants: people who came here by choice. Suppose Selina's environment had been unyielding, and a sense of rootedness, however vague, had not materialized. This is the environment of Morrison's *The Bluest Eye*. There young Pecola Breedlove's father is not a benign poet, as Selina's father, Deighton Boyce, was, but rather an incestuous rapist. Robbed of becoming themselves, girls in Morrison's novel are removed from their past and their futures. In the course of their development, they neither remain with girls nor turn to men. Rather, they are left completely alone. Selina's "too old" eyes, we believe, will come to focus on a cohesive--if raw and unpleasant--history. In Morrison's novel Pecola's eyes are without vision; they are the haunting eyes of madness.

In *The Bluest Eye* Morrison concerns herself with all the possibilities of Othering: the parents who make the Other out of their children, the men who make the Other out of women, the patriarch who makes the Other of his child, the social class that makes the Other out of social difference, the race that makes the Other out of a different color, and so on. Accepting this Otherness is a recipe for disaster--directly so for African-Americans, implicitly so for whites; tragedy inevitably results when African-Americans take their identities from whites, and when females take their identities from the dictates of males. The ultimate tragedy in the novel is Pecola's splitting within the self; cruelly Other-ized throughout the novel, in that she has two selves who converse with each other. The possibility of a coherent self-image, a reasonable reflection, is dashed.

Unlike Silla Boyce, who attempted to confine her daughter to the house and, in effect, to herself, Pauline Breedlove breaks the coherent mirror reflection and sees her daughter not only as different, but as an alien Other, ironically, because Pecola is like herself. The mirror-stage, as Lacan elucidated it, reassures the child who sees in the reflection that the inchoate body actually is a whole self. This mirrored reflection, in fact, establishes a physical self. This stage has a clear function in growth, for it provides recognizable form to the primordial terror of the dependent, inchoate, disembodied image of the earliest months of life. This specular image both verifies and distinguishes (and alienates) the self.

However, recognizing oneself eventually enables recognition of another as potentially compatible. Infants also look to their mothers to provide compatible emotional mirrors. Later, they look to the culture to provide meaningful reflections of themselves. It is here that girls of all races in western culture develop an anxiety as they grow. What do their mirrors tell them? The mirror, mirror on the wall inevitably has the voice of a patriarch. It is no surprise, then, that so many girls have internalized the belief that an esthetically pleasing image is a necessary condition for receiving love and security. And if the mirror has unkind things to say to white girls, it has still unkinder things to say to black girls, who, as Barbara A. White once noted, "are barred even from the traditional compensation of womanhood, that is, from being a *valued* sex object" (165). Thus, Pecola Breedlove spends "[l]ong hours...looking in the mirror, trying to discover the secret of the ugliness."[8] She is made Other by the reflection she sees in her mother, in her immediate environment, and in her culture at large.

Pernicious social constructions, when combined with individual psychology and bleak circumstance, set in motion an intergenerational concatenation of disastrous encounters with life. Like the stepmother queen in "Snow White and the Seven Dwarfs," girls and women who seek the security of a loyal mirror (an impossible luxury for all females, just as is the perfect family life in the Dick and Jane primer) meet only an escalating anxiety that ends in self-destruction. "Snow White" is a tale that instills the virtues of beauty and acquiescence, a girl's guide to a successful life in a patriarchal society. Inverting the story, Morrison has Pauline look for her reflection in the revered, idealized blondes of Hollywood films. Pecola is a rude reminder to her of the impossibility of this fantasy. As an infant, though, the child seeks a positive reflection in her mother. D.W. Winnicott, much influenced by Lacan's essay on the mirror stage, noted that the baby, looking upon the mother's face, sees himself or herself: "In other words," he wrote, "the mother is looking at the baby and *what she looks like is related to what she sees there*."[9] The baby's self-esteem is in trouble if the baby sees only a troubled, uncongenial visage looking back at her.

Such malevolent reflections are exactly what Pecola sees. From the beginning, Pauline Breedlove reflected to her daughter her own sense of inferiority that, in turn, Pecola radiated back to her. This mother-daughter mirror reflects images of sometimes-self and sometimes-Other in both the mother's and the daughter's struggle to know who each is, an effort that stretches across generations. Thus, Pauline seeks her own missing mother as she looks at Pecola. "So when I seed it [the baby]," Pauline narrates, "it was like looking at a picture of your mama when she was a girl. You know who she is, but she don't look the same."[10] The intergenerational mirror already has betrayed Pauline; she reflects this infidelity, what Lacan calls "primordial Discord," to her daughter. The image that Pecola returns weights her mother's fantasies even more: Pecola serves as a constant and stubborn reminder of Pauline's blackness and limitations. To Pauline, the new Pecola is a mere "black ball of hair."[11] Willing to talk to her when Pecola was in her womb, Pauline experiences Pecola in the world as Other. It was better to hold an image of Pecola than to embrace the real girl. Pecola herself later mockingly re-enacts these pre-birth conversations when she talks to her supposedly blue-eyed self in the mirror. In this way Pecola eradicates her black self. This self had not proved to be viable: Pecola, like the child she herself bears, was, figuratively speaking, stillborn. Instead of growing up and out, Pecola grows down and in.

But there is another Other in the story, one who presumably attains a better fate. Claudia MacTeer, whom we assume to be an adult who escaped, narrates portions of the sections Autumn, Winter, Spring, and Summer. She seeks some sort of reconciliation with the world, something that will enable her to achieve an eventual adulthood consonant with herself just as she is. This drive for consistency is behind her destruction of the white baby dolls she receives for Christmas. Keenly aware of herself as different--non-white, non-adult, non-moneyed, and so on--she nevertheless resists being clothed in whiteness, which she regards as a systematic layering over herself. Claudia, recalling her nine-year-old self, remembers her black girl's body as a site of pleasure and delight: "[W]e felt comfortable in our skins."[12] She resents being taught to feel discomfort with her body and her skin hue. She rebels against a limiting maturity, in which the images of oneself in the large cultural mirror tend to be unfriendly and unnerving. Like an infant discovering the reassuring cohesiveness of a mirrored reflection, Claudia as a child experiences a sense of wholeness and internal compatibility, a relative lack of othering at the personal level. She learns and keeps the language of resistance. Finally, in relating the story to us, she has the words that bear witness, words that fail Pecola, who lapses into a silent, private, and internal conversation.

Silence for girls and women is part of a strategy of retreat reserved for those times when the words of others are used in menacing ways. Forced to look upon such a world in the course of their education, girls drive themselves more deeply inward, and steer themselves away from public participation. Especially for a black girl, achieving what Lacan called "dialectical synthesis" between the internal self and external reality is difficult; for example, it requires reconciliation of the disparity between appreciating one's black female body and knowing it is reviled in the world.[13] With Claudia, however, the problem of the "organism and its reality" in Lacan's mirror is reversed: the self that she can imagine is less terrifying than the self that her society assigns to her. Claudia's particular "dialectical synthesis" must concern a reconciliation of the opposing factions of visibility and invisibility, a rapprochement that is especially difficult in a society that is determined to assign meaning and decide how she will be visible.

The story Claudia tells is her foray against silence and invisibility, at the same time that it discusses ineradicability of those conditions for most, including Pecola. In the end, completely bereft of community as she admires the reflection of her nonexistent blue eyes, which, among other things, have come to be associated with acquiring womanhood, all Pecola has is what she does not have.[14] She is driven inward, and studies images for some sign of herself. Her alien reflection and her alienated life have made turning inward the only option. Because it is not connected to a relational world, the inward search can uncover only an imitation self, a distorted, discordant version of the real thing. She is Othered: emotionally abandoned, dropped from school for carrying her father's child, and removed by her mother to the edge of town, a place far off "the hem of life."[15] Like Snow White, who was left alone by the huntsman ordered by the Queen to kill her, Pecola is abandoned not just at the edge of the kingdom, but also, metaphorically speaking, at the edge of adulthood.

So much pain, and no outlet to relieve it. Perhaps this is why Michelle Cliff's Clare Savage, a timorous and hapless Jamaican girl in the novel *Abeng*, is transformed into a revolutionary who makes the ultimate sacrifice in *No Telephone to Heaven*. In *Abeng* twelve-year-old Clare recognizes that she, as a light-skinned black, is somehow outside her culture. Taught the etiquette of "passing," she feels fraudulent and inauthentic. Consequently, she finds herself identifying with Others: she reads accounts of the Holocaust, particularly the lives of Anne Frank and Kitty Hart. Still, as a girl having a difficult time growing up in a complex culture, Clare's main difficulties have to do with being female. When Clare shoots her grandmother's bull by mistake, attitudes toward her action, as Clare realizes, are based on her gender: "She had stepped out of line, no matter what, in a society in which the lines were unerringly drawn. She had been caught in rebellion. She was a girl. No one was impressed with her."[16] Her transgression was behaving in a manner inappropriate for a female.

In the sequel to *Abeng,* Clare is a member of a band of guerrillas that plans an attack on a Hollywood film company on location in Jamaica, an impoverished land that the filmmakers see only in terms of its exotic and romantic possibilities. To the filmmakers, it is a setting, a backdrop that exists for their commercial needs; Jamaica itself is Other. The revolutionaries determine to thwart this exploitative construction of Otherness. To them, these intruders are the Other. Someone betrays these guerrillas, however, and in the ensuing fight, Clare is killed.

In *No Telephone to Heaven*, Clare lives her life as Other; first in her own family, then in Kingston, and later in New York, where her father, who is determined to "pass," forbids her to connect or identify in any way with the struggle of African- Americans in the civil rights movement. Clare again is Other as a graduate student in England, the "mother" country, a country that rejects her with the assured, firm subtlety of her own mother. As a child, her imagination, like the imaginations of the restricted, "privileged" white girls, sought to convert her into a successful Other. Recalling her childhood, Clare notes that she "'[m]ade believe. Made believe a lot. From the movies...books...the 'real' world. Pretended I was Pip in *Great Expectations*--my favorite book. Pretended I was...Peter Pan. Even Columbus, God help me.'"[17] Even the enemy, the ultimate Other, had its use to a girl growing up whose rigid, confining culture forces her to devise strategies for getting out.

Both of Cliff's novels end in blood. After killing the bull in *Abeng*, Clare, for disciplinary reasons, is sent to live with a refined woman who brags that she has "not one drop of the blood."[18] The novel ends after Clare gets her first menstrual period. Clare, the outsider, the perpetual Other, through her menstrual blood has an unassailable link to virtually every woman on earth. She cherishes this shared womanhood; it's a refreshing contrast to her usual experience of rupture with girls and with women. Throughout the novel, an omniscient narrator had been telling us about chapters of Jamaica's history, but this blood shifts the focus to personal history. *No Telephone to Heaven* also ends in blood, the blood of warfare, political blood. Clare moved from connection to differentiation and, finally, disconnection. In her, the personal and the political develop into very different constructs. In the first novel Cliff insisted on the gender category, while in the second, she collapsed it. Among the many questions and debates that this can lead us to is this one, what should we value more: the blood that connects or the blood that disrupts?

Unlike the repression and the struggle against being Other-ed that consumes black girls, for suburban white middle-class girls, vicarious contact with the Other, usually constructed as the forbidden, represents a way out of repression and constricting "good girl" ego ideals. In her insightful study *Young, White, and Miserable: Growing Up Female in the Fifties*, Wini Breines suggests that for some resisting white girls, identification with the Other was a means of coping with a sharply limited situation; such identification was a way, as she puts it, "to subvert dominant notions of femininity."[19] Among these many notions alive today is the dissembling of the female, a process deemed necessary for feminine success, particularly for these white middle and upper middle class girls.[20] Strong, vocal girls at ages eight through eleven must transform into nice, pleasant ones who strive to be perfect and utter nary a cross word. Hence, we have the appeal of the Other, someone seen as free of these psychological, spiritual, and moral confines.

Unfortunately, white girls' constructions of Otherness do not grant the Other equal subjectivity (cross-cultural encounters rarely do); rather, since segregation allows little direct knowledge of the Other, this Other is imaginatively re-created as a hedge against boredom and restrictions. The Other, then, is part reality and part fantasy. It is these hybrid properties of the real and the imaginary that enable the construction to function as a catalyst for growth beyond the status quo. For many white girls, creation of the Other is a recapitulation of D.W. Winnicott's "transitional object" of infancy. Throughout human development, it is objects outside the self that stimulate growth. The transitional object in particular represents a balance--or, in my view, the potential for balance--between what is within oneself and what is without. A catalyst for growth, the object is present in existential form, but the infant creates it, regards it as an original discovery. This object is the juncture of cognition and imagination. In its best forms, however, this transitional object is an expression of a genuine appreciation of difference, something distinguished from and outside of the narcissistic realm of the self. Accordingly, the transitional object provides a means for differentiation as well as escape from narcissism. The transitional object theory suggests an ability both to incorporate and to distinguish difference. I am suggesting that suburban girls' fantasies of otherness is their way of rejecting a chauvinistic, "privileged," and restrictive way of life for one that is richer personally and deeper democratically.

How was it for girls in the 1950s? Implicit in isolating white girls in the suburbs, as Breines points out, was the idea of maintaining sexual purity. An interest in the Other often was an expression of sexual curiosity. This interest, once it was perceived in the dominant culture, was viewed as a threat to established values. In the 1950s, as Breines shows, middle-class white girls who rejected dominant values had no choice but to utilize and adapt male versions of rebellion and disaffection. For these girls, the attraction of outsiders, of "hoods" and "greasers," of movie stars like James Dean and Marlon Brando in roles of alienation and working-class defiance, and of black and black-inspired music was profound. Males who were inappropriate as boyfriends and potential mates and who represented an alternative to their bland teenage world played a significant role in girls' psychic lives. Ethnic, class, and racial differences had meaning in the lives and minds of heterosexual, middle-class white girls. Difference was ignored and denied in both adult and teenage mainstream culture, but it was alive, even thriving, for many teenage girls.[21]

The hypocrisy rife in the suburbs where appearances mattered, fostered a yearning for that which was perceived as authentic. This romanticizing of the Other by white girls created a new matrix for these girls to recreate themselves in imaginative new ways. White girls used the Other as a way to move outside of a culture that stymied and stultified them. Even when black music was appropriated and sanitized for a mass white audience, an allegiance remained to its black roots. As Breines puts it, "That the music was derived from black culture and made by black people, a population discriminated against and kept separate, even invisible to many white teenagers, was part of its appeal."[22] To be a fan of the rock musicians was to make a statement against conformity and expectations, to "love" someone inappropriate. It also was a means to experiment, albeit in fantasy form, with alternative versions of heterosexuality. The more remote, impossible, inappropriate, and impractical the love object the better. This connection to popular culture was and is significant, for many white girls fantasized themselves as at least part black. And, in a sense, they were part black. For, as Ralph Ellison, remarked in 1970, "On this level [popular culture] the melting pot did indeed melt, creating such deceptive metamorphoses and blending of identities, values, and life-styles that most American whites are culturally part Negro-American without even realizing it."[23]

Do white girls today express through the Other a genuine interest in another culture or is it merely "voyeuristic use as an escape from one's own"?[24] A sticky question. But it is worth noting that in contemporary fiction, many women writers, black and white, do reposition the Other. They reclaim the other from the margins to a central position; the Other holds a prominent focal point in their work. All of this leads to an inevitable question: what would America be like without the Other? Toni Morrison, in her *Playing in the Dark,* persuasively suggests that the white cultural concerns of the United States--autonomy, authority, newness, and difference--are "shaped by, activated by, a complex awareness and employment of a constituted Africanism."[25] The slave population functioned, she argues, as the means of measuring white difference and privilege, an idea that can be traced through literature and whose detritus informs our work and actions today. This "parasitical nature of white freedom" exists in all literature, even when African Americans are not directly present or mentioned; it is part of the American collective and creative unconscious. The neurotic character of so much of American fiction--a fiction yoked in extremes--may be owing to this unacknowledged relationship. We attempt to integrate the Other through self-reflexive appropriation. In white writers' hands, Morrison says, "images of blackness can be evil *and* protective, rebellious *and* forgiving, fearful *and* desirable--all of the self-contradictory features of the self."[26] Whiteness, on the other hand, constitutes an abstract omnipotence.

Ralph Ellison expressed it another way, in a time before theories of difference dominated. In a 1970 essay he argued that American culture is a hybrid, and could not exist without Blacks. African Americans, he argued, have shaped not only popular culture, but language, literature, and politics, particularly the politics of a protean democracy seeking to perfect itself. In this context blacks are the moral reminders of unfulfilled promises. Ellison saw both ghettos and "shaky suburban communities," as he called them, sharing similar fates. Certainly for their denizens--the white girls of one place and the black girls of another--there is a creative recognition of the Other born out of need. The Other in both cases is a product of what is best and worst in our society; both are reminders of what must be made possible. And even in the use and abuse of the Other we can see girls on both sides of the divide expressing "curiosity, wonder, adventure, and relating to the Other (and to the self) as unknown and strange."[27] By resisting "thinking as usual,"[28] black girls and white girls have the potential to find in an appropriate other subversive new ways of being in the world.

NOTES

1. Wini Breines, *Young, White, and Miserable: Growing Up Female in the Fifties* (Boston: Beacon, 1992), 23.

2. Toni Morrison, *The Bluest Eye*. Afterward by Morrison (New York: Plume, 1994).

3. Claude Levi-Strauss, *Structural Anthropology*, trans. Claire Jacobson and Brooke Grundfest Schoepf (New York: Basic, 1963), 229.

4. *The Bluest Eye*, 210.

5. Paule Marshall, "Shaping the World of My Art," *New Letters* 40 (1973), 107.

6. Paule Marshall, *Brown Girl, Brownstones* (New York: Feminist Press, 1981), 307.

7. Ibid., 288.

8. Barbara A.White, *Growing Up Female: Adolescent Girlhood in American Fiction* (Westport, CT: Greenwood, 1985), 45.

9. D. W. Winnicott, *Playing and Reality* (New York: Basic Press, 1971).

10. Ibid., 125.

11. Ibid., 124.

12. Ibid., 74.

13. Lacan, "The mirror stage as formative of the function of the I as revealed in psychoanalytic experience," in *Ecrits: A Selection*, trans. Alan Sheridan (New York: Norton, 1977), 1-7.

14. In a therapy session, one of Winnicott's patients who had endured many losses in her life formulated the statement: "All I have got is what I have not got." Of the statement, Winnicott writes: "There is a desperate defense against the end of everything" (24).

15. *Playing and Reality*, 17.

16. Michelle Cliff, *Abeng* (Trumansburg, NY: Crossing Press, 1984), 149-50.

17. Michelle Cliff, *No Telephone to Heaven* (New York: Vintage, 1988), 173.

18. *Abeng*, 142.

19. Breines, 12.

20. See Carol Gilligan, Nona P. Lyons, and Trudy J. Hanmer, *Making Connections: The Relational Worlds of Adolescent Girls at Emma Willard School* (Cambridge, MA: Harvard, 1990); Special Issue: Women, Girls & Psychotherapy: Reframing Resistance, *Women & Therapy: A Feminist Quarterly,* 11 (1991); Lyn Mikel Brown and Carol Gilligan, *Meeting at the Crossroads: Women's Psychology and Girls' Development* (New York: Ballantine, 1992).

21. Breines, 130.

22. Breines, 154.

23. Ralph Ellison, "What America Would Be Like Without Blacks" in *Going to the Territory* (New York: Random, 1986), 108.

24. Breines, 159.

25. Toni Morrison, *Playing in the Dark: Whiteness and the Literary Imagination* (Cambridge: Harvard UP), 1992.

26. *Playing*, 59.

27. Z. D. Gurevitch, "The Other Side of Dialogue: On Making the Other Strange and the Experience of Otherness," *The American Journal of Sociology* 93 (1988), 1180.

28. Ibid, 1180.

11

The Theater of the New World (B)Orders: Performing Cultural Criticism with Coco Fusco, Guillermo Gómez-Peña and Anna Deavere Smith

Jennifer Drake

In his 1990 essay "The New Cultural Politics of Difference," Cornel West suggests that a new kind of cultural worker is in the making: artists and critics who respond creatively "to the precise circumstances of our present moment" through cultural practices that critically engage issues of "exterminism, empire, class, race, gender, sexual orientation, age, nation, nature, and region" (19). West argues that cultural work informed by this new cultural politics of difference does not simply contest dominant ideologies; does not necessarily agitate for its inclusion in mainstream canons and institutions; and it is not primarily interested in the kind of avant-garde 'activism' that shocks conventional art audiences. Rather, West notes:

The new kind of critic and artist associated with the new cultural politics of difference consists of an energetic breed of New World *bricoleurs* with improvisational and flexible sensibilities that sidestep mere opportunism and mindless eclecticism; persons from all countries, cultures, genders, sexual orientations, ages and regions with protean identities who avoid ethnic chauvinism and faceless universalism; intellectual and political freedom-fighters with partisan passion, international perspectives, and, thank God, a sense of humor that combats the ever-present absurdity that forever threatens our democratic and libertarian projects and dampens the fire that fuels our will to struggle.[1]

A (very) short list of critics and artists working in this mode would include the writers Ntozake Shange, Bharati Mukherjee, Leslie Marmon Silko, Audre Lorde, Gloria Anzaldúa, and Susan Howe; the critics Paul Gilroy, Lucy Lippard, Norma Alarcón, and José David Saldivar; the performance artists Holly Hughes, Marlon Riggs, James Luna, Suzanne Lacy, Mel Chin, Guillermo Gómez-Peña, Coco Fusco, and Anna Deavere Smith; visual artists Jimmie Durham and Faith Ringgold; musicians Me'Shell Ndege Ócello and Café Tacuba; conceptual artist and philosopher Adrian Piper; and film-maker Trinh Minh-ha. The work of these artists consistently refuses monoculture as it redefines the "experimental" in relation to the grassroots and the "postmodern" in relation to histories of marginalized cultural production. It questions both separatism and assimilation as models for resisting domination. In both form and content, this art reconceptualizes "America" and "American" so as to remind "Americans" that we have all been uprooted; we are all potential border-crossers; and we are all the products of more than one culture.

West's improvisational and flexible New World *bricoleuer* takes one particular shape in MacArthur award-winning Guillermo Gómez-Peña's 1988-1989 Border Brujo performances, as well as in Gómez-Peña's critical writing of the early 1990s.[2] Gómez-Peña translates West's New World *bricoleuer* as a hybrid border-crosser:

The hybrid is cross racial, polylinguistic, and multicontextual. From a disadvantaged position, the hybrid expropriates elements from all sides to create more open and fluid systems. This figure is from the grassroots yet experimental, radical but not static or dogmatic. The hybrid fuses 'low' and 'high' art, the indigenous and the high-tech, the problematic notions of self and other, the liquid entities of North and South. An ability to understand the hybrid nature of culture develops out of the experience of dealing with a dominant culture from the outside. The artist who understands hybridity in this way can be at the same time an insider and an outsider; a citizen of multiple communities; an expert in border crossings. He/she performs multiple roles in multiple contexts. At times he/she can operate as a crosscultural diplomat, a coyote (smuggler of ideas), or a media pirate. At other times he/she assumes the role of nomadic chronicler, cultural reinterpreter, or political trickster. He/she speaks from more than one perspective, to more than one community, about more than one reality. His/her job is to trespass, bridge, interconnect, translate, remap, and redefine. (217)[3]

Artist-critic Coco Fusco evokes both West's New World *bricoleuer* and Gómez-Peña's hybrid border-crosser in her 1993 description of the wide variety of artistic practices and perspectives flourishing in the late 1980s and 1990s, particularly among artists of color:

It appears that we have worked away from the once widely held belief that artists of color must all be engaged in what Stuart Hall has called an act of imaginative recovery of a singular, unifying past in order for their work to be valid. No longer bound to a sense of having to restrict one's focus, materials, or genre, many contemporary artists of color move back and forth between past and present, between history and fiction, between art and ritual, between high art and popular culture, and between Western and non-Western influence. In doing so, they participate in multiple communities.[4]

West, Gómez-Peña, and Fusco, then, all suggest that recent creative work by artists and writers from many communities has stressed hybridity as a contemporary cultural reality and as a formal strategy, or structural logic, for their work. Unlike the more acceptable "celebration of diversity" demonstrated by the addition of "different voices" to canons, exhibitions, or anthologies, this still-burgeoning body of work challenges Eurocentric and monocultural modes of seeing, writing, listening, thinking, and knowing.

Performance art, that marginalized and hybrid form, has been a productive site for this cultural work during the past decade because it draws together radical and oppressive histories of cultural production. As Fusco explains in "Performance and the Power of the Popular," contemporary performance artists of color work at the convergence of performance traditions whose connections have not yet been fully articulated or explored. These traditions include: European and Euro-American avant-gardist movements such as Dadaism, Surrealism, the Black Mountain College and 1960s Happenings; 1970s ephemeral, body-based, often feminist performance art, intended to test physical limits and expose social taboos; African-American and Native-American drumming, dancing, and performative rituals and the American laws written to prohibit these performative traditions; the late nineteenth-century mimicry and commodification of black and native performance traditions for white mass entertainment; early Modernist interest in, and exoticization of, the performance practices of non-Western peoples; the history of vernacular performance poetries and storytelling traditions; and the wide variety of other community-based and community-building arts practices. This is a rich and embattled terrain for making art that investigates the nature of democracy and the role of art and artists in the American democratic project. Certainly, as Carol Becker has noted, the recent "culture wars" and censorship battles, and the attempted disemboweling of the National Endowment for the Arts, "were actually disagreements about the nature of democracy, which point of view would be allowed to be expressed."[5]

Read together, Guillermo Gómez-Peña's and Coco Fusco's controversial 1992 performance, "Two Undiscovered Amerindians Visit..." and Anna Deavere Smith's highly-acclaimed *Twilight: Los Angeles, 1992* provide a complex example of how the new cultural politics of difference informs contemporary cultural production. Smith's interest in performing the eloquent stutters and missteps that together create American character(s) offers one democratic alternative to the colonialist performance history of ethnographic display that Gómez-Peña's and Fusco's piece so effectively theorizes and enacts. In very different ways, both pieces work against the "fictional narrative of Western culture 'discovering' the negation of itself in something authentically and radically distinct."[6] Gómez-Peña's and Fusco's satiric representation of "Otherness" and Smith's refusal to represent "otherness" in relation to a fixed center dramatize the *mutual* and *ongoing* transformation of cultures and persons in the New World.

REPORTER: Excuse me could you tell me what you think of Christopher Columbus?
WOMAN A: You mean the film or the Broadway musical?
MAN A: He was the first illegal alien in the Americas, *que no?*
WOMAN B: He discovered this country and that's a great thing.
MAN B: I'm Italian. I identify with him completely.
WOMAN C: Uh, didn't he begin the slave trade?
KID: I saw him on TV the other day. He's boring.[7]

"Two Undiscovered Amerindians Visit..," a 1992 performance by Fusco and Gómez-Peña, is a satiric representation of "otherness" based on the widespread cultural practice of exhibiting indigenous peoples from Africa, Asia, and the Americas to predominantly white Western audiences. A chronology of this practice compiled by Fusco and Gómez-Peña cites examples from the fifteenth through the twentieth centuries, beginning in 1493, with an Arawak Indian brought from the Caribbean to Spain by Columbus, and ending with the Minnesota State Fair's 1992 exhibition of a black woman midget billed as "Tiny Teesha, the Island Princess."[8] Fusco argues that the 500-year history of such ethnographic exhibits might be thought of as "the origin of intercultural performance in the West," initiating white/pop culture's ongoing dependence on constructing an authentic "ethnic Otherness as essentially *performative* and located in the body."[9] In creating a critical reenactment of this particular performance tradition, Fusco and Gómez-Peña insist that performance artists of color and their audiences acknowledge this history and its still-current effects on the reception of contemporary art.

Juxtaposed with official celebrations of Columbus' quincentenary, "Two Undiscovered Amerindians Visit..." took the form of a traveling "ethnographic exhibit." Venues included the Edge 1992 Biennial in Madrid, Spain; the Whitney Museum in New York; Covent Garden in London; the Smithsonian's National Museum of Natural History; the Australian Museum of Natural History in Sydney; and the Field Museum of Chicago. Fusco and Gómez-Peña presented themselves as recently discovered 'Guatinaui' Amerindians from an island in the Gulf of Mexico that "had somehow been overlooked by Europeans for five centuries."[10] Led to and from their cage on leashes, the Guatinauis spent their days performing "traditional tasks" such as lifting weights, sewing voodoo dolls, working on the computer, and watching television. For a small donation, Fusco would dance to rap music and Gómez-Peña would tell "authentic" Amerindian stories in a nonexistent language. Guards were on hand to feed them, and to speak with visitors since the Guatinauis "did not speak English." At the Whitney Museum performance, visitors were allowed a peek at Guatinaui male genitals for five dollars. A panel near the cage displayed a detailed chronology of exhibits of non-Western peoples; another panel simulated an encyclopedia entry about Guatinaui and its people, and included a map of the island.

Fusco has written that the human exhibitions on which "Two Undiscovered Amerindians Visit..." is based "dramatize the colonial unconscious of American society,"[11] the flip side of our democratic narratives. The museum, site of many such exhibitions and site of the "Two Undiscovered Amerindians Visit..." performances, has been one cultural institution that has perpetuated colonial models of relationship by creating narratives of "authentic ethnic others." Museums purport to represent the world by taking objects out of their specific contexts, making them stand in for complex cultures and cultural practices, and developing systems of classification and relationship that override the object's living history. As James Clifford has noted, "The collector discovers, acquires, salvages objects. The objective world is given, not produced, and thus historical relations of power in the work of acquisition are occulted. The *making* of meaning in museum classification and display is mystified as adequate *representation*. The time and order of the collection erase the concrete social labor of its making." According to Clifford, then, the history of collections "is central to an understanding of how those social groups that invented anthropology and modern art have *appropriated* exotic things, facts, and meanings."[12] By performing "Two Undiscovered Amerindians Visit..." in museums, Fusco and Gómez-Peña mimic, critique, and enact the cultural practice of making meaning through museum classification and display. In this way, they engage histories of appropriation, exoticization, and objectification at a key institutional site.

Paul Gilroy has suggested that "To be inauthentic is sometimes the best way to be real."[13] This is the strategy that Fusco and Gómez-Peña explore as one challenge to the history of collecting and displaying "authentic" "exotic" objects. The cultural expression of inauthenticity, as one possible use of a hybrid aesthetic, takes stereotypes seriously. Stereotypes are (in)authentic history; they are lies with real power; they are real because they participate in making the real. Arguing that stereotypes as well as pop culture images locate histories that must be claimed and contested, Fusco points out that "the strategy of reworking cultural stereotypes [is] a very different objective from that of the imaginative retrieval of 'original cultural forms,' or that of creating entirely new paradigms devoid of historical traces."[14] In "Two Undiscovered Amerindians Visit...," Fusco and Gómez-Peña also heed Homi Bhabha's call to shift interventions into colonial discourse from "the *identification* of images as positive or negative, to an understanding of the *processes of subjectification* made possible (and plausible) through stereotypical discourse."[15] To work *with* cultural stereotypes in order to understand and expose "the processes of subjectification made possible and plausible through stereotypical discourse" is to struggle with the ways in which colonial discourse assumes a white, Western viewer. As Bhabha notes, colonist discourse also defines "otherness" as bodily, visible, and therefore knowable to that viewer.

Through the satiric performance of a particular, fictive, "native" culture, "Two Undiscovered Amerindians Visit..." offers a critique of the equations between seeing and knowing, knowing and owning, that produce the so-called other as a discoverable object. As Bhabha observes, "Colonial power produces the colonized as a fixed reality which is at once an 'other' and yet entirely knowable and visible. t resembles a form of narrative in which the productivity and circulation of subjects and signs are bound in a reformed and recognizable totality....that is structurally similar to realism."[16] When Fusco and Gómez-Peña create an *inauthentic* performance of otherness by *satirically* re-enacting the cultural practice of displaying "natives" for European and Euro-American audiences, they challenge patterns of reception based on realism's truth-claims and draw upon the possibilities of "the holes in the representational, the holes in the visible."[17]

This visual doubleness, the contradiction between creating a cultural other and believing that the other is entirely knowable, creates the performance's tension. Fusco and Gómez-Peña act like stereotypical "natives" engaging in authentic native activities. Their audiences, in turn, re-enact (and very occasionally reflect critically upon) the "discovery" of native cultures. Even while acting out these oppressive cultural scripts, Fusco and Gómez-Peña disrupt them by foregrounding the artist's role as cultural actor, *and by playing the Guatinauis as cultural actors*. As contemporary artists critically engaging a particular performance history, Fusco and Gómez-Peña act to transform culture. The Guatinauis also transform culture as they listen to the music of another culture (rap), invent languages, engage computer technologies, and make fools of audience members who believe that the Guatinauis are "real."

The "Two Undiscovered Amerindians Visit..." performance works precisely because its complex commentary on "reality," "performance," and "(in)authenticity" does not always work. In other words, many audience members failed to see how the performance satirized ethnographic stereotypes of "native" cultures; they also failed to see Fusco and Gómez-Peña as artists engaged in an interactive performance that *included audience reactions* as part of the subject at hand. Many audience members handled the uncomfortably "real" spectacle of caged Guatinauis through familiar Western humanistic and scientific discourses about the visibly different bodies of others. They assumed a naturalist's or anthropologist's role, approaching the "Guatinauis" as specimens to be viewed and discussed. This is, of course, typical museum behavior, and is related to watching traditional documentaries and nature shows as well. While viewers rarely questioned the authenticity of the faux map and text that accompanied the performance, they often pointed out the inauthenticity of Fusco's and Gómez-Peña's "too light" skin and Fusco's dance to rap music. In addition, many white Americans and Europeans reacted to the hybridity of the cage environment by "speculating in front of us about how we could possibly run a computer, own sunglasses and sneakers, and smoke cigarettes."[18]

While the hybridity of the performance distressed many white viewers, as it disrupted their preconceptions of "authentic otherness," Fusco observes that "regardless of whether they believed or not, Latinos in the United States and Europe and Native Americans never criticized the hybridity of the cage environment and the costumes for being 'unauthentic.'" She continues with these stories:

One Pueblo elder from Arizona who saw us in the Smithsonian went so far as to say that our display was more 'real' than any other statement about the condition of Native peoples in the museum. 'I see the faces of my grandchildren in that cage,' he told a museum representative. Two Mexicans who came to see us in England left a letter saying that they felt that they were living in a cage every day they spent in Europe. A Salvadoran man in Washington stayed with us for an extended period, pointing to the rubber heart suspended from the top of the cage, saying 'That heart is my heart.'[19]

While conducting interviews for *The Couple in the Cage*, a documentary about the performance and the performance histories it engages, Fusco found that most white audience members read the fiction as "real" and the inauthenticating disruptions as "false." Most Latino/a and Native American audience members read the performers' inauthenticity and cultural hybridity as more "real" than the cultural stereotypes perpetuated by the rest of the museum's exhibits. Even viewers who saw the performance as art often actively engaged the fiction, easily taking on the colonizer's role by, for example, paying money to feed the Guatinauis bananas or to see them dance. Media coverage of the exhibition often focused on the moral implications of "misinforming the public" and threatening the truth-function of museum exhibits, as did other "official" responses to the performance.

As Fusco observes, "the cage became the metaphor for our condition, linking the racism implicit in ethnographic paradigms of discovery with the exoticizing rhetoric of 'world beat' multiculturalism." Read within ethnographic paradigms of discovery, as in museums of science and natural history, the Guatinauis' "inauthentic" cultural hybridity confuses audiences. To make sense of these "discrepancies," audiences attribute inaccuracy to the representation rather than to their own familiar cultural narratives and visual habits. Encountered in an art museum and read as groovy multicultural bordercrossing exotics, as postmodern art, the Guatinauis are appropriated to a Eurocentric discourse emphasizing the freedom to choose identity and its expression over the power to choose identity and its expression. Such readings obscure the function of the cage in these performances, privileging how one is entitled to shape one's sense of self as well as one's culture.[20] Official American stories that emphasize entitlement, freedom, and discovery, that equate the clearly visible with the real, and that whitewash racism and white supremacy, profoundly shaped the reception of Fusco's and Gómez-Peña's performance work.

The variety of interpretative modes, as well as the predominance of literal interpretations, give credence to Fusco's argument that patterns of reception must be historicized by recognizing the heritage of "regulation and economic exploitation by outsiders" which actually produced a fissure between those inside and those outside of mainstream culture, each responding to seeing each other differently.[21] By suggesting that patterns of reception must be historicized, Fusco also suggests that oppressive ways of reading and seeing difference are learned. Through Anna Deavere Smith's work, I want to explore the necessary hope that "we" can develop methods of seeing and reading so that "otherness" might be read "otherwise."

Both "Two Undiscovered Amerindians Visit..." and *Twilight: Los Angeles, 1992* suggest that "European and non-European cultures were transformed by their 'new' and closer relationship to one another in the 'New World.' For the most part, the relationship was one of exploitation, appropriation, oppression, and repression. But it is also true that something came into and is coming into being: something neither 'primitive'/'tribal' nor European modern."[22] This "something" can be read, awkwardly and tentatively, in the stutters and struggles of Anna Deavere Smith's characters to speak about the violences that occurred in Los Angeles in 1992. Smith's interest in performing the eloquent stutters and missteps that together create American character(s) offers one democratic alternative to the colonialist performance history of ethnographic display that Gómez-Peña's and Fusco's "Two Undiscovered Amerindians Visit..." so effectively theorizes and enacts.

As an artist interested in representing United States culture as a hybrid multiculture created and recreated through exchange and appropriation, respect and oppression, MacArthur award-winning playwright and Stanford professor Anna Deavere Smith mines a variety of art-making traditions. Smith's performances might be productively compared to cultural forms as diverse as Brechtian theater, Cubist (and therefore African) visual art, West African age-grade festivals, Faith

Ringgold's story-quilts, talk shows, oral histories like John Langston Gwaltney's *Drylongso* and Studs Terkel's numerous books, and sociodramatic techniques of conflict resolution. Smith also cites the work of Ntozake Shange, Allen Ginsberg, and George Wolfe as influences, and points to a Johnny Carson interview with Sophia Loren as critical to the development of her approach to character.[23] *Twilight: Los Angeles, 1992* is an installment in Smith's ongoing documentary theater project, *On the Road: A Search for American Character.* Since 1982, Smith has been interviewing people, often in the context of a specific event or conflict occurring within a particular community.[24] From these taped interviews, Smith shapes a 'solo' performance that is multifocal and many-voiced. Many of these performances have remained local, meeting the goals of assisting the community in its exploration of an issue or the negotiation of conflict; bringing people into the same room, the theater, who would not normally come together; and making theater accessible to people who do not usually attend. However, Smith's 1992 performance, *Fires in the Mirror*, an exploration of the violence that occurred in August 1991 between the African-American and Hasidic Jewish communities of Crown Heights, Brooklyn, touched a national nerve and catapulted her work to national attention. This visibility prompted the Los Angeles Mark Taper Forum to commission a similar performance based on the violence that occurred in the wake of the April 1992 acquittal of the LAPD officers accused of beating Rodney King.

While researching *Twilight: Los Angeles, 1992* Smith interviewed about two hundred people, but each live performance can include only about twenty-five characters. Since the performance itself is "on the road," Smith varies the material she uses in each performance; the book version of *Twilight: Los Angeles, 1992* includes material presented at the Taper in 1993 and at the New York Shakespeare Festival in 1994. Characters include well-known players in American public life, such as scholars Cornel West and Homi Bhabha, Los Angeles Mayor Tom Bradley, Congresswoman Maxine Waters, former Senator Bill Bradley, and former LAPD chief Daryl Gates. Other characters include survivors of police brutality Rudy Salas, Jr., and Michael Zinzun; community activists Theresa Allison and Chung Lee; Rodney King's aunt, Angela King; LAPD sergeant Charles Duke; an anonymous juror in the Simi Valley trial; LAPD district attorney Gil Garcetti; television writer Joe Viola; appliance store owner Richard Kim; former liquor store owner Mrs. Young-Soon Han; gang truce activists and ex-gang members Allen Cooper and Twilight Bey; truck driver Reginald Denny; lumber salesman Julio Menjivar; the Reverend Tom Choi; former head of the Black Panther Party, Elaine Brown; and the late artist Betye Saar.

By including such a wide variety of voices and perspectives in *Twilight*, Smith makes a political art based on the democratic ideal of full representation. At the same time, as what bell hooks has called a "critical ethnographer," Smith's performance practice "represents individual experience in ways that...*metonymically refer to, but can never grasp,* an entire culture."[25] By including such a wide variety of voices and perspectives, which suggests that we still cannot have heard the whole story, and by incorporating Smith's presence as interpreter and editor of the material, *Twilight* attempts full representation even as it critiques the possibility of full representation. Smith's process resembles the ethnographic practice of participant observation, which "obliges its practitioners to experience, at a bodily as well as an intellectual level, the vicissitudes of translation" and "requires arduous language learning, some degree of direct involvement and conversation, and often a de-rangement of personal and cultural expectations."[26] However, rather than writing a seamless narrative synthesizing the "data" she gathers, Smith's actions as author-authority-writer resemble what James Clifford has called the surrealist moment in ethnography:

The cuts and sutures of the research process are left visible; there is no smoothing over or blending of the work's raw data into a homogeneous representation. To write ethnographies on the model of collage would be to avoid the portrayal of cultures as organic wholes or as unified, realistic worlds subject to a continuous explanatory discourse...To think of surreal-ism as ethnography is to question the central role of the creative 'artist,' the shaman-genius discovering deeper realities in the psychic realm of dreams, myths, hallucinations, automatic writing. This role is rather different from that of the cultural analyst, interested in the making and unmaking of common codes and conventions. Surrealism coupled with ethnog-raphy recovers its early vocation as critical cultural politics. (146-7)

Smith's version of critical ethnography emphasizes the negotiation of meanings, displacing the traditional ethnographer's desire for fixed definitions with the surrealist-ethnographer's exploration of juxtaposition. Smith's ethnographic practice also shifts emphasis from the act of observation to the process of listening aurally and kinetically, which emphasizes her subjects' speech acts and gestures over her own visual and linguistic performances as participant-observer.

Smith is especially interested in people's words, spoken rhythms, speech patterns, and talk-driven gestures; these linguistic markers sound out how people struggle for language, especially when trying to speak about race in the United States. As Priscilla Wald observes, "disruptions...caused by unexpected words, awkward grammatical constructions, rhetorical or thematic dissonances...mark the pressure of untold stories" (1).[27] Disrupted speech marks the pressure of negotiat-ing between conforming to cultural prescriptions for "sense" and "story," and the refusal of comprehensibility that is part of the struggle to say it differently, to say something known and felt and inchoate. While Smith's interviewees struggle with "lousy language" so as to talk about their roles in specific multicultural and violent events (Los Angeles 1992, Crown Heights, Brooklyn 1991) her speech-based embodiments of these varied characters suggest ways to engage difference and Otherness without dominating, appropriating, or assimilating. Smith's strategies for gathering and performing her material suggest that communication, connection and empathy can begin to happen when language breaks down, so that we *have* to listen carefully. Only then can we start to work with and beyond "the damage the search for sameness has done for us."[28] Smith believes that speech is a physical act and that language, gestures, the struggle for words, is the locus of identity. She seeks for American character in the ways that people speak. Her performances display her interest in the difficulty people have in talking about race and difference, the lack of words for this ongoing American conversation. For Smith, "American character is alive inside of syntactical breaks. The break from the pattern is where character lives, and where dialogue, ironically, begins, in the *uh,* in the pause, in the thought as captured for the first time in a moment of speech, rather than in the rehearsed, the proven." Smith's performances offer these stutters in a character's monologue, these breaks and juxtapositions in the performance's dialogue, as moments of possibility, as moments where both character and audience can experience "authorship...say something that is like poetry. The process of getting to that moment is where 'character' lives." If character resides in the process of using language, and if embodied speech reveals what is invisible about a person, then Smith's performances work on the premise that language might be "a photograph of what was unseen about society just as it reflects what is unseen in an individual."[29]

Syntactical breaks, the speaker's rough handling of words in order to speak at all, foreground the inadequacy of our already-memorized cultural scripts to the ongoing (and conflictual) projects of self-identification and cross-cultural dialogue. For example, official scripts rigidify "difference" so that dialogue can only happen within American subgroups but not between them, or require that persons assimilate to a monolingual, monocultural "America" in order to participate publicly in the cultural conversation. Rather than these self-centered processes of constructing conversation, Smith's compositional method "begin(s) with the other and comes to the self." Smith articulates the connection between her method and social change like this:

I am interested in how inhibitions affect our inability to empathize. If I have an inhibition about *acting* like a man, it may also point to an inhibition I have about *seeing* a man or *hearing* a man....If only a man can speak for a man, a woman for a woman, a Black person for all Black people, then we, once again, inhibit the *spirit* of theater, which lives in the *bridge* that makes unlikely aspects *seem* connected. The bridge doesn't make them the same, it merely *displays* how two unlikely *aspects* are *related.* These relationships of the *unlikely...*are crucial to American theater and culture if theater and culture plan to help us assemble our obvious differences.[30]

Smith's performative deployment of an empathy that depends upon inarticulateness and unlikely connection suggests an approach to representation that bell hooks attributes to "critical fictions." In "Narratives of Struggle," hooks writes that many critical fictions use "languages in ways that open up a text to multiple audiences," so that readers "cannot approach work assuming that they already possess a language of access, or that the text will mirror realities they already know and understand." As such, hooks continues, "readers must learn to 'see' the world differently if they want to understand this work. This is the fundamental challenge of critical fictions. They require that the reader shift her paradigms and practice empathy as a conscious gesture of solidarity with the work."

Like the written critical fictions hooks describes, Smith's performance work requires that she, and her audiences, struggle to read and see "otherwise." For both hooks and Smith, "imagination can enable us to understand...realities that in no way resemble where we are coming from."[31] Both women insist that the imagination can work against the will to possess the "otherness" of a text or a stranger. For Smith, "the *other* is not an imaginative construction of an internal psychic function, a Lacanian other; but rather, the *other* is an actual figure in the world who is enmeshed in some critical way in the complex social event she addresses."[32] As such, Smith searches for her characters in the *movement* between self and other rather than through the Stanislavskian technique of searching for characters within oneself and one's own experiences. While the Stanislavski method bridges the differences between actor and character "by endowing both with the experiences of the actor...Smith asks the actor to observe and maintain these differences so when the actor becomes the character, he/she must travel over to the other, and become a person different from his/her self."[33] As Lyons and Lyons suggest, "The difference between assimilating one's own psyche into the fictional experience of a character and inhabiting the discourse of the other is telling...Smith deliberately attempts to resist the temptation to internalize the other...and reconfigure that image as an aspect of her own interiority."[34] Inhabiting the discourse of the other requires a willingness to empathize, to see anew, to bridge differences while respecting them, to experience the other's words and gestures viscerally. Inhabiting the discourse of the other is not the same as appropriating or "eating" the other[35]; rather, others are partners in negotiating the distances between "me" and "you," or "us" and "them."

Smith's search for character offers a model of social relationship based on dialogue, empathy, and difference: traveling towards otherness by listening to what people say, do not say, how they sound and move when they speak. This model of social relationship rejects the metaphorics of (20/20) vision in favor of kinetics, sound, and speech. Smith's light tan skin, androgynous clothing, acting ability, and limited use of props, a hat here, a scarf there, deliberately deprive audiences of our usual overdependence on visual signifiers to "read" a person and determine our interaction with that person. Faced with limited visual information, we have to listen to each character's words and rhythms. Language and voice, the form and content of the word, become sites for empathetic connection based on an often *unexpected* commonality of feeling rather than preconceived visual notions about who we will listen to and agree with. Audiences have a chance to really hear multiple voices, to recognize themselves in unexpected places, to experience surprising selves through unlikely connections.

As Smith juxtaposes characters' voices, gestures, and perspectives, slipping from character to character, insight grows in the moments between the voices and between the words spoken by each voice. Meaning is made through an authorial presence, a particular body possessed by her characters, the particular intelligence that fashioned the performance's framework, but this authorial presence also signifies the slippage of Smith's authority. In other words, Smith conjures characters and events through embodying the *characters'* spoken acts of authorship, not her own. At the same time, Smith does not hide her authorial role in collecting, organizing, and performing these speech acts, and so creates a productive tension between the assembled characters' polyphony and the acoustical/material unification that Smith's physical presence onstage provides. Smith's performances mediate differences and build bridges by exposing how the characters' speech acts "constitute performances in which the individual figures characterize themselves, with varying degrees of self-consciousness, to Smith and before Smith...Smith, as actor, represents that self-constituting act as she shows that process to the audience, casting the spectators (including the people she portrays) into the role of witnesses."[36] Audiences witness how these acts of self-constitution contextualize each other, and it is precisely the tension between the similarities and the differences in the stories told that creates the community being portrayed, and its conflicts, its truths:

This is contemporary America, a land of such diversity that no one tolerates difference, a land of such bizarre eclecticism that everyone must know one's place...In order to begin the great project of racial, gender, and generational reconciliation, we must sign a temporary peace treaty. Perhaps the key here is the recognition that we are all partially guilty and that most of us are partially disenfranchised...Like at a family reunion, we must face these issues frontally but with respect, without indicting anyone, without calling names. Our cultural institutions can perform an important role: They can function as laboratories to develop and test new models of collaboration and 'free zones' for intercultural dialogue.[37]

Clearly, "Two Undiscovered Amerindians Visit..." and *Twilight: Los Angeles, 1992* struck a nerve with American audiences: the Guatinauis received mixed to negative reviews as a performance piece, with mainstream media coverage focusing on the "trick" that Fusco and Gómez-Peña were playing, while reviews of *Twilight* were quite enthusiastic, often using words such as "epic," "heroic," and "masterpiece." Since both performances, and audience reactions to them, tell us something about who and where we are as Americans, these differences in audience reaction are worth a closer look. As Fusco suggests, "performance has historically been and continues to be about the unconscious, both individual and collective."[38] *Twilight* appealed to Americans in a way that "Two Undiscovered Amerindians Visit..." did not because Smith's performance appears to be more populist, more democratic, than Fusco's and Gómez-Peña's razor-edged intervention into the history of intercultural performance. While "Two Undiscovered Amerindians Visit..." acts like art and/or like scientific-historical fact, depending on the venue, *Twilight* resembles familiar forms of contemporary popular culture such as the talk show. By satirizing the formation and institutionalization of official knowledge about non-European and nonwhite cultures, Fusco and Gómez-Peña alienated people who may already feel disenfranchised in museum spaces; audiences fall for the fiction by falling back on colonialist modes of interpretation encouraged by official museum culture, and then are shamed by representatives of the institution for having learned these forms of discourse so well. *Twilight*, on the other hand, includes and implicates the audience in its representation of American multiculture, and so creates a dissonance in which dialogue happens, or could happen. While both performances demonstrate that, as Gómez-Peña puts it, "our cultural institutions can function as laboratories to develop and test new models of collaboration and 'free zones' for intercultural dialogue," Smith's performance received rave reviews because the audience experienced the beginnings of intercultural dialogue from within the multicultural American community. "Two Undiscovered Amerindians Visit," though an effective satire of colonialist modes of perception, divided "us" and "them," in part because audiences often overlooked, or questioned, the cultural hybridity of the Guatinauis and themselves. American audiences fall for the hopeful ending, or what seems like the hopeful ending, every time.

bell hooks has written that the performance work of Anna Deavere Smith and Coco Fusco (and therefore, by implication, Gómez-Peña) "appears to be specifically designed to disrupt mainstream white sensibilities."[39] While hooks' statement does not adequately account for the complex ways that strategies of inauthenticity and juxtaposition, for example, might work disruptively for many members of a multicultural American audience, it does partially contextualize the differences in the mainstream (white) media's reactions to "Two Undiscovered Amerindians Visit..." and *Twilight*. White Americans reading for sameness, looking to identify with whites and whiteness, would feel much more comfortable with the democratic variety of white voices and perspectives in *Twilight* than with the role of colonizer that the interactive script of "Two Undiscovered Amerindians Visit..." required them to play. And because Smith mines the connection between everyday speech and identity while deemphasizing the visual, white Americans reading for sameness would also be more likely to identify with at least a few characters from *Twilight* who do not otherwise fit their demographic profile. This identification with whites/whiteness, as well as identification across racial and cultural differences, makes white audience members comfortable with *Twilight* and comfortable with themselves. Despite the violence that the performance represents, white Americans may feel like they are playing their best selves in a familiar script about democratic America, and so can safely take seriously the ways in which *Twilight* challenges that script.

In contrast, "Two Undiscovered Amerindians Visit..." makes audiences, and especially white audience members, stand face-to-face with their own oft-denied racism and democracy's failures, as well as with the kind of violence that made the United States multicultural in the first place. Because these two performances represent distinct aspects of multicultural America, and use different representational strategies to do so, *Twilight: Los Angeles, 1992* and "Two Undiscovered Amerindians Visit..." together show how performance art, "this territory of multiple perceptions, and of the unpredictable, is a perfect place from which to continue to test the limits of the promise of democracy and tolerance: great ideas to which this country aspires, but which it has such tremendous difficulty actually living up to."[40]

NOTES

1. Carol Becker, ed., *The Subversive Imagination: Artists, Society, and Social Responsibility* (New York: Routledge, 1994), 36.

2. Many of Guillermo Gómez-Peña's essays and performance texts are collected in *Warrior for Gringostroika* (St. Paul, MN: Graywolf Press, 1993) and *The New World Border: Prophecies, Poems, and Loqueras for the End of the Century*.

3. *Warrior for Gringostroika*, 217.

4. Coco Fusco, *English is Broken Here: Notes on Cultural Fusion in the Americas* (New York: New Press, 1995).

5. Gómez-Peña, Guillermo, "The Free Art Agreement/El Tratado de Libre Cultura" in *The Subversive Imagination: Artists, Society, and Social Responsibility*, ed. Carol Becker (New York: Routledge), 1994, xii.

6. *English is Broken Here*, 49.

7. From "Radio Pirata: Colon Go Home!, a live broadcast by Coco Fusco and Guillermo Gómez-Peña, aired on National Public Radio in 1992-1993.

8. *English is Broken Here*, 41-43.

9. *English is Broken Here*, 44.

10. *English is Broken Here*, 39.

11. *English is Broken Here*, 47.

12. James Clifford, *The Predicament of Culture: Twentieth-Century Ethnography, Literature, and Art* (Cambridge: Harvard UP), 1988.

13. Paul Gilroy, "'To Be Real:' The Dissident Forms of Black Expressive Culture," in *Let's Get It On: The Politics of Black Performance*, ed. Catherine Ugwu (Seattle: Bay Press and The Institute of Contemporary Arts, 1995), 29.

14. Coco Fusco, "Performance and the Power of the Popular," *Let's Get It On: The Politics of Black Performance*, ed. Catherine Ugwu (Seattle: Bay Press and The Institute of Contemporary Arts, 1995), 161.

15. Homi Bhabha, "The Other Question: Difference, Discrimination and the Discourse of Colonialism," in *Out There: Marginalization and Contemporary Cultures*, ed. Russell Ferguson, Martha Gever, Trinh T. Minh-ha, Cornel West (New York: The New Museum of Contemporary Art and MIT Press, 1990), 71.

16. *English Is Broken Here*, 76.

17. Peggy Phelan, *Unmarked: The Politics of Performance* (New York: Routledge, 1993), 177.

18. *English is Broken Here*, 56.

19. *Ibid.*, 56.

20. *Ibid.*, 39, 68.

21. Fusco, "Performance and the Power of the Popular," 160.

22. Michelle Wallace, "Modernism, Postmodernism, and the Problem of the Visual in African-American Culture," in *Out There: Marginalization and Contemporary Cultures*, eds. Russell Ferguson, Martha Gever, Trinh T. Minh-ha, Cornel West. (New York: The New Museum of Contemporary Art and MIT Press, 1990), 48.

23. On Smith's affinities with the age-grade festivals of West Africa, see Sandra Richards' "Caught in the Act of Social Definition: *On the Road* with Anna Deavere Smith," p. 43. See Richards' essay, p. 40, for the Johnny Carson/Sophia Loren connection. Richards also connects Smith's work with "a tradition of political clowning that has largely been lost in the United States" (42), and suggests the Brechtian connection in her choice of descriptors such as 'estrangement' and 'distancing.' She coins the provocative phrase 'postmodern theater for development,' suggesting that the use of theater in Third World countries to introduce new technologies has affinities with the use of theater in "elite Western settings where the problem is not technological but social underdevelopment" (46). Charles and James Lyons, in their essay "Anna Deavere Smith: Perspectives on her Performances within the Context of Critical Theory," suggest the connection with Cubist collages, as well as Duchamp's found art and Louise Nevelson's assemblages (45). They also discuss Smith's work in terms of Brechtian theater traditions (59-61). However, Smith has had few encounters with Brecht's work; for a discussion of her performances as Brechtian in this context,

see Carl Weber's interview with Smith, "Brecht's 'Street Scene,'On Broadway, of all Places? A Conversation with Anna Deavere Smith." See Barbara Lewis' interview with Smith, "The Circle of Confusion: A Conversation with Anna Deavere Smith," for mention of Ntozake Shange (55), Allen Ginsberg (59), and George Wolfe (61).

24. In "Caught in the Act of Social Definition: *On the Road* with Anna Deavere Smith," Sandra Richards gives the following examples of Smith's *On the Road* perform-ances: "She interviewed San Francisco-Bay Area women for the symposium 'Bay Area Women in Theater.'..With the University of Pennsylvania and the Five Colleges at Amherst, Smith explored issues related to feminism and racism. Crossroads Theatre in New Bruns-wick commissioned a show on black theater and black identity, while San Francisco's Eureka Theatre wanted to probe realities behind the public mystique of 'the city by the Bay'" (36). Sandra Richards, "Caught in the Act of Social Definition: *On the Road* With Anna Deavere Smith," *Acting Out: Feminist Performances*, eds. Lynda Hart and Peggy Phelan (Ann Arbor: UMI Press, 1993) 35-53.

25. "Performance Practice as a Site of Opposition," 214.

26. Clifford, 24.

27. Priscilla Wald, *Constituting Americans: Cultural Anxiety and Narrative Form* (Durham: Duke U P, 1995).

28. Smith in John Lahr, "Under the Skin," *New Yorker* 28 June 1993, 93.

29.Anna Deavere Smith, *Fires in the Mirror* (New York: Anchor/Doubleday, 1993), xxxix-xi, xxxi.

30. Ibid., xxviii-xxix.

31. bell hooks, "Narratives of Struggle," in *Critical Fictions: The Politics of Imaginative Writing*, ed. Philomena Mariani (Seattle: Bay Press, 1991), 58.

32. Charles Lyons and James Lyons, "Anna Deavere Smith: Perspectives on her Performance within the Context of Critical Theory," in *Journal of Dramatic Theory and Criticism* 9 (1994), 51.

33. Monica Muñoz-Corte, "The Works of Anna Deavere Smith: An Exploration of Otherness." OnlineWorldWideWeb. 21 Feb.,1996, 3.
Available http://www.mcnair.berkeley.edu/ 95Journal/MonicaCortes.html

34. Lyons and Lyons, 49.

35. For a discussion of 'eating the other,' see bell hooks' "Eating the Other: De-sire and Resistance" in *Black Looks: Race and Representation* (Boston: South End Press, 1992).

36. Lyons and Lyons, 46.

37. Gómez-Peña, "The Free Art Agreement," 219-220.

38. "Performance and the Power of the Popular," 174.

39. bell hooks, "Performance Practice as a Site of Opposition," in *Let's Get It On: The Politics of Black Performance*, ed. Catherine Ugwu (Seattle: Bay Press and The Institute of Contemporary Arts, 1995), 219.

21. Fusco, "Performance and the Power of the Popular," 174-5.

PART III

PRAXIS

12

Curriculum Reform, Women's Studies, and Women of Color

Arlene Sgoutas

Transforming higher education for a diverse society depends both on the knowledge taught in the classroom and how that knowledge is constructed. Responding in part to the diversity of the student population in colleges and universities[1] and in part to the gaps in knowledge, efforts are now being made to offer a more inclusive curriculum. Creating an inclusive curriculum begins by answering the following three questions: First, what is the present content, scope and methodology of a discipline? Second, how would the discipline need to change to reflect the roles, contributions and perspectives of those excluded? And thirdly, what responsibilities do various departments have in creating a curriculum that accurately reflects the histories and experiences of all women and ethnic groups? This essay will explore the answers to these questions in order to explain why the future of curriculum reform[2] is dependent on the experiences and voices of women of color.[3] The essay begins with an overview of curriculum reform through Women's Studies courses, programs, and projects. Then, a review of the lessons learned is followed by suggestions for the next step in the continuation of feminist curriculum reform. In this section, an examination of the relationship between Women's Studies and ethnic studies is given. The essay concludes with the importance of curriculum transformation and a focus on how to incorporate research and teaching about women of color into the undergraduate curriculum.[4] In the final analysis it is concluded that, as the agents of change, women of color are central to creating a gender balanced, multicultural curriculum.

Until the advent of contemporary feminist inquiry, disciplines and their curricula maintained and transmitted only the issues and concerns of the white Western male. Male domination over the curriculum assumes that the male experience represented "a whole society," thus projecting its assumptions onto all social groups.[5] Rendered invisible, women were regarded as neither valuable, legitimate subjects nor significant contributors to the knowledge based in those disciplines. The introduction of gender as a category for analyzing social experience questioned the traditional disciplinary approach and brought significant changes to the study of women. Leading the way were Women's Studies programs whose initial attempts to change academic offerings focused on the concern to uncover and reclaim women and their experience.[6] Curriculum reform efforts began to generate courses and materials that focused on women's traditions, history, culture, values, vision and perspectives. Moreover, these courses examined power relations as they are produced and reproduced in our life. Unfortunately, the result was that the experience of white, middle-class women provided the norm at the exclusion of other women.

In the following section, a closer examination of the widespread introduction of Women's Studies courses and programs as part of the curriculum in higher education is followed by an evaluation of its impact on the curriculum. While feminist scholars enlarged and challenged the assumptions of the traditional disciplines, many lessons were learned and challenges presented in addressing the short-sightedness of an exclusive curriculum. To address the gaps in curriculum reform, race became an important analytical tool for investigating and understanding the differences among women. By taking gender and race in their fullest historical and cultural contexts and developing an understanding of the complexities of these experiences and their relatedness, curriculum transformation projects were forced to address their white-privileged structures. Future projects realized that only by concentrating on the issues and experiences of women of color and collaborating with new, emerging programs could the hope of a truly inclusive curriculum be fulfilled.[7]

The recognition of the invisibility of women, as well as the identification of sexism in traditional knowledge, led to the search for missing women and then to an understanding of women's experiences, perspectives, and voices.[8] Within traditional systems of knowledge, the universality of the white, male experience excluded women's experiences and perspectives. When women were included, sex stereotypes and traditional attitudes toward women prevailed. Since these disciplines developed in times when culturally-constructed gender roles were perceived as natural and inevitable, women were presented only in the context of their roles as mothers, wives, and homemakers. This limited view of the female experience resulted in a call for the creation of a space in which learning for, on, with and by women could be generated. The result was change not only in the understanding of women's roles in society but also in attitudes towards women and in gender relations. Another result was a higher awareness of the impact of gender and sex stereotyping on women's daily lives and choices. Instrumental to these changes were the efforts made by Women's Studies programs, their achievement in challenging the dominant knowledge in various disciplines and fields of research and their assistance in creating and sustaining curriculum reform projects.

Women's Studies pioneered procedures for infusing the curriculum with the perspective and voices of those excluded from mainstream scholarship. As a formal area of teaching and research, Women's Studies first appeared in higher education in 1969. Fueled by the women's movement and the growth in the number of female students and faculty members in colleges and universities, Women's Studies programs were the first to provide intellectual leadership for transformation projects on campus. Faculty with ties to Women's Studies devised two strategies for achieving a gender-balanced curriculum.

Of these two strategies, one advocated the continuance of the groundbreaking research and criticism, challenging the androcentric paradigms that rendered women invisible. The other strategy emphasized the integration of content on women and gender into the curriculum in various departments. "Integrating" or "mainstreaming" women into a course merely implies adding examples or sections about women into an established, accepted and unchangeable body of knowledge centered within an existing male framework. While there are some feminist scholars who see value in integration, most prefer autonomy. Those who favor the latter worry that integration projects compromise Women's Studies by modeling it to fit into the patriarchal systems of knowledge. Instead, a transformation must take place that will do away with patriarchal assumptions about culture and society. Included in this approach to reform is the incorporation of feminist approaches to learning. Thus, female scholars were rethinking not only what but how we teach.[9] One way to evaluate these two strategies is feminist phase theory.

Feminist phase theory identifies five common phases of thinking about women: male scholarship, compensatory scholarship, bifocal scholarship, feminist scholarship, and multifocal or relational scholarship.[10] Each phase of feminist theory requires an examination of the level of consciousness about the exclusion of women and the steps needed to include women in the major fields or disciplines within the curriculum. For example, male scholarship has "no consciousness that the male experience is a 'particular knowledge' selected from a wider universe of possible knowledge and experience." [11] Thus, at this stage no effort is made to add women into the traditional structure. On the other hand, in multifocal or relational scholarship, the level of consciousness is high and scholars are aware of particularity but also identify common denominators of experience. Efforts are made to "fuse women's and men's experience into a holistic view of human experience." At each stage, issues of content and conceptualization of the disciplines are explained. Therefore, feminist phase theory shows "where one has been, where one is, and where one might be going" This classification system of changes in curriculum phases and individuals occurs as a series of intersecting circles, undergoing changes in response to one another.

The usefulness of feminist phase theory goes beyond evaluating content and focus of research and scholarship to measuring shifts in participating faculty's level of conceptualizing the inclusion of women in their discipline:

Feminist phase theory is an approach to evaluation that is consistent with the academic goals and intellectual content of feminist studies. It enables an evaluator to check curricula, syllabi, or faculty conceptualizations against the various phases of feminist scholarship in order to determine the content, structure and methodology of a discipline in relation to gender. This evaluation model has already demonstrated its clear applicability to content analyses of published texts, in which both copy and visuals can be related to each phase.[12]

The various levels of feminist phase theory are thus used as a measuring stick of how the inclusion of women is conceptualized and how researchers and scholars incorporate perspectives and materials on women. The result is to encourage women's experience to be learned as it is lived, expanding human knowledge exponentially.

In order to incorporate basic feminist scholarship within traditional fields of knowledge, Women's Studies programs initiated scores of curriculum transformation projects in colleges and universities throughout the country. The forerunner in the field of feminist curriculum transformation is The Arizona Project. This four-year cross-disciplinary program at the University of Arizona was sponsored by the National Endowment for the Humanities and was directed toward senior faculty, including department chairs, in the social sciences and humanities. The project developed integration strategies that included summer seminars, colloquia and lectures by visiting scholars. By the end of the project the participants had prepared revised syllabi for approximately 80 courses. In addition, a number of them found their own research profoundly affected by their work in the project. The project had to confront the resistance of male faculty members to feminist scholarship. One of the criticisms, however, is that the program was not multicultural in its approach. The Western States Project on Women is another example of a curriculum transformation program. Conducted by the Southwest Institute for Research on Women at the University of Arizona, the project was funded with a two-year grant from the Ford Foundation. The purpose of the project was "to encourage the integration of new scholarship on women into the curriculum primarily by making grants to four-year institutions for faculty development projects." [13] The collection of resources from the projects were reported in a two-volume collection. These resources included but were not limited to, essays, reports, and syllabi.

These projects, among many others, taught reformers that curriculum transformation is a long-term project that requires a combination of elements, the most important of which are course content, faculty development, and institutional support. The first of these elements, course content, involves course revision with a focus on restructuring syllabi. Rethinking and revising syllabi calls for more than the mere addition or subtraction of materials, but for reconceptualizing the lessons, research problems, methods of study and outcomes. For many subjects this may involve broadening their courses to take an interdisciplinary approach to topics. A revised syllabus will reconstruct the canon so as to introduce new materials, but also include women as authors of valued and authoritative works. This inclusion of authors might make many academics, as well as students, uncomfortable with adopting their works since their approach to issues and subjects will differ from white male authors. Still, it is essential to gain awareness and respect for women's intellectual contributions, whatever the subject and whether or not they present an explicit feminist perspective, and to accept them as part of the authoritative canon of literature in every field. Be aware that many women's writings may not fit neatly into the established pigeonholes and paradigms of the field. Not reflected in a course syllabus, however, is pedagogy, classroom dynamics and techniques, and how and what the instructor values or emphasizes in research and discussion. Therefore, teaching methods, language and style are all important.

The second element, faculty development, looks at the concern over the quality of teaching and how traditional ways of teaching may no longer serve the needs of an increasingly diverse student body. Faculty development involves the introduction of new scholarship through the preparation of monographs and guides to relevant topics and source material, workshops, summer institutes and conferences. Previous transformation projects had faculty meet in an interdisciplinary faculty seminar on feminist scholarship followed by a day-long conference on curriculum change and a one-year program for visiting consultants who gave public lectures and advised faculty on the reconstruction of their courses. All of this involved additional research and preparation on the part of the participating faculty. Central to the Arizona Projects' success was that participants engaged in additional guided reading and held consultations with feminist specialists in their individual disciplines about the relationship of the new scholarship on women to their pedagogy and research. The third element, institutional support, refers to the type and level of commitment by university faculty senate, administrator groups and other university actors to greater inclusiveness in the curricula. Types of support vary anywhere from individual faculty members incorporating the "new" scholarship into lectures, course syllabi, and their own research to university funding for conferences that introduce the concepts of multiculturalism. Other types of support are public statements by university officials on the need for change, and most importantly perhaps, is financial support given to ethnic and Women's Studies programs. Levels of institutional support range from creating and requiring more Women's Studies courses as part of the core curriculum or the inclusion of a diversity requirement for graduation or completion of a departmental major[14] to the adoption of an *ad hoc* curricular transformation. The type of reform proposed must be considered in the context of the institution. The commitment level of that reform will become clear once it is put into motion.

Early efforts at feminist curriculum reform taught us how change takes place and what change means. The Arizona and Western States projects, along with others, created spaces and times, forums and strategies for educators to talk about methodology as well as content, pedagogy and research. Moreover, these projects exposed faculty to new materials and knowledge within their fields, as well as new critical scholarship on gender. This discovery provided many with a means for renewal and an opportunity to change the way they teach and learn. During these initial programs, hard lessons were learned. This section will outline some of those lessons, along with suggestions for the next phase of curriculum revision.

While the success of curriculum reform will vary from place to place, three lessons are clear. The first two lessons deal with factors for success. First, the success of efforts to transform the curriculum are dependent on the initial and sustaining support given by faculty. Thus, it is important to identify those who are not only best positioned to change the curriculum, but also willing to take the risk. Female untenured faculty are often in truly vulnerable situations, so that the level of involvement in projects and its ramifications on one's job security and possibilities for professional advancement have to be considered. An alternative is to cultivate tenured faculty as well as temporary faculty and those not on a tenure-track who are sometimes at lower risk. Once the wheels are in motion, progressive faculty are key to retaining control and moving along the process of curriculum reform.

Major changes in courses usually require a secure position within a department or considerable departmental support. If there is no support within the individual department, then Women's Studies program can perhaps offer a course that could later be cross-listed. However, it is important to note that all faculty do have some leeway with their courses to include the new scholarship. Faculty could therefore choose appropriate courses for revision and initiate changes incrementally.

Second, the success of curriculum integration is mostly found in upper-division and other specialized courses, Women's Studies courses and new courses, rather than in the basic courses of the traditional disciplines. Introductory courses that normally embody a traditional set of concepts are among the most resistant to change. Likewise, core courses are also difficult to make more inclusive of gender and race, despite the efforts of professional groups to develop materials that focus particularly on integrating the study of women into the introductory curriculum. It is more advantageous to promote the alternative perspective as a training tool for students in critical thinking and analysis. Thus, one who is trained to recognize the influence of gender bias will in turn learn to think for themselves and develop a more critical point of view.

A third lesson to learn from early reform advocates is that curriculum transformation is a lengthy process involving a series of trade-offs. The choice may be to abandon the hope of broad-scale reform in exchange for the growth of special women's programs. However, program supporters should not compromise too soon and should remember that small victories often lead to larger changes. Realizing that the transformation of curriculum and of knowledge itself is an enormous project, compromised successes can be won without losing the integrity of the original proposal. In this initial stage, one objective is to teach, generate broad support and create a critical mass of truly knowledgeable students, faculty, and administrators. To meet this objective, the evolution of curriculum transformation requires a grounding in the new scholarship and therefore requires knowledgeable scholars.[15] Their knowledge of the gender-based scholarship is critical to meeting a second objective, to transform curricular perspectives rather than simply trivialize feminism.[16]

Having learned the lessons, what needs to be done to further the process of reform? Should curriculum reform continue to be based upon a feminist, trans-formative vision? What about other populations commonly excluded or left at the margins of scholarly discourse? How should faculty in Women's Studies work conjunction in with colleagues in African-American, Hispanic, and other ethnic and gay and lesbian studies to develop cooperative ventures that foster inclusiveness across categories of oppression? While the initial goal was to include the experi-ence of women in the curriculum, it has now broadened and become more carefully defined. New directions in Women's Studies scholarship have emphasized the differences and diversity among women. With this step came the opportunity for women of color scholars to share their experiences and knowledge thus providing information from a multiple-context perspective. As a result, not only were the doors opened on the realities of women of all backgrounds, but a new pathway was set in providing a truly inclusive curriculum. Rethinking both what and how we teach has become more complex and more challenging and the experience of successful projects is therefore all the more valuable.

Curriculum reform is a continuous, evolutionary process. To meet its goal, curriculum transformation now needs to be achieved through Women's Studies from a multiethnic perspective to create a gender-balanced and multicultural curriculum.[17] Therefore, confronting women of color brings significant transformations of content and emphasis to a course. Two systems of oppression, racism and sexism, intersect to form the context for the experience of women of color. Learning about their lives and their oppression raises awareness and understanding of the experiences of all women either explicitly or implicitly. Rather than asking how to integrate women of color into the established curriculum, the question should be what kind of curriculum do women of color want? This distinction is crucial because "as women of color in the academy establish themselves within a changing curriculum, they give back to their disciplines a knowledge of the complexity of identity, of fluid boundaries of class, race, ethnicity and sexuality."[18] Therefore, women of color need to play if not a central, then at least a not peripheral role in directing and planning transformation initiatives.

During this stage, faculty development continues to be an important part of the process. Building faculty knowledge of new interdisciplinary scholarship from feminist and ethnic scholarship is an integral and critical part of this stage in transformation of the curriculum. Regarding course content, faculty might want to consider the use of multicultural media as text. Most important is the inclusion of women of color[19] among the authorities of course readings.[20] Finally, more women of color should be among the tenured faculty in higher education.

A rather unique experiment in higher education curriculum transformation is the Ford Foundation's Mainstreaming Minority Women's Studies Program. In this program there were 13 transformation projects in all, each addressing the exclusion of women's multiple realities based on race, ethnicity, and class, as well as sexual preference, age, physical ability and other often overlooked categories used to marginalize and exclude. The projects collaborated with Women's Studies and racial-ethnic studies programs and scholars in planning and implementing projects to incorporate research and teaching about women of color into the undergraduate curriculum. The program addressed the issue of how to theorize about race, ethnicity, and gender, while also fostering the connections and coalition work between these two departments. As a result, the program created the opportunity for racial-ethnic studies and Women's Studies faculty to engage in future dialogues. A growing body of "new" scholarship and the increasing number of scholars active in its production resulted in the creation of new programs, units, and departments. Similar to Women's Studies, these programs tended to be peripherally related to higher education institutions. The decision to build a separate program as opposed to mainstreaming the new scholarship on race, class and gender has several implications. This section will look at some of these implications, the potential for collaboration among Women's Studies and ethnic studies program and the role of women of color in curriculum reform.

One of the ongoing lessons in curriculum transformation is that if you do not mainstream new scholarship into the curriculum, then the success of programs depends on the existence of a strong Women's Studies program. This fact, along with the increase in "new" or "special" programs, raises three questions. As courses are generated, which department will sponsor them? Do faculty need to pledge allegiance to one program over another? What impact does the distribution of funds and resources have on the relationship between these new programs? Before answering these questions, however, a closer look at the contributions of both Women's Studies and ethnic studies, independent of each other and together, will be given.

The history and importance of Women's Studies in the process of curriculum transformation has been stated in previous sections. What has not been noted is that in the field of Women's Studies, there is a growing awareness of the need to integrate and diversify courses and materials across the lines of race. Women's Studies faculty have recognized that building an inclusive curriculum means both working to build Women's Studies into the curriculum, as well as doing the work and thinking that makes Women's Studies multicultural and multiracial. Once this need for Women's Studies to be multiracial is recognized, it can play a significant role in opening the canon to include women of color.

One of the new emerging units in universities today, ethnic studies, promotes interdisciplinary research and teaching in Afro-American studies, American-Indian studies, Asian-American studies, Chicano studies, and in cross-cultural and comparative race and ethnic studies. Through its courses, ethnic studies encourages participatory, experiential, diverse and student-centered learning, in addition to empowering students of color to move beyond being objects of study towards being subjects of their own social realities, with voices of their own. Moreover, students are encouraged to examine their inherited political/economic and social/cultural positions. In the same manner, faculty are encouraged to recognize that each student brings a particular way of knowing that can be used so that these individual truths can be interwoven into course content. Knowledge, then, becomes a social construction, one constituted on students' own terms, as well as in concert with others so that students can analyze their own social, cultural, historical, political and economic contexts. Racial and ethnic studies, like Women's Studies, have helped to open the doors to underrepresented groups and to the incorporation of their knowledge in the curriculum.

The importance of these programs cannot be overstated. Women's Studies and ethnic studies programs support the teaching, scholarship, and graduate training that produces the knowledge necessary for reform, as well as the next generation of scholars/activists rooted in the new scholarship. With this next generation comes the assurance that the use of new theories and methods will be at the foundation of their classes, scholarship and efforts at reform. Further, academics no longer will have to conform to the traditional standards of scholarly discourse to be accepted in their fields before they can begin to challenge traditional assumptions.

In summary, both programs have already had an impact on interested faculty and administrators. Taken together, it seems that the two departments, including its students and scholars, should collaborate to incorporate scholarship on women of color into Women's Studies courses, as well as into other courses in the liberal arts. Sadly, this type of collaboration is not always the case.

In its attempt to include diversity training in its core curriculum, universities often create an environment of competition and resentment among these programs. There are several sources for conflict and tensions in meeting diversity requirements. One source of conflict is a diversity requirement that is satisfied in either department rather than both. This situation causes units to compete for students. Thus, programs are very protective of the programs they sponsor and careful not to lose their ownership. This fact leads to another source for conflict, cross-listing. The advantages of cross-listing are clear; it shows unity, draws from both cultures, and encourages minority students to take courses. However, cross-listing is often problematic since courses are sponsored by the unit that pays and may not always easily fit into the other department's requirements. For example, a course listed in ethnic studies at the sophomore level may not be easily cross-listed with a Women's Studies course required at a higher level. Therefore, ethnic studies (the department where the course is housed) has the choice of whether or not to put the course at a higher and thus more advanced level. If the decision is made not to do this, then Women's Studies most likely will not create a new course simply to offer it at the higher level. This situation is problematic for Women's Studies since programs do not want competing courses, but on the other hand want to offer a course that is in demand. Moreover, administratively cross-listing is economically problematic.[21]

Personal choice is often involved when dealing with the tensions between departments and issues of cross-listing. For nonwhite males, the answer is a bit more universal. Most nonwhite males stay with ethnic studies programs. The exception is for gay males whose scholarship is more connected with Women's Studies and perhaps not as welcomed in ethnic studies. Likewise, gay/lesbian scholarship is more easily integrated into traditional disciplines than in ethnic studies. These divisions often cause a split between women of color and nonwhite male scholars. Given the potential for conflict, how do departments and the individuals within them work together? There are several opportunities for collaboration.

One way to collaborate is during the course proposal stage. While developing courses not currently available, departments can seek input from other programs. These courses are in turn more likely to be cross-listed since they are not viewed as competition for an existing course. On the same level, faculty can combine classes, make presentations, and present guest lectures. A second avenue of collaboration is through research centers housed outside the two programs. For example, women's research centers have worked in conjunction with racial and ethnic studies programs to mainstream minority Women's Studies.[22] While collaboration may be uneasy at first, departments can learn with and from each other. The alternative is overlapping work, distanced co-existence, and harmful antagonism.

All of these measures are dependent on the politics of departments and the individuals involved. Budgetary concerns, administrative priorities, and faculty support all play a role. Too often departments at the margins are made to compete for a small piece of the pie. These programs are typically fragile and structurally vulnerable. Therefore, tight budgets lead to less cooperation and a tendency to compromise more easily. Given the amount of individual interaction between departments, oftentimes problems stem not from departments but rather from personalities. Taken together, the frustration within units, personality conflicts, and a lack of understanding leave units at odds. The solution is obvious: departments must be given adequate resources and funding to promote healthy growth. The result would be a greater call to create a supportive forum across "special studies" program. If there are no programs in existence, then coalitions among individuals can be formed to build a base and work locally to change knowledge and systems.

Women's Studies and ethnic studies both play a critical role in the overall effort of curriculum development. In order to expand the diversity efforts of curriculum reform, it is crucial for each department to have more outreach. This outreach can be accomplished through brown bag monthly lunches, invitations to potentially interested but uninformed colleagues, and to the circulation of newsletters and lists. Once implemented, this stage of reform begins to generate courses and materials that examine power relations as they are produced and reproduced in institutions of higher education.

There are many benefits to curriculum reform beyond the changes in course content and in the political, intellectual, and personal transformations that this process inspires. Among these benefits is the exposure to scholarship that offers useful approaches to addressing issues of gender and racial equity.[23] In a multi-gendered, multi-racial world, learning to live with diversity is as critical for young men and women as mastering the course content of their disciplines. Sensitizing students to the issues of racism and sexism and the strategies to responding maturely to these problems improve the overall campus climate. The Mainstreaming Minority Women's Studies Program helped focus on positive measures to influence the quality of campus life at a time of growing dissension and an increase in problems of racial and diversity disharmony on United States campuses. The program showed us that educating the college student of the early 21st century will mean taking on the antiracist, anti-sexist work of educating the whole person.[24]

Reform efforts also assist universities in building a larger community that incorporates all its members. The only foreseeable roadblocks to the creation of this community are the domination of conservative forces and patriarchal attitudes that have negative opinions toward Women's Studies and ethnic studies. There may even be direct confrontations with entrenched faculty members who have their own agendas and do not welcome new ideas from unexpected sources. Fortunately, there are those who are continuously looking for ways to accommodate change and invoke renewal into our disciplinary and institutional structures. Over time the various faculty discussion groups, guest lecturers and lunchtime chats are difficult to ignore. Intense efforts on campus to encourage interaction and understanding across all groups, hand-in-hand with the agenda of curriculum reform, offer hope for a gender-balanced, multiracial, and culturally integrated curriculum in higher education today.

NOTES

1. In the United States, the enrollment of women and minorities in higher education is on the rise. At the same time, the demand for Women's Studies and ethnic studies programs has also grown. For further perspectives on this theme, see *Teaching What You're Not*, ed. Katherine J. Mayberry (New York: New York U P, 1996); Richard Guarasci, Grant H. Cornwell and Associates, *Democratic Education in an Age of Difference: Redefining Citizenship in Higher Education* (San Francisco, CA: Jossey Bass, 1997);, *Creating an Inclusive College Curriculum: A Teaching Sourcebook from the New Jersey Project*, eds. Ellen G. Friedman, Wendy K. Kolman, Charley B. Flint, and Paula Rothenberg (New York: Teachers College Press, 1996).

2. The terms "curriculum reform" and "curriculum transformation" are used interchangeably in this essay.

3. The phrase "women of color" implies the existence of the race and ethnicity of white women as well as women who are members of groups that are racial minorities.

4. The scope of this paper is limited to the experience of curriculum transformation programs within select universities in the United States. The emphasis of these programs was at the undergraduate level and included courses in the core as well as in various disciplines. Such consciousness raising programs and changes may also occur as early as kindergarten through all levels and varieties of education. For example, *Women's Studies Quarterly* devoted an entire issue to faculty development and curriculum transformation in community colleges; see "Curriculum Transformation in Community Colleges: Focus on Introductory Courses," *Women's Studies Quarterly* 24 (1996).

5. For example, this view assumes that black women adapt to the same standards as white (male) society rather than evaluating themselves according to their own standards and values. Also see *Feminism & Methodology: Social Science Issues*, ed. Sandra Harding (Bloomington: Indiana U P, 1987), 34.

6. For an excellent history of the development of the Women's Studies in the United States, see Marilyn Jacoby Boxer, *When Women Ask the Question: Creating Women's Studies in America* (Baltimore: John Hopkins U P, 1998). See also.*Women's Studies in Transistion,* eds. Kate Conway-Turner, Suzanne Cherrin, Jessica Schiffman, and Kathleen Doherty Turkel (Newark: U of Delaware P, 1998).

7. For a collection that reflects this new approach, see *New Frontiers in Women's Studies: Knowledge, Identity, and Nationalism*, eds. Mary Maynard and June Purvis (London: Taylor & Francis, 1996).

8. There are several resources that analyze the techniques, processes, implications and effects of curriculum reform. Among them are Deborh S. Rosenfelt, "'Definitive' Issues: Women's Studies, Multicultural Education and Curriculum Transformation in Policy and Practice in the United States" *Women's Studies Quarterly* 22 (1994), 26; Deborah Mahlstedt and Arvid Bloom, "Towards a Model for Facilitating Curriculum Transformation." *Transformations*, 3 (1992), 67; Peggy McIntosh, "Interactive Phases of Curricular Re/vision: A Feminist Perspective." Working Paper No. 124. Wellesley, MA: (Wellesley College Center for Research on Women, 1983); Betty Schmitz, "Women's Studies and Projects to Transform the Curriculum: A Current Status Report." *Women's Studies Quarterly* 11 (1983), 7-19; Marilyn R. Schuster and Susan R. Van Dyne, "Feminist Transformation of the Curriculum: The Changing Classroom, Changing the Institution." Working Paper No. 125. Wellesley, MA: Wellesley College Center for Research on Women, 1983; and *Toward a Balanced Curriculum: A Sourcebook for Initiating Gender Integration Project*, eds. Bonnie Spanier, Alexander Bloom, and Darlene Boroviad (Cambridge, MA: Schenkman, 1983).

9. For a discussion of feminist teaching, see Shirley C. Parry, "Feminist Pedagogy and Techniques for the Changing Classroom," *Women's Studies Quarterly* 34 (1996), 45-54.

10. Mary Kay Thompson Tetreault, "Classrooms for Diversity: Rethinking Curriculum and Pedagogy," in. *Multicultural Education: Issues and Perspectives*, eds. James A. Banks and Cherry A. McGee Banks (Needham Heights, MA: Allyn and Bacon, 1993), 129. For further discussion of feminist phase theory, see Mary Kay Thompson Tetreault, "Feminist Phase Theory: An Experience-Derived Evaluation Model," *Journal of Higher Education* (1985), 363-384.

11. Tetreault, 368; 370; 366; 380.

12. Tetreault, 380.

13. Myra Dinnerstein and Betty Schmitz, eds, *Ideas and Resources for Integrating Women's Studies into the Curriculum, Vol. I.* Western States Project on Women in the Curriculum (The Southwest Institute for Research on Women, 1986), ix.

14. Revising graduation requirements, however, may come at some risk. These risks are outlined in Lynne Goodstein, "The Failure of Curriculum Transformation at a Major Public University: When `Diversity' Equals `Variety,'" *NWSA Journal* 6 (1994), 82-102, and in the following responses to her article: Paula Rothenberg, "Rural U.: A Cautionary Tale," *NWSA Journal* 6 (1994), 291-298, and Elizabeth Kamarck Minnich, "Prisoners of Hope: Even When We Have Tried to Go Further than It Turns Our We Yet Can, We Have Not Simply Failed," *NWSA Journal*, (1994), 299-307. An option to this strategy is to offer honor sections for those students who are serious about the new courses.

15. This point is argued extensively in Goodstein, Rothenberg and Minnich.

16. As curriculum transformations broaden to include race, it is important to have them grounded in multicultural and gender scholarship.

17. For a report on one project, see *Full Circle: The Women of Color in the Curriculum Project* (Madison: University of Wisconsin Madison Women's Studies Research Center with the University of Wisconsin System Office of Multicultural Affairs, 1995).

18. Fiol-Matta, Liza and Mariam K. Chamberlain, *Women of Color and the Multicultural Curriculum: Transforming the College Classroom* (New York: The Feminist Press, 1994), 3.

19. There is no one view that can speak for all women of color.

20. The Center for Research on Women at Memphis State University publishes a bibliography that is an excellent review of research about women of color. Other women of color publications and journals can be found in *Feminist Periodicals*.

21. For example, a course offered on female composers through the music department may cover the lives of the composers simply because they are female. However, a similar course offered through Women's Studies might take a different view, infusing feminist theory.

22. Programs were launched in the 1980s to incorporate research and teaching about women of color into the mainstream curriculum and its various disciplines. For specific examples see Chamberlain, ix-xiii.

23. Unfortunately, a wide range of social research reflects the prevalence of traditional racist and patriarchal attitudes which then reinforces commonly held views. From childhood, we learn that such things as sex and race bring differences in power and privilege, and that these are acceptable. The idea that difference justifies domination is deeply embedded in society and defended as "natural." Therefore, the assignment of power and privilege based on the distinctive characteristics of some directly results in the inequality of power and privilege. In the classroom, analysis of power relations challenges myths of

individual merit as the basis for power and success and helps to dismantle internalized notions of race, class and sex inferiority and incapacity.

    24. Fiol-Matta and Chamberlain, 8.

13

Librarians and Women's Studies Programs

Arglenda Friday

A great deal of potential exists for creating a powerful partnership, as well as a symbiotic relationship between academic librarians and Women's Studies scholars. Following a brief history of the development of the relationship between librarians and Women's Studies programs, this essay will focus on how the primary responsibilities of academic librarians can mesh with the growth and development of research and writing by Women's Studies scholars. The primary academic duties and activities of librarians include, but are not limited to: (1) collection development; (2) supporting faculty and the academic community by providing library and bibliographic instruction to students and preparing bibliographies and other reference tools; and (3) engaging in scholarly research, writing and publishing. The objective of this paper is to explain the roles of academic librarians in order to identify opportunities and avenues for librarians to work more closely with feminist scholars to increase the quality and quantity of materials by and about women and people of color. In addition, this paper will cite techniques librarians can use with Women's Studies teaching faculty and scholars to augment current research and scholarship efforts in these areas.

Historically, certain occupations have become identified with one sex to the degree that all members are commonly associated with the characteristics of that sex. Teachers, social workers, nurses, secretaries and librarians work within the constraints of professions sex-typed as female. Within such professions, however, the organizational pyramid usually dictates that men dominate the pinnacle while women prevail at the base. The women's and civil rights movements improved pay equity and increased the number of management positions for female librarians and more men entered the "predominantly female" profession, but in general female librarians continue to outnumber males by far.[1]

Sex-role stereotyping of librarianship also can be applied to feminist studies. Because both are female-intensive disciplines, there are generally more obstacles to achieve professional status and acceptance as "respectable" in the academy.[2] Librarians generally have to campaign harder for faculty status, while Women's Studies faculty often have to justify the continued existence of their programs. By forming alliances with feminist scholars, female librarians can exert a positive influence on scholarship and contribute to research, while also improving opportunities for the advancement of librarianship and wider recognition and acceptance of Women's Studies.

Most librarians are members of the American Library Association (ALA), founded in 1876. The ALA currently has over 56,000 members (most of whom are female), and a budget in excess of $32 million. With over 57 regions and a host of committees, divisions, subgroups, and affiliations, it is one of the largest and most diverse associations of professional women and minorities.[3] The ALA has several divisions, round tables, and committees whose members can use their expertise and sheer numbers as clout to promote and support Women's Studies in many ways, including collection development, influencing the publication choices of the major vendors and academic presses, and in the cataloging and creating of library subject headings and terminology for women's issues.

These ALA subgroups include the Association of College and Research Libraries division (to which most academic librarians belong), and a number of organizations concerned with promoting ethnic and women's issues. The major subgroups are Women's Studies, Afro-American Studies sections, Minority Concerns and Cultural Diversity group, Ethnic Materials Information Exchange Round Table, and ethnic group affiliations such as the Chinese American Librarian Association, REFORMA (Hispanic librarians), American Indian Librarians, and the Black Caucus. Like the parent organization, they are all charged with promoting and improving library service and librarianship in a culturally diverse organization.[4] The ALA also created several committees and sections for advancing the interests of women librarians following the turbulent 1960's. The Committee on Pay Equity, Feminist Task Force, Committee on the Status of Women in Librarianship, Social Responsibilities Round Table-Gay and Lesbian Task Force, and Women's Studies Section are a few of the responses to the movement.[5] The primary role of each of these organizations is to advance the interests of women librarians by focusing on issues affecting them, such as pay equity and career opportunities, and to improve the status of women.

Women's Studies was introduced into American colleges and universities in the late 1960's; however, library professionals did not seriously consider the need for creating a forum for discussing women's issues within the specific context of academic and research libraries until almost two decades later. The Women's Studies Section of the Association of College and Research Libraries, a division of ALA, was created at the 1983 ALA Midwinter Conference, when several women involved in other ALA women's groups decided to create a forum to discuss Women's Studies within the specific context of academic and research libraries.[6] It should be noted that the ACRL is a large division representing over 3500 university and college libraries (medical, law, departmental and special collections) and over 1200 community colleges or one-eighth of the total of 37,000 United States libraries in ALA. Thus, there is a strong presence of female librarians in these institutions of higher learning.

The ACRL Board of Directors approved establishing a Women's Studies Discussion Group (WSDG) for the 1984 Annual Conference. By 1985, the WSDG had grown to nearly 200 members and, in 1986, the ACRL Board approved the WSDG petition to become the fourteenth Section of ACRL. It was renamed the Women's Studies Section (WSS) and the first meeting of the new section, WSS, was held at the 1988 ALA Midwinter conference. Membership has grown rapidly, with almost 1000 members in 1996. As with ALA, the primary activities of this section include collection development, library instruction and service, and net-working in Women's Studies. In addition to the primary activities, committees within the section also focus on communications, publications, technical services, and social issues and education.

To perform their duties, most librarians have a subject specialization in addition to a knowledge of general reference materials. The interdisciplinary nature of Women's Studies creates unique opportunities for infusing resources by and about women throughout the collection by focusing on increasing book purchases about women and minorities in all disciplines. For example, the health sciences specialist can select items on women's health issues, while the philosophy and business specialists can do the same with their budget allocations. Similar acquisi-tion patterns can be encouraged with diversity materials to increase the quantity of materials by and about women of color in the Women's Studies section and the interdisciplinary subjects. While librarians can use their budgets to increase the number of items about women in the collection, gaining visibility and circulation of these materials is another issue. Strategic placement and location of materials may pose challenges in the implementation of the mass infusion objective in that the interdisciplinary scope of Women's Studies requires a broad range of subject coverage in collection development. The librarian's primary goal should be to include items about women and ethnic groups in all collections, irrespective of the location. Library support for collection development varies in that some systems (1) interfile materials and information about women or specific ethnic groups with the regular collection, (2) others have separate collections and budgets for Women's Studies, and (3) a few fund separate library collections and women's resource centers.[7]

The majority of academic libraries offer a combination of support. Most materials on women are usually interfiled with the regular library collection. Many large academic institutions also support a separate library in a women's resource center. The center is often created and funded by the Women's Studies program with a liaison relationship with the Women's Studies librarian or subject specialist.

Regarding Women's Studies librarians, there appear to be more subject specialists in Women's Studies than librarians employed primarily for the Women's Studies library or resource centers. In addition, because of the broad subject coverage required for Women's Studies, it has been equally difficult to identify positions for "women of color" librarians, although there is a slow but steady growth in the number of Multicultural Services Librarians or Coordinators. While this person is frequently more responsible for diversity and outreach programs for women and minorities rather than collection development, there are usually opportunities for expanding this role to buy and select materials in all formats for women and people of color.

Irrespective of the location of the collections, librarians can exert a strong influence on the location and placement of materials by and about women of color. To a large extent, they can also determine the format, videos, books, journals, or other materials. Books and materials are usually purchased through the library Acquisition Departments that have contractual agreements with major university presses and publishers. A majority of materials by and about women of color are published by small and independent presses; therefore, purchases from these sources may be limited unless librarians specify feminist presses for their purchases or if Acquisitions can make contracts or special arrangements to do business with the small vendors.

Smaller publishers, such as Small Press Distributors, Inc., a nationwide nonprofit distributor of literary small presses, publish booklets such as *Multicultural Series Checklists* along with booklists for specific ethnic groups. L-S Distributors, and Small Press Distributors have long provided a primary avenue for locating resources by and about women, women of color, and minorities. If librarians can be encouraged to use and share this catalog with teaching faculty in Women's Studies and other disciplines, they can make faculty more aware of other resources and alternative materials for possible inclusion in course readings. Feminist presses regularly produce groundbreaking volumes and are often first to articulate new political issues, to showcase new literary talent, and to bring in writing from outside white, heterosexual middle-class circles. Although there has been marked improvement in the visibility and exposure of the products of small feminist presses, small press books are still slighted by the standard reviewing media. Librarians have been making contributions in this arena by compiling bibliographies and resource guides and manuals that identify these presses and major authors.[8]

Support of small presses can also create a domino effect in that, by supporting small and feminist presses, librarians keep them in business and help them expand operations which, in turn, provide more avenues for publication of feminist scholarship and research. Likewise, purchasing items from diversity and multicultural or ethnic presses promotes their growth and development as well. It should be noted that a growing number of academic and university presses and large publishing houses have begun to publish a number of works by female authors, and print excellent catalogs featuring works by and about women and people of color (including materials from and about developing countries in Africa and Latin America). However, librarians are in a position to use their budget allocations and collection development book profiles to petition university presses for research by and about women and minorities.

Most academic librarians are liaisons for the teaching faculty and departments for which they are subject specialists. Responsibilities in this area may include attending and having input in the department college faculty meetings, working directly with the teaching faculty on collection development, conducting library and bibliographic instruction for research and writing courses, and occasionally team-teaching classes for certain programs. In addition, librarians can assist professors with diversity and gender issues in other ways by keeping faculty members and department chairs abreast of new books, journals, and articles related to women of color and diversity. By showing a presence at this level, the librarian will be more knowledgeable of the course curricula and thus be in a better position to make recommendations for titles in the subject areas and to specific faculty for the course syllabi.

Evelyn Hayes explores teaching faculty knowledge and perceptions of libraries and librarians and notes a number of ways both groups can benefit from a symbiotic relationship while also improving the quality of education for the student clientele.[9] This position should be especially appealing to women's and ethnic studies programs as a win-win proposition. If the teaching faculty understand the library budget and collection development process, and the librarians understand the areas of specialization of the faculty, both groups can create a mutually beneficial relationship. Team-teaching research courses with faculty is another often overlooked area where librarians and teaching professors can enhance the symbiotic relationship. Co-facilitation is one of many issues for consideration in feminist restructuring of academic disciplines, but they fail to include librarians in the discussion. As information specialists and feminists, librarians can help professors locate relevant references and materials for curriculum development and help their students conduct meaningful research on women and people of color.[10] Given the broad coverage of Women's Studies courses, librarians could team-teach in a number of disciplines.

Librarians can also complement Women's Studies programs in the more traditional role of library instructor by helping teaching faculty instruct students on basic library research and skills.[11] When the first courses on women were introduced into American college and universities in the late 1960s, instructors went to libraries to find fragments of information to use in their teachings. Shortly thereafter, these professors were generating new scholarship on women, producing thousands of books, hundreds of journals, and tens of thousands of courses. Unfortunately, earlier research on women required considerable effort as standard data sources generally did not include women or women of color as separate entries. In spite of the improvements made at the Library of Congress, subject searches can be a tricky process, especially in Women's Studies, and even more so in research on women of color. As an interdisciplinary field, Women's Studies necessarily crosses a wide number of overlapping subject areas in the academic curriculum. Because Women's Studies draws upon theories and issues relevant to many different disciplines, pertinent materials will be found within a variety of resources and throughout the collection of academic libraries, depending upon the particular interest of the researcher. Therefore, it is important for librarians to work closely with students and researchers in women's and ethnic studies to be able to provide a general knowledge of the overall organization of the library, along with specialized knowledge of some of the lesser known reference tools to locate materials by and about women of color.

The growing interest in different perspectives of women's issues raised by women of color, African Americans, Puerto Ricans and Hispanics (Latinas or Chicanas), Asian-Americans, American Indians, and women of other ethnic origins-has resulted in the need for more refinement of the library resources search process. It has also led to a need to broaden the scope of the search net to include ethnicity and gender perspectives within the different academic disciplines. Therefore, bibliographic instruction is another way librarians can take a more active role in the infusion of diversity into the women's curriculum by incorporating gender and ethnic specific materials into the orientation sessions offered to most undergraduate classes. Because bibliographic instruction is usually offered to all lower division English Composition and General Education classes, librarians can expose freshman and sophomores to female and minority authors and works early in the academic careers of most students.

During the library orientation exercises, librarians can use examples with women and women of color as potential topics for research, thus helping students view these topics as viable and researchable. In addition, librarians can create research guides and instructional materials about women of color, such as *Guide to Research in Multicultural Studies* or *Guide to Resources in African American Studies* or *Asian-American Studies* or *Native American Studies or Chicano Resources*, or even *Researching American Women of Color*. In general, librarians can promote scholarly research on women of color in library and bibliographic instruction by highlighting more reference sources that emphasize works of women, and by preparing research and guides for students to use in their search strategies. Active cooperative instruction programs can serve to bring libraries into the mainstream of academic life. These will create effective opportunities not only for librarians to listen to faculty and learn what their information needs actually are, but also to inform them of how the library supports their study, teaching, and research.

Scholarly publications are vital to the acceptance and maintenance of academic programs and the faculty teaching in those disciplines. Librarians and teaching faculty in Library Science and Women's Studies, two female-dominated programs, could unite forces in this arena for a mutually beneficial relationship.[12] The enormous impact of feminist scholarship on academic research and writing is evidenced by the growing number of books and articles to support the panoply of Women's Studies courses. Most of the books written by women, particularly female librarians, are bibliographies and guides to information sources.[13] One example of a collaborative effort of academic librarians, ACRL and a Women's Studies program in a city college, is a guide to collections in New York.[14]

Other scholars have thoroughly investigated the possibilities for the mutual transformation of Women's Studies scholarship and the academic disciplines without a single reference to librarians or the role of librarians in the research transformation.[15] Even guides and references on Women's Studies by feminist scholars tend to ignore the logical liaisons that can be formed between feminist scholars and female librarians. For example, Schmitz cites several projects and excellent resources in her guide and bibliography on integrating Women's Studies into the curriculum, but makes no mention of library resources or the role of librarians in the infusion process.[16]

Institutions and scholars have long accepted women's and ethnic studies as integral and ongoing parts of the regular curriculum and are now focusing on redefining concepts and theories. The same institutions, however, have also been remiss in considering librarians as an integral part of the research process. For example, Joanna deGroot and Mary Maynard in a series of essays explore different ways of conducting feminist research in the 1990's in response to the "idea that there can be a universal feminist approach or a generally valid framework for feminist analysis or politics."[17] Their exploration includes challenges of diversity, gender studies, postmodernism, and feminist scholarship. However, none of their strategies incorporates the potential contributions of feminist librarians on the agenda.

The situation regarding accreditation for Ethnic Studies programs and promotion of research and scholarship on minorities and women of color is similar to Women's Studies and library science. Many teaching faculty have commented, off the record, that they would like to include more books about women and people of color in their courses, but that there is little *scholarly* material available for inclusion in the syllabi. While there has been an increase in the number of books and articles by and about African-American women and Latinas, most writings by and about women of color are concentrated in such literary sources as poetry and fiction. Even fewer works or scholarly articles are written about Native-American and Asian-American women. In general, references to women of color are all too often relegated to chapters, sections, or paragraphs in books, and occasional articles in journals about women, minorities or a specific ethnic group.

Librarians can use their positions as information specialists to promote scholarly research on women of color in the academic community and the publishing arena. They can do joint research and publishing with Women's Studies scholars. For example, the education librarian can encourage faculty in the College of Education to incorporate materials in their syllabi that emphasize different learning styles of persons of color, women, and international students. Or a health science librarian can alert the teaching faculty to new books on "culture and health." They can then combine their research and efforts to publish on these topics. If, as in some academic institutions, there is a Multicultural Services Librarian, this person can help coordinate outreach research efforts with subject specialist librarians.

Librarians can also encourage the faculty to motivate their students to conduct more scholarly research about women of color. This suggestion would probably be particularly well suited for instructors of English Composition and freshman writing courses in which there may be less demand for citations from more "scholarly" articles that reflect rigorous research methodology and in-depth discussion of theoretical issues. In a similar manner, graduate students of color could be encouraged to undertake survey research on and theoretical analysis of issues germane to women and people of color for their masters theses or research papers. With better usage of available data and statistical information provided in a number of government reports and documents, students and teachers should be able to produce more scholarly research on peoples of color. Irrespective of the combination, joint efforts between librarians and Women's Studies scholars and their students, could produce a wealth of scholarly research and publications on women and women of color.

Feminist librarians have made substantial contributions to Women's Studies in the mass production of bibliographies, guides and references to works on and about women in general and women of color in particular. There is also a burgeoning literature on internet resources on Women's Studies.[18] The meteoric rise in electronic resources also provides opportunities for librarians to identify materials for research on women of color. There are a growing number of electronic tools for Women's Studies, and different ethnic groups; however, none of the sources is dedicated totally to women of color. Again, most of the sites are relatively broad in coverage. Women of color are, collectively, one of the fastest growing "minority" groups in America. Scholars, teaching faculty, and students in Women's Studies need to be able to conduct scholarly research and writing about women of color. Librarians can be of great assistance in the research process and development of search strategies in this area. Librarians can also serve as catalysts for improving scholarship in Women's Studies by encouraging book vendors and publishing houses to support and promote publication of materials by and about women of color. Finally, the burgeoning market of electronic reference tools also creates a wealth of opportunities for expanding this market.

NOTES

1. Betty Irvine, *Sex Segregation in Librarianship: Demographic and Career Patterns of Academic Library Administrators* (Westport, CT: Greenwood Press, 1985); Suzanne Hildenbrand, eds., *Reclaiming the American Library Past: Writing the Women In* (Norwood, NJ: Ablex Publishing Company, 1996).

2. Roma Harris, *Librarianship: The Erosion of a Woman's Profession* (New Jersey: Ablex Publishing Corporation, 1992).

3. Jacqueline Barrett, ed., *Encyclopedia of Women's Associations Worldwide* (Detroit: Gale Research International, 1993).

4. See the following as indicative of the profession's sensitivity to traditionally underserved groups: Call Gough and Ellen Greenblatt, eds., *Gay and Lesbian Library Service* (Jefferson, N.C.: McFarland, 1990); Kathleen de la Peña McCook, ed., *Women of Color in Librarianship: An Oral History* (Chicago: American Library Association, 1998); Donald E. Riggs and Patricia A. Tarin, eds., *Cultural Diversity in Librarians* (New York: Neal-Schuman, 1994).

5. Barrett, 269.

6. *ALA Handbook of Organizations, 1996-1997* (Chicago: American Library Association, 1996).

7. Beth Stafford, ed., *Women's Studies Programs and Library Resources* (Phoenix, AZ: Oryx Press, 1990).

8. Catherine Loeb, Susan Searing, and Esther F. Stineman, eds., *Women's Studies: A Recommended Core Bibliography, 1980-1985* (Littleton, CO: Librarians Unlimited, 1987).

9. Evelyn Hayes, "Librarian-Faculty Partnerships in Instruction," in *Advances in Librarianship*. ed. Irene Godden (San Diego, CA: Academic Press, 1996), 219.

10. For a guide to such information seeking by librarians, see Nancy Kushingian, "Researching Women's Lives and Issues," *Database* 20 (December, 1999): 18-26; "Seek and You Shall Find," *American Libraries* 30 (May, 1999), 104.

11. For an empirical study of the interdisciplinary problems faced by Women's Studies scholars and the solutions used by the scholars as well as the librarians who work with them, see Lynn Westbrook, *Interdisciplinary Information Seeking in Women's Studies* (Jefferson, N.C.: McFarland, 1999).

12. Michele Paludi and Gertrude A. Steuernagel, eds., *Foundations for a Feminist Restructuring of the Academic Disciplines* (New York: Haworth Press, 1990). Also, see C.D. Hurt, "The Future of Library Science in Higher Education: A Crossroads for Library Science and Librarianship," in *Advances in Librarianship,* ed. Irene Godden, (San Diego, CA: Academic Press, 1992).

13. See Sarah Carter and Maureen Ritchie, *Women's Studies: A Guide to Information Sources* (Jefferson, NC: McFarland, 1990); Betty Schmitz, *Integrating Women's Studies into the Curriculum: A Guide and Bibliography* (New York: Feminist Press, 1985).

14. Women's Resource Group of the Greater New York Metropolitan Area Chapter of the Association of College and Research Libraries and the Center for the Study of Women and Society of the City University of New York . *Library and Information Sources on Women: A Guide to Collections in the Greater New York Area* (New York: Feminist Press, 1988).

15. Domna Stanton and Abigail Stewart, eds., *Feminisms in the Academy* (Ann Arbor: University of Michigan Press, 1995).

16. Betty Schmitz, *Integrating Women's Studies into the Curriculum: A Guide and Bibliography* (New York: Feminist Press, 1985).

17. Joanna deGroot and Mary Maynard, *Women's Studies in the 1990s: Doing Things Differently?* (New York: St. Martin's Press, 1993), 149.

18. Mary Glazier, "Internet Resources for Women's Studies," *College and Research Libraries News*, 55 (1994), 139-43.

Bibliography

Abraham, Julie. *Are Girls Neccessary? Lesbian Writing and Modern History.* New York: Routledge, 1996.

Ackelsberg, Martha. "Communities, Resistance, and Women's Activism: Some Implications for a Democratic Polity." In *Women and the Politics of Empowerment.* Ed. Ann Bookman and Sandra Morgen. Philadelphia: Temple University Press, 1988.

Ackelsberg, Martha. "Women's Collaborative Activities and City Life: Politics and Policy," In *Political Women.* Ed. Janet A. Flammang. Beverly Hills, CA: Sage, 1984.

Acker, Joan. "Feminist Goals and Organizing Processes." In *Feminist Organizations: Harvest of the New Women's Movement.* Ed. Myra Marx Ferree and Patricia Yancy Martin. 137-144. Philadelphia: Temple University Press, 1995.

Alarcón, Norma. "Chicana's Feminist Literature: A Re-vision Through Malintzin/or Malintzin: Putting Flesh Back on the Object." In *This Bridge Called My Back: Writings by Radical Women of Color.* Ed. Cherríe Moraga and Gloria Anzaldúa. New York: Kitchen Table: Women of Color Press, 1983.

Anzaldúa, Gloria. *Borderlands/La Frontera: The New Mestiza* San Francisco: Spinsters/Aunt Lute, 1987.

_____. "Speaking in Tongues: A Letter to Third World Women Writers." In *This Bridge Called My Back,* Women of Color Press, 1981. 165-173.

Barrett, Jacqueline, ed. *Encyclopedia of Women's Associations Worldwide.* Detroit: Gale Research International, 1993.

Becker, Carol, ed. *The Subversive Imagination: Artists, Society, and Social Responsibility.* New York: Routledge, 1994.

Bernstein, Susan David. "Confessing Feminist Theory: What's I Got to Do with It?" *Hypatia* 7 (1992).

Beverley, John. "The Real Thing (Our Rigoberta)" *Modern Language Quarterly* 57 (1996).

Bhabha, Homi. "The Other Question: Difference, Discrimination and the Discourse of Colonialism." In *Out There: Marginalization and Contemporary Cultures.* Ed. Russell Ferguson, Martha Gever, Trinh T. Minh-ha, Cornel West. New York: New Museum of Contemporary Art and MIT Press, 1990.

_____. *The Location of Culture*. London: Routledge, 1994.

Blinde, Patricia Lin. "The Icicle in the Desert: Perspective and Form in the Works of Two Chinese-American Women Writers." *MELUS* 6 (1979).

Boneparth, Ellen. "Resources and Constraints on Women in the Policymaking Process: State and Local Arenas" In *Political Women*. Ed. Janet A. Flammang. Beverly Hills, CA: Sage, 1984.

Breines, Wini. *Young, White, and Miserable: Growing Up Female in the Fifties*. Boston: Beacon Press, 1992.

Britten, Alice A. "Close Encounters of the Third World Kind: Rigoberta Menchú and Elisabeth Burgos's *Me llamo Rigoberta Menchú.*" *Latin American Perspectives* 22 (1995).

Brodzki, Bella and Celeste Schenck. *Life/Lines: Theorizing Women's Autobiography*. Ithaca, NY: Cornell University Press, 1988.

Caraway, Nancie. *Segregated Sisterhood: Racism and the Politics of American Feminism*. Knoxville: University of Tennessee Press, 1991.

Castillo, Ana. *The Massacre of the Dreamers.* Albuquerque: University of New Mexico Press, 1994.

Cha, Theresa Hak Kyung. *Dictee*. New York: Tanam Press, 1982.

Clark, Suzanne. *Sentimental Modernism*. New York: Oxford UP, 1990.

_____. "Rhetoric, Social Construction and Gender: Is it Bad to be Sentimental?" In *Writing Theory and Critical Theory*. Ed. John Clifford and John Schilb. New York: Modern Language Association, 1994.

Cliff, Michelle. *No Telephone to Heaven*. New York: Vintage, 1988.

_____. *Abeng*. Trumansburg, NY: Crossing Press, 1984.

Clifford, James. *The Predicament of Culture: Twentieth-Century Ethnography, Literature, and Art*. Cambridge: Harvard UP, 1988.

Collins, Patricia Hill, *Black Feminist Thought: Knowledge, Consciousness, and the Politics of Empowerment*. New York: Routledge, 2000

_____. "The Social Construction of Black Feminist Thought" in *Signs: Journal of Women in Culture and Society* 14 (1989).

"Cultural Mis-readings by American Reviewers." In *Asian and Western Writers in Dialogue: New Cultural Identities*. Ed. Guy Amirthanayagam. London: Macmillan, 1982.

Daniels, Arlene Kaplan. *Invisible Careers: Women Civic Leaders from the Volunteer World*. Chicago: University of Chicago Press, 1988.

Davies, Carol Boyce, *Black Women, Writing and Identity: Migrations of the Subject*. London: Routledge, 1994.

deGroot, Joanna, and Mary Maynard. *Women's Studies in the 1990s: Doing Things Differently?* New York: St. Martin's Press, 1993.

Dhairyam, Sagri, "Racing the Lesbian, Dodging White Critics," In *The Lesbian Postmodern*. Ed. Laura Doan. New York: Columbia UP, 1994.

Dinnerstein, Myra, and Betty Schmitz, eds. *Ideas and Resources for Integrating Women's Studies into the Curriculum.* Vol. 1 Western States Project on Women in the Curriculum. The Southwest Institute for Research on Women, 1986.

D'Souza, Dinesh. *Illiberal Education: The Politics of Race and Sex on Campus*. New York: Random House, 1991.

Duberman, Martin, Martha Vicinius, and George Chauncey, Jr., eds. *Hidden From History: Reclaiming the Gay & Lesbian Past*. New York: Meridian, 1989.

duCille, Anne. "The Occult of True Black Womanhood: Critical Demeanor and Black Feminist Studies." *Signs: Journal of Women in Culture and Society* 19 (1994).

Ellison, Ralph. "What America Would Be like Without Blacks." In his *Going to the Territory*. New York: Random House, 1986.

Espiritu, Yen Le. "Colonial Oppression, Labour Importation, and Group Formation: Filipinos in the United States." *Ethnic and Racial Studies* 19 (January 1996).

Esquivel, Laura. *Like Water for Chocolate: A Novel in Monthly Installments with Recipes, Romances, and Home Remedies.* Trans. Carol Christensen and Thomas Christensen. New York: Doubleday, 1989.

Feng, Pin-Chia. *The Female Bildugsroman by Toni Morison and Maxine Hong Kingston: A Postmodern Reading.* New York: Peter Lang, 1998.

Ferree, Myra Marx, and Beth B. Hess. *Controversy and Coalition: The New Feminist Movement.* Boston: Twayne, 1985.

Flammang, Janet A. "Filling the Party Vacuum: Women at the Grassroots Level in Local Politics," In her *Political Women*. Beverly Hills, CA: Sage, 1984.

Foucault, Michel, *The History of Sexuality: An Introduction*, Vol. 1, New York: Random House, 1978.

Funderburg, Lise. *Black, White, Other: Biracial Americans Talk about Race and Identity.* New York: William Morrow, 1994.

Fusco, Coco. *English Is Broken Here: Notes on Cultural Fusion in the Americas.* New York: The New Press, 1995.

_____. "Performance and the Power of the Popular." In *Let's Get It On: The Politics of Black Performance*. Ed. Catherine Ugwu. Seattle: Bay Press and Institute of Contemporary Arts, 1995.

Fuss, Diana. *Essentially Speaking: Feminism, Nature & Difference.* New York: Routledge, 1989.

Garber, Judith. "Defining Feminist Community: Place, Choice, and the Urban Politics of Difference," In *Gender in Urban Research*. Eds. Judith A. Garber and Robyne S. Turner. Thousand Oaks, CA: Sage, 1995.

Gilroy, Paul. "To Be Real: The Dissident Forms of Black Expressive Culture." In *Let's Get It On: The Politics of Black Performance*. Ed. Catherine Ugwu. Seattle: Bay Press and Institute of Contemporary Arts, 1995.

Glazier, Mary. "Internet Resources for Women's Studies," *College and Research Libraries News* 55 (1994), 139-143.

Gómez-Peña, Guillermo. *The New World Border: Prophecies, Poems & Loqueras for the End of the Century.* San Francisco, CA: City Lights, 1996.

Gurevitch, Z. D. "The Other Side of Dialogue: On Making the Other Strange and the Experience of Otherness." *American Journal of Sociology* 93 (1988).

Harding, Sandra. *Whose Science? Whose Knowledge?: Thinking from Women's Lives.* Ithaca, NY: Cornell University Press, 1991.

Harris, Roma. *Librarianship: The Erosion of a Woman's Profession.* Norwood, NJ: Ablex, 1992.

Hayes, Evelyn. "Librarian-Faculty Partnerships in Instruction." In *Advances in Librarianship*. Ed. Irene Godden. San Diego, CA: Academic Press, 1996.

Hedges, Elaine, and Shirley Fisher Fishkin, eds. *Listening to Silences: New Essays in Feminist Criticism.* New York: Oxford University Press, 1994.

Hine, Darlene Clark. "Rape and the Inner Lives of Black Women in the Middle West: Preliminary Thoughts on the Culture of Disemblance." In *Unequal Sister: A Multicultural Reader in U.S. Women's History*. Ed. Vicki Ruiz and Ellen Carol DuBois. New York: Routledge, 1990.

Hong Kingston, Maxine. *The Woman Warrior: Memoirs of a Girlhood Among Ghosts.* New York: Vintage Books, 1975.

hooks, bell. *Ain't I a Woman: Black Women and Feminism.* Boston: South End Press, 1981.

_____. *Feminist Theory: From Margin to Center.* Boston: South End Press, 1984.

_____. "Narratives of Struggle." *Critical Fictions: The Politics of Imaginative Writing.* Ed. Philomena Mariani. Seattle: Bay Press, 1991.

_____. *Talking Back: Thinking Feminist, Thinking Black.* Boston, MA: South End Press, 1989.

_____. *Yearning: Race, Gender and Cultural Politics.* Boston, MA: South End Press, 1990.

Irvine, Betty. *Sex Segregation in Librarianship: Demographic and Career Patterns of Academic Library Administrators.* Westport, CT: Greenwood Press, 1985.

JanMohamed, Abdul R. "Sexuality on/of the Racial Border: Foucault, Wright, and the Articulation of 'Racialized Sexuality.'" In *Discourses of Sexuality: From Aristotle to AIDS.* Ed. Domna C. Stanton. Michigan: University of Michigan Press, 1992.

Jelinek, Estelle C. *Women's Autobiography: Essays in Criticism* Bloomington: Indiana University Press.

Kaminer, Wendy. *Women Volunteering: The Pleasure, Pain, and Politics of Unpaid Work from 1830 to the Present.* Garden City, NY: Anchor, 1984.

Kauanui, J. Kehaulani and Ju Hui "Judy" Han. "'Asian Pacific Islander': Issues of Representation and Responsibility." In *The Very Inside: An Anthology of Writing by Asian and Pacific Islander Lesbian and Bisexual Women.* Ed. Sharon Lim-Hing. Toronto: Sister Vision Press, 1994.

Kim, Elaine H. "Beyond Raildroads and Internment: Comments on the Past, Present, and Future of Asian-American Studies." In *Privileging Positions: The Sites of Asisa-American Studies.* Ed. Gary Okihiro, Marilyn Alquizola, Dorothy Fujita Rony and K. Scott Wong. Pullman: Washington State University Press, 1984.

Kingston, Maxine Hong. "Cultural Mis-readings by American Reviewer." In *Eastern and Western Writers in Dialogue: New Cultural Identies.* Ed. Guy Amirthanayagam London: Macmillan, 1982.

_____. *The Woman Warrior: Memoirs of a Girlhood Among Ghosts.* New York: Vintage Books, 1975; rpt. 1989.

La Duke, Winona. "In Honor of Women Warriors," *Off Our Backs,* February, 1981.

Loeb, Catherine, Susan Searing, and Esther F. Stineman. *Women's Studies: A Recommended Core Bibliography, 1980-1985.* Littleton, CO: Librarians Unlimited, 1987.

Lorde, Audre, *Sister Outsider: Essays and Speeches.* Freedom, CA: The Crossing Press, 1984.

Lowe, Lisa. *Immigrant Acts: On Asian-American Cultural Politics.* Durham: Duke University Press, 1996.

Lugones, Maria. "On the Logic of Pluralist Feminism." In *Feminist Ethics.* Ed. Claudia Card, Lawrence, KS: Kansas University Press, 1991.

Lugones, Maria. "Playfulness, World-Traveling and Loving Perception." In *Lesbian Philosophies and Cultures.* Ed. Jeffery Allen. Albany: SUNY Press, 1990.

Lyons, Charles, and James Lyons. "Anna Deavere Smith: Perspectives on Her Performance within the Context of Critical Theory." *Journal of Dramatic Theory and Criticism* 9 (1994).

MacLear, Kyo. "Not in So Many Words: Translating Silence Across 'Difference.'" In *Fireweed: A Feminist Quarterly of Writing, Politics, Art and Culture* (1994).

Madison, D. Soyini, *The Woman that I Am: The Literature and Culture of Contemporary Women of Color.* New York: St. Martin's Press, 1994.

Marshall, Paule. *Brown Girl, Brownstones.* Afterword by Mary Helen Washington. New York: Feminist Press, 1981.

_____. "Shaping the World of My Art." *New Letters* 40 (1973).

Martin, Theodora Penny. *The Sound of Our Own Voices: Women's Study Clubs, 1860-1910*. Boston: Beacon Press, 1987.

Maslow, Abraham. *Motivation and Personality*. 2nd ed. New York: Harper and Row, 1970.

McCarthy, Kathleen D.. "Parallel Power Structures: Women and the Voluntary Sphere." In *Lady Bountiful Revisted: Women, Philanthropy, and Power*. Ed. Kathleen D. McCarthy. New Brunswick, NJ: Rutgers University Press, 1990.

Menchú, Rigoberta. *I Rigoberta Menchú: An Indian Woman in Guatemala*. Ed. Elisabeth Burgos-Debray. Trans. Ann Wright (London: Verso, 1984).

Minh-ha, Trinh T., "Feminism and the Critique of Colonialist Discourse Conference." In *Making Face, Making Soul / Haciendo Caras: Creative and Critical Perspectives by Women of Color*. Ed. Gloria Anzaldúa. San Francisco: Aunt Lute, 1990.

_____. "Not You/Like You: Post-Colonial Women and the Interlocking Questions of Identity and Difference" in *Making Face, Making Soul/Haciendo Caras: Creative and Critical Perspectives by Women of Color*. Ed. Gloria Anzaldúa. San Francisco: Aunt Lute Foundation, 1990.

_____. *Woman, Native, Other: Writing Postcoloniality and Feminism* Bloomington: Indiana University Press, 1989.

Mohanty, Chandra Talpade, Ann Russo, and Lourdes Torres, eds. *Third World Women and the Politics of Feminism*. Bloomington: Indiana University Press, 1991.

Moraga, Cherríe, *Loving in the War Years*. Boston: South End Press, 1983.

Morrison, Toni. *The Bluest Eye*. New York: Plume, 1994.

_____. *Playing in the Dark: Whiteness and the Literary Imagination*. Cambridge: Harvard University Press, 1992.

Nelson, Barbara, and Najma Chowdhury. "Redefining Politics: Patterns of Women's Political Engagement from a Global Perspective," In *Women and Politics Worldwide*. New Haven, CT: Yale University Press, 1994.

Niranjana, Tejaswini. *Siting Translation: History, Post-Structuralism, and the Colonial Context* Berkeley: University of California Press, 1992.

Olsen, Tillie. *Silences*. New York: Delta/Seymour Lawrence, 1965.

Owens, Louis. "Other Destinies, Other Plots; An Introduction to Indian Novels." In *Other Destinies: Understanding the American Indian Novel*. Norman: University of Oklahoma Press, 1992.

Paludi, Michele, and Gertrude A. Steuernagel, eds. *Foundations for a Feminist Restructuring of the Academic Disciplines*. New York: Haworth Press, 1990.

Parker, Alice. "Writing Against Writing and Other Disruptions in Recent French Lesbian Texts." In *Feminism and Institutions: Dialogues on Feminist Theory*. Ed. Linda Kauffman. Oxford: Basil Blackwell, 1989.

Phelan, Peggy. *Unmarked: The Politics of Performance*. New York: Routledge, 1993.

Posnock, Ross. "Before and After Identity Politics." *Raritan* 15 (1995).

Quinby, Lee. "The Subject of Memoirs: *The Woman Warrior's* Technology of Ideographic Selfhood." In *De/Colonizing the Subject*. Ed. Sidonie Smith and Julia Watson, Minneapolis: University of Minnesota Press, 1992.

Rich, Adrienne. *Of Woman Born: Motherhood as Experience and Institution*. New YorkL Norton, 1976; rpt. 1986.

_____. *On Lies, Secrets, and Silence: Selected Proses 1966-1978*. New York: Norton, 1979.

Roberts, Sam. *Who We Are: A Portrait of America Based on the Latest US Census*. New York: Times Books, 1994.

Rodriguez, Clara E. and Hector Cordero-Guzman. "Placing Race in Context." *Ethnic and Racial Studies* 15 (1994).

Salazar, Alonzo. "Young Assassins of the Drug Trade." *NACLA Report on the Americas* 27

(May-June 1994).

Schmitz, Betty. *Integrating Women's Studies into the Curriculum: A Guide and Bibliography*. Old Westbury, NY: The Feminist Press, 1985.

Simmons, Diane. *Maxine Hong Kingston*. New York: Twayne, 1999.

Smith, Anna Deavere. *Fires in the Mirror*. New York: Anchor/Doubleday, 1993.

Smith, Sidonie. "Maxine Hong Kingston's *Woman Warrior*: Filiality and Woman's Autobiographical Storytelling" *Feminism: An Anthology of Literary Theory and Criticism*. Ed. Robyn R. Warhol and Diane Price Hernl. New Brunswick, NJ: Rutgers University Press, 1991.

_____. *Subjectivity, Identity, and the Body: Women's Autobiographical Practices in the Twentieth Century*. Bloomington: Indiana University Press, 1993.

Spillers, Hortense. "Notes on an Alternative Model-Neither/Nor," In *The Difference Within*. Ed. Elizabeth Meese and Alice Parker. Philadelphia: John Benjamins, 1989.

Stafford, Beth ed. *Women's Studies Programs and Library Resources*. Phoenix, AZ: Oryx Press, 1990.

Stanley, Sandra Kumanoto, *Other Sisterhoods: Literary Theory and U. S. Women of Color*. Urbana: University of Illinois Press, 1998.

Terry, Jennifer. "Theorizing Deviant Historiography." *Differences* 3 (1991), 55-74.

Tetreault, Mary Kay Thompson. "Classrooms for Diversity: Rethinking Curriculum and Pedagogy." In *Multicultural Education: Issues and Perspectives*. Ed. James A. Banks and Cherry A. McGee Banks. Needham Heights, MA: Allyn and Bacon, 1993.

Verba, Sidney, Kay Lehman Schlozman, and Henry E. Brady. *Voice and Equality: Civic Voluntarism in American Politics*. Cambridge MA: Harvard University Press, 1995.

Wald, Priscilla. *Constituting Americans: Cultural Anxiety and Narrative Form*. Durham, NC: Duke University Press, 1995.

Walker, Alice. "In Search of Our Mothers' Gardens." In *The Norton Anthology of Literature by Women: The Traditions in English*. Ed. Sandra M. Gilbert and Susan Gubar. 2nd ed. New York: Norton, 1996.

Wall, Cheryl A., ed. *Changing our own words: Essays on Criticism, Theory, and Writing by Black Women*. New Brunswick: Rutgers University Press, 1989.

Wallace, Michelle. "Modernism, Postmodernism, and the Problem of the Visual in African-American Culture." In *Out There: Marginalization and Contemporary Cultures*. Ed. Russell Ferguson, Martha Gever, Trinh T. Minh-ha, Cornel West. New York: The New Museum of Contemporary Art and MIT Press, 1990.

Watts, Margit Misangyi. *High Tea at Halekulani: Feminist Theory and American Clubwomen*. Brooklyn: Carlson, 1993.

White, Barbara A. *Growing Up Female: Adolescent Girlhood in American Fiction*. Westport, CT: Greenwood, 1985.

Williams, Patricia. *The Alchemy of Race and Rights: Diary of a Law Professor*. Cambridge: Harvard University Press, 1991.

Winnicott, D. W. *Playing and Reality*. New York: Basic, 1971.

Wolfe, Leslie R, and Jennifer Tucker. "Feminism Lives: Building a Multicultural Women's Movement in the United States." In *The Challenge of Local Feminisms: Women's Movements in Global Perspective*. Ed. Amrita Basu. Boulder, CT: Westview, 1995.

Wong, Sau-ling Cynthia. "Autobiography as Guided Tour? Maxine Hong Kingston's *The Woman Warrior* and the Chinese-American Autobiographical Controversy." In *Multicultural Autobiography*. Ed. James Robert Payne. Knoxville: University of Tennessee Press, 1992.

Woolf, Virginia. *A Room of One's Own*. New York: Harcourt Brace Jovanovich, 1929.

Yamada, Mitsuye. "Asian Pacific American Women and Feminism." In *This Bridge Called My Back: Writings By Radical Women of Color*. Ed. Cherríe Moraga and Gloria Anzaldúa. New York: Kitchen Table Women of Color Press, 1981.

Young, Iris Marion. "Gender as Seriality: Thinking about Women as a Social Collective" *Signs* 19 (1994).

Yung Judy. *No Chinese Stranger*. New York: Harper & Row, 1975.

_____. *Unbound Feet: A Social History of Chinese Women in San Francisco*. Berkeley: University of California Press, 1995.

Zimmerman, Marc, "*Testimonio* in Guatemala: Payeras, Rigoberta, and Beyond," *Latin American Perspectives* 18 (1991).

Zinn, Maxine Baca, Lynn Weber Cannon, Elizabeth Higginbotham, and Bonnie Thornton Dill. "The Costs of Exclusionary Practices in Women's Studies." *Signs* 11 (1986).

Zinn, Maxine Baca and Bonnie Thornton Dill, eds. *Women of Color in U.S. Society*. Philadelphia: University of Pennsylvania Press, 1994.

Index

Contributors

NANCY BACKES is an assistant professor of English at Cardinal Stritch University in Milwaukee where she teaches writing and literature. Although she specializes in American literature, she also has published on popular culture topics and on contemporary women's theater. Her major area of concentration is age studies, and she is currently working on a book that historically, racially, and ethnically examines the age of fifteen in American girlhood.

JANET K. BOLES is professor of political science at Marquette University where she teaches courses on the politics of race, gender, and ethnicity and women in American politics. She is the author of *The Politics of the Equal Rights Amendment*, editor of *American Feminism* and *The Egalitarian City*, and coauthor with Diane Long Hoeveler of *The Historical Dictionary of Feminism*.

PATTI L. DUNCAN is assistant professor of Women's Studies at Portland State University. Her dissertation, "A History of Un/Saying: Silence, Memory, and Historiography in Asian-American Women's Narratives," explores the uses of silences as methods of resistance in texts of Asian Pacific women writers, and was completed at Emory University's Institute for Women's Studies.

JENNIFER DRAKE holds degrees from Brown University and SUNY-Binghamton. Currently she is an assistant professor of English and Women's Studies at Indiana State University, where she teaches courses in women's literature, multicultural United States literatures, and creative writing. She is coeditor of *Third Wave Agenda: Being Feminist, Doing Feminism* (1997), and has written essays on the work of women artists such as Bharati Mukherjee, Adrian Piper, Lorna Simpson, and Ani DiFranco.

ARGLENDA FRIDAY holds degrees from Howard University, the University of Maryland, and is currently a doctoral student at Florida State University. She also serves as the Diversity Coordinator and Reference Librarian at San Jose State University, where she teaches courses in Women's Studies, Public Administration, and library science.

LANCE GRAHN is associate professor and Chair of the Department of History, Marquette University. His publications include *Let My People Live: Faith and Struggle in Central America* (Eerdmans, 1988) and *The Political Economy of Smuggling: Regional Informal Economies in Early Bourbon New Granada* (Westview, 1997). His National Endowment for the Humanities-funded work in Latin American studies with Milwaukee-area secondary school teachers has twice garnered him the North Central Council of Latin Americanists' Professional Teaching Award. He currently serves on the American Historical Association's Teaching Prizes Committee, the Executive Committee of the Consortium of Latin American Studies Programs, the Executive Committee of the Latin American and Caribbean History Section of the Southern Historical Association, and the governing board of the Wisconsin Humanities Council.

NINA MANASAN GREENBERG specializes in the fields of critical theory, feminist theory, and Women's Studies. She has published articles in the *Chaucer Review*, the *CEA Critic*, and was an assistant professor of English at the University of Central Florida. She currently is working as a freelance editor in New York City.

ROSETTA R. HAYNES is an assistant professor of English at Indiana State University, where she teaches courses in African-American and American literatures. Her research interests include nineteenth-century African-American and American literatures, particularly the cross-cultural aspects of women's writings. She received her Ph.D. in English from Cornell University.

DIANE LONG HOEVELER is professor of English and Coordinator of the Women's Studies Program at Marquette University. She is author of *Gothic Feminism* (1998), *Romantic Androgyny* (1990), and coauthor with Lisa Jadwin of *Charlotte Bronte* (1997). She has also coauthored the *Historical Dictionary of Feminism* (1996) with Janet Boles, coedited the MLA's *Approaches to Teaching Jane Eyre* (1993) with Beth Lau, and coedited *Comparative Romanticisms: Power, Gender, Subjectivity* (1998) with Larry Peer. Most recently, she has edited Emily Brontè's *Wuthering Heights* for Houghton Mifflin (2001), and coedited *Approaches to Teaching Gothic Fiction* with Tamar Heller (forthcoming MLA, 2003). She specializes in teaching Romanticism, Gothicism, and Women's Literature. In addition, she currently serves as President of the American Conference on Romanticism (2000-2002), and has organized six national conferences on women's studies.

LAURA H. ROSKOS coordinates the Graduate Consortium in Women's Studies at Radcliffe College. She earned her Ph.D. in the Modern Studies Program at the

University of Wisconsin-Milwaukee, where she also taught literature in the Women's Studies and peace studies programs. A former VISTA volunteer, she spent over 12 years as a community activist and organizer in Milwaukee's central city. She is currently at work on a book entitled *The Life of the Party: A Genealogy of the Community Impulse in Literature.*

ARLENE SGOUTAS received her Ph.D. from the Graduate School of International Studies at the University of Denver, where she now teaches courses on international women's issues, social movements, and feminist theory. Her research interests lie in studying the patterns of women's global organizing and the gender dimensions of international relations.

MARY SULLIVAN-HALLER received her Ph.D. at SUNY-Stony Brook, where she wrote a dissertation entitled "A Rhetoric of Revision: Ethical Discourse and the Idea of Women's Literature." She has served as assistant to the Director of Writing Programs at Stony Brook, and assistant professor of English at Mount St. Vincent College.

TONI-MICHELLE C. TRAVIS is associate professor of Government and Politics at George Mason University. Her latest book with Karen Rosenblum is *The Meaning of Difference: American Constructions of Race, Sex and Gender, Social Class, and Sexual Orientation.* She specializes in research on race and gender issues in political participation and urban politics. As a political analyst on Virginia and national politics, she hosts the television program, "Capitol Region Roundtable." She has also served as president of the Women's Caucus of the American Political Science Association and the National Capital Areas Political Science Association.

JORGE VALADEZ was raised in Laredo, Texas, a town on the United States-Mexico border. He obtained his Ph.D. in Philosophy from Yale University and has taught at Marquette University and Our Lady of the Lake College in San Antonio, Texas. His research interests include alternative epistemologies and metaphysics, pre-Columbian philosophy, and social and political philosophy. He is currently completing a book on the philosophical foundations of multicultural democracies.